LAST LETTERS

Seize brumaire 2 9bre 1793.

Ce sont les derniers caractères que ma main
tracera. Dans peu d'heures je ne serai plus.
Je suis condamné à mort.

Va, femme que j'ai toujours tendrement chérie,
je meurs plein de tendresse pour toi. Je ne te dis
pas de m'oublier; je connais ta belle ame,
ton cœur si tendre; non, tu ne m'oubliera
jamais. Mais vis pour nos pauvres enfans.
Rappelle moi à leur souvenir. Que je leur serve
d'exemple. Qu'ils soient meilleurs que moi.
Elève les dans l'exercice des vertus. Mes biens
sont confisqués; ils sont si peu de chose, que
ce ne sera pas une grande perte pour eux.
Elève les dans l'amour du travail. Reporte
sur eux toute l'amitié que tu avais pour moi.
Adieu, mille fois adieu. Essuye tes larmes
et ne t'occupe que de nos enfans.

Durfresnille

OLIVIER BLANC

LAST LETTERS

PRISONS and PRISONERS
of the
FRENCH REVOLUTION

1793-1794

Translated by
ALAN SHERIDAN

Michael di Capua Books
Farrar, Straus and Giroux
New York

FRONTISPIECE
The last letter of Gabriel Rochon de Wormeselle

To the memory of Paul Blanc

CONTENTS

PART II

Last Letters   85

❧

INTRODUCTION

While going through boxes 111–195 in the W series of the Archives Nationales, a series of papers supposed to have belonged to the public prosecutor of the Paris Revolutionary Tribunal, I came to realize that, among the thousands and thousands of unpublished documents to be found there, the most moving were the letters written by men and women condemned to death a few hours or even a few minutes before their departure for the scaffold. These letters, most of which were intercepted by the courts and handed over to Fouquier-Tinville, ended up stuck into files without any apparent order. Those published in this book represent only a small proportion of those final, moving farewells. All those men and women, who, sometimes a week or so earlier, were dining peacefully at their family table or were on their way to the theatre when arrested, nevertheless had time to accustom themselves to the idea of their imminent death.

Of the hundred and fifty letters or farewell notes that I have selected, a hundred and thirteen have never before been published: some of the others were published shortly after the Revolution, but are not generally known, with the exception of the fine letters written by Marie-Antoinette and Mme Roland, which I felt could not be excluded from such a book.

Their number and diversity necessitated some criteria of selection and some decision as to their mode of presentation. I tended to choose the unpublished rather than the published, letters rather than notes, which were usually very short. The letters speak for themselves. Nevertheless it seemed to me to be useful to try to reconstruct something of the context, the atmosphere in which these letters were written. I have usually provided a short account of the writers' personal history, the crimes with which they were charged, the circumstances of their arrest and condemnation. I have also tried to describe what life was like in the Paris prisons of Year II, which numbered about forty in all, often set up at short notice in such buildings as schools, private houses, barracks, monasteries, or lunatic asylums.

In 1793–4, close on seven thousand persons entered these often sinister places. Apart from the minority of common criminals, there were three sorts of prisoners. There were those who had been condemned by the Revolutionary Tribunal, usually to the *gêne* or to the *fers*.[1] A larger number were individuals charged and held in custody, whose investigation was in progress and who had not yet appeared before the Revolutionary Tribunal. Their stay in prison varied from forty-eight hours to six months and they were accused of a wide range of crimes. These included the hoarding of commodities or precious metals, financial crimes in general, as well as such direct offences against public order as federalism, treason, corruption, emigration, undeclared correspondence with persons abroad, and even writings or statements tending to bring institutions or the people's elected representatives into disrepute. Lastly, there was a third category of prisoner: the 'suspect', that is to say, those who, unlike those charged with crimes, had not yet been arrested, a judicial formality that marked the beginning of the period of confinement.

It was soon the suspects who were to form the bulk of the prison population after the passing by the Convention on 17 September 1793 of the famous law that bears their name.

This new law laid down a very wide definition of suspects that made it possible to reach all the enemies of the Revolution with the utmost ease. All those who, by their behaviour, their associates, what they said or what they wrote, showed themselves to be 'advocates of tyranny or federalism and enemies of liberty' were defined as suspects. Those who did not have legal means of support and those who, having relations abroad, had failed to demonstrate their loyalty to the Revolution were suspect. Lastly, those who had emigrated and who had nevertheless been acquitted before the law was passed were suspects!

The law relating to suspects that marked the arrival of the Terror seems to have been mainly intended to bring a rapid halt to counter-revolutionary action and its concerted manoeuvres to destabilize the regime. To begin with, such destabilization could be economic, for the opponents of the Revolution soon realized that it would be more effective to attack the government in the economic and financial fields, rather than by armed intervention. Although the realization of these plans was defective, the idea was correct enough. Indeed, since

1789, the currency was strongly secured by the national wealth: the confiscated lands and wealth of the crown, the clergy, the émigrés and those convicted of being enemies of the Revolution. But the realization of capital through the sale of this property was slow and difficult: the buyers, including speculators, deferred their payments by spreading them over a longer period of time, gambling on the rapid fall of the assignat. Many a property confiscated in 1791 was sold off in 1795 at half its true value!

Since the expected government revenues were not enough to supply the state with the money it needed, assignats were issued on a massive scale to cover, first, everyday expenditure, then, after 1792, the war. At the same time, taxes were no longer being collected and patriotic gifts or contributions, wealth taxes and other forced loans were failing to bring in the revenue expected of them. To cap it all, the civil servants in the Treasury and those working in the administration of government finances generally were often loyal to the *ancien régime* and did their best, if only through inertia, to sabotage the new order.

In 1791, the counter-revolutionaries were planning to damage the economic and financial situation still further. On their own or through their financial agents (notaries, bankers, etc.), they tried to take advantage of the slow workings of the Assembly, whose legislation, though still restrictive and repressive, did not succeed in stopping the outflow of capital and the continual rise in the price of commodities.

It was often, therefore, for their involvement in illegal or fraudulent financial practices that the suspects were arrested, usually after being denounced by one of their associates. But their aims were not always solely political. For many, it was a matter of preserving their possessions and their capital. In order to prevent the confiscation and sale of the family heritage, and to be able to go on receiving their incomes, many rich émigrés secretly returned to France and tried to obtain forged residence certificates and so get their names removed from the list of émigrés.[2] The public prosecutor of the Revolutionary Tribunal, Fouquier-Tinville, was well aware of this:

Many émigrés have come back to France; by using forged residence certificates they enjoy property that was the Nation's security. People are not afraid to declare that the absolutions granted them by corrupt municipalities or administrations have caused the Republic a loss of over two thousand million *livres* (there are eighty-five *départements*; if you take only eighty-three for the émigrés, and count only five émigrés per *département* and suppose that they own on average four million each, you will soon arrive at

over two thousand million) . . . We must therefore conclude that if
there are buyers for these forged certificates, there are necessarily
sellers and that these sellers are to be found at the very heart of the
public services.[3]

Very often, these émigrés, who took advantage of their return to
France to recover the movables of relations or friends who had fled,
had already placed in safety abroad a not inconsiderable part of their
possessions – ingots, silver, goldsmiths' work, etc. Indeed a great
deal of jewellery sold abroad is still to be found in certain foreign
collections.

This left the families' immovable property. To prevent it being
sold, one had to prove one's uninterrupted residence in France from
the promulgation of the first laws on emigration. Once one's papers
were in order, thanks to forged certificates, the optimists bought
back their property (or those of their relations or friends), which had
passed into national ownership, in depreciated assignats, while the
pessimists hastened to sell estates, farms or furniture at the best prices
they could get.

At the same time, everybody continued to send money abroad.
One made use of *passeurs* when precious stones or metals were
involved, certain stockbrokers in the case of bonds that were nego-
tiable abroad and certain notaries when it was a matter of drawing up
accommodation bills in favour of individuals who had remained in
France and ran no risk, devoted servants, for example.

Rich suspects, who expected to be condemned and foresaw the
inevitable seizure of their property, were clever enough to effect a
transfer of ownership just in time.

Thus we find on a Paris notarial register, dated 29 Pluviôse Year II,
an obligation contracted by Citizeness de Billens in favour of
Citizeness Dufresne.[4]

That day, Baronne de Billens, who had been held in the Conciergerie for a month, was given her indictment, summoning her to
appear the following day before the Revolutionary Tribunal. The
Republic inherited only a tiny fraction of her fortune, which had
been transferred in time to Citizeness Dufresne, who was forced in
turn to transfer it to a new, mysterious third party.

In this way, by means of a few signatures, considerable sums of
money eluded the hands of the revolutionaries. But things did not
always happen so easily. We know the case of the Duc du Châtelet,
who possessed a very large fortune and had no direct heirs. Held in
solitary confinement, he could be certain of death. His nephews and
nieces went to extraordinary lengths to obtain a deed of assignment

of his fortune before his condemnation. He himself attempted suicide, for, as long as he was not condemned, a member of his family who had not emigrated could inherit. Condemned to death in 17 December 1793, all these manoeuvres failed and his property was finally seized by the state.[5]

Among the 'suspects' who filled the prisons of the Terror, a number were there for speculating on the sale of national assets.[6] Speculation in all its forms delivered staggering blows to the young Republic. It operated at every level: from the mere exchange of a hundred-*livres* assignat for half its value in cash on the steps of the Palais-Royal to the higher reaches of the civil service, especially in the deals made between the civil service and the military transport companies. The Abbé d'Espagnac, director of one of these companies, is one of the most celebrated examples (see p. 80).

But, above all, a large quantity of false assignats spread like an epidemic, thus increasing the general mistrust of an already weakened currency. Manufactured in Germany or in England, they often crossed from Switzerland into the French frontier *départements*.[7] They then went their way, changed into cash or distributed profusely by the royalists. Several of those condemned were accused of just such a crime: the Marquise de Forceville, arrested for passing twenty-four thousand forged *livres* to the former *fermier général* Duvaucel; the Comte d'Angivilliers, condemned for receiving a large quantity sent from London by Louis XVI's former minister, Bertrand de Molleville;[8] the Marquis de l'Aigle and his niece, the Comtesse de Durtal, guillotined for the same crime. There can be no doubt that forged assignats and famine represented at the time far more dangerous enemies than the whole coalition of powers put together.

If we are not clear today why certain suspects were arrested, it is because the financial acts of which they were suspected were often themselves somewhat obscure.

Thus there were several thousands of detainees, living in constant terror of betrayal, of a confession extracted from someone close to them, of the discovery of some document (a forged certificate, an undeclared letter from abroad, forged currency, etc.) that might at any moment transform them from suspects into prisoners and condemn them to the scaffold.

I have devoted the first part of this book to the prisons, to the memories associated with them and to some of their inmates. Unpublished correspondence, police reports and extracts from prisoners' 'memoirs' have helped me to reconstruct what on the whole must have been a gloomy atmosphere.

The second part is more directly concerned with a few individuals whose last letters were intended for their families. Some of them are quite unknown. In such cases I have tried to give some information, gleaned from police and court files, concerning their lives, the motives for their arrest and sometimes their last moments. In the case of the more famous of those whose last letters I reproduce, I refer the reader to other, more detailed studies.

My aim is to let the documents and the facts speak for themselves, but I would be happy if such archives could be of service to others and thus contribute to a better understanding of the history of *mentalités* in the late eighteenth century.

PART ONE

THE PRISONS OF THE TERROR
AND THEIR INMATES

BEHIND THE WALLS

Who were the prisoners?

At a time when the nobility was suspect *a priori*, many of its members were seeking the most ingenious ways of hiding or disguising their identity. Like other opponents of the Republic, they sought refuge with their friends and neighbours and changed their names as often as they thought necessary. In a way, what Chateaubriand was later to write already had a measure of truth:

By an agreed disguise, a mass of people changed their identities: each bore his pseudonym or borrowed name hanging about his neck, rather as the Venetians, at the Carnival, carry in their hands a little mask to warn people that they are masked. One was reputed to be an Italian or a Spaniard, another a Prussian or a Dutchman; I was Swiss. A mother passed herself off as her son's aunt, her father as his daughter's uncle; the owner was merely a manager . . .[9]

It was the same in the prisons of the Terror. To complicate matters further, certain police files available to us today have lost their contents and several prison records have disappeared, destroyed when the Hôtel de Ville was burnt down in 1871. Of those that we are lucky enough to possess, many are of questionable value owing to illegible handwriting or to the practice, on the part of many of the prisoners, of using pseudonyms (Rouvroy de Saint-Simon calls himself 'Bonhomme', Caumont-La Force 'Boucher', Lambert 'Scarra') or certain of their more rarely used family names.[10] Lastly, there was an organized trafficking in prison registers, especially at La Force, on which, for a certain sum of money, one could arrange not to have one's name appear.

This confusion obviously complicated the researches of the authorities and, today, does not make the historian's task any easier. To this should be added another difficulty. Many of the detainees do not tell the truth about their titles or the profession that they claim to practise. One must, therefore, be extremely prudent when dealing with the information to be found in the archives. A certain Bonnard, who declares himself to be a farmer at Villiers-la-Garenne, omits to say that he held power of attorney for the Duc des Deux-Ponts. Rabourdin, apparently a simple country priest, was the financial agent at Neuilly of the Duchesse de Choiseul-Praslin. Egré, alias Cornet d'Egré, a brewer at Suresnes, manufactured forged assignats. Behind a merchant, a former financier was hiding. Behind a servant, a concierge or a brothel-keeper might be a former countess or a woman of the haute bourgeoisie. It would, therefore, be advisable to resist any attempt at a rigorous typology of the prisoners.[11]

Although the large majority of the prisoners were men, there were nevertheless many women. This is rather surprising for a period when women enjoyed no political rights. Their number began to increase steadily after the passing of the law of suspects in September 1793. From then on, it was enough to be the mother or daughter of an émigré to find oneself in prison. But it was above all when they were suspected of transmitting money abroad through financial agents that they were arrested. The wives of émigrés were in a similarly precarious situation – some had already taken the precaution of seeking a divorce in order to deflect the effects of the law on émigrés' property.[12]

Among these women, some had played a more active role in the counter-revolutionary movement; one thinks especially of Mme de Beaufort, Mme de Rochechouart, and Mme de Bonneuil. Who remembers now that they risked their lives ten times over to defend a friend, but especially to save a fortune. Utterly fearless, they haunted the corridors of the committees, seduced the deputies, corrupted the police administrators, before finally being arrested and imprisoned.

The indictments were usually handed out to the detainees in the late evening. They would appear in court within forty-eight hours: many of them had already applied to Fouquier for the documents necessary to their defence and for an interview with their lawyers.

Accepted by the Revolutionary Tribunal, these lawyers, nicknamed '*défenseurs officieux*' (unofficial defenders), were supposed to help the detainees prepare their defence. Their job was to gather favourable evidence and to collect the documents necessary to their client's case, documents that sometimes had to be brought from the provinces.

In fact, many of these 'defenders', whose services cost dear, were of no great help. When they were abolished by decree, one detainee, Lambertie, confessed to Fouquier that he 'was very pleased to be delivered from that haddock, that monster', who had been given him at the Abbaye and who had 'tricked me into believing that he had taken steps on my behalf that he had never taken'.[13]

Among the list of those who acquired national assets during the Revolution and Directoire are the names of several such 'vultures', such as La Fleutrie, who became very rich indeed at the expense of their unfortunate clients.

More conscientious was the barrister who acted for the queen and for Charlotte Corday, Citizen Chauveau-Lagarde. Arrested in turn, he wrote this letter to the members of the Revolutionary Tribunal:

> Citizens,
>
> I have in my possession a quantity of documents entrusted to me by clients whom it was my task to defend before our abolition and which may, by throwing light on their cases, save their innocence. I beg you to have me conducted to them so that I may put them in order and deposit them with the public prosecutor, who will restore them to their rightful owners. They are a sacred property and it is above all my duty to dispossess myself of them.
>
> When the time comes to think of myself, it will be only to solicit your justice; from my own point of view, I should like this done as soon as possible, whatever fate awaits me.
>
> 16 Messidor, Year II of the one
and indivisible Republic.[14]

Many prisoners did without the services of a barrister, preferring to address Fouquier directly. Citizen Souque, who was fearful of coming before the Tribunal, did not hesitate to ask the prosecutor frankly for his advice as to 'the steps to be taken to avoid appearing in those proceedings, which,' he said, 'could just as easily do without me'.

The pragmatic Bourrée de Corberon, former president of the *Parlement*, had the idea of pinning to the request that he addressed to Fouquier a fifty-*livres* assignat 'to cover the initial costs'. In the Archives Nationales, the note is still attached to the letter.[15]

There are numerous, very moving, self-justificatory memoranda by detainees whose ultimate fate we know. Ménage-Pressigny had the same text copied out more than thirty times: was it his intention to send a copy to each of the members of the Tribunal?[16]

Young La Pallu also wrote a great deal, and his letters increased in number when he finally realized that his case was going badly. We see him trying desperately to get witnesses of his own choice to appear at his trial: 'Don't forget me, I beg you!' It was all in vain. He was executed.[17]

The son of the naturalist Buffon wrote endless self-justificatory memoranda, invariably evoking the memory of his father. It was all to no avail.

When the investigation was in progress, some tried to justify themselves . . . out of a sense of honour. In the pamphlets or posters distributed outside, they sometimes blamed the institution or the people's elected representatives, as in the cases of Mazuel or Olympe de Gouges.[18]

To save their lives, other, not so clever individuals, did not hesitate to denounce their former friends or their co-detainees. One poor woman wanted to convince Fouquier of the guilt of a woman in a nearby cell: 'She won't say what her name is. She says she's the sister of the Comte d'Aria (*sic*). She pretends she's an imbecile, or drunk . . .'[19]

The papers piled up on Fouquier's desk. They came from far and wide. There was the woman L'Herbette, who wrote on the subject of her guillotined husband; her portrait in miniature had been taken from him: 'Since I think my face can be of interest only to those who know me, I dare to hope that you will not refuse to return it to me.' And she offered to pay the cost of the gold frame to the Republic.[20]

Hertault de Lammerville died before coming to trial, yet the prison keeper asked Fouquier if 'in order to proceed with the confiscation of his property, which has already been partly seized', his trial might nevertheless take place.[21]

Reports and denunciations followed one another. One individual was arrested for shouting out in the street several times, '*Merde pour la Nation*',[22] while another was 'suspected of being suspect'.

A great many of the documents read by Fouquier or his secretaries bear in the margin in red ink the words 'attached to file X', under the name of the individual concerned.

This minimal, almost non-existent defence left the detainees little hope of escaping a fatal outcome. What course was left to them? Escape? But was it possible to escape from the prisons of the Terror and especially from the Conciergerie?

There were, it is true, a few escapes. Several documents in the archives refer to prisoners who failed to turn up at the roll-call. But they were very few in number and rarely important figures, who were too well guarded to try their luck.

In notes left by a certain warder, Louis Larivière, we find the account of an escape in which Fouquier-Tinville himself played a role. On certain evenings at nightfall, Fouquier was in the habit of stalking the corridors of the Conciergerie, as if looking for someone or something. On one such evening, he caught sight of a warder moving silently along the wall.

'Hey,' he called out, 'where are you going?'

'I've just come off work,' stammered the warder, 'and I'm going to have a little rest.'

'Do you know me?'

'Who does not know the eminent public prosecutor of our Tribunal?'

'Do you know where I live?'

'Yes, I've seen you come out of the house, and anyway I was sent one day to take a note to your address.'

'Then you will go to my house and tell my wife not to expect me for supper. I have work to do here and will be home late.'

'But,' said the warder, timidly, 'they might not let me out at this time.'

Fouquier then led him to the first gate and yelled:

'Let him through – he's on court business.'

The order was transmitted from gate to gate, and the warder passed through unchallenged. Soon he found himself outside the Palace. The porters had not recognized him, but they thought he must be a 'new' one. And, in any case, one did not question the orders of Fouquier-Tinville.

When, late that night, the prosecutor arrived home, he found his wife in a very worried state. She had not eaten and had tried to keep supper warm as she waited for her husband. The messenger had never turned up at their home in the Place Dauphine.

Next morning, a furious Fouquier went to the Conciergerie, where he learnt something that was not calculated to improve his temper: a girl, accused of complicity with the émigrés, had just disappeared, the day before she was due to appear in court.

'We've looked for her everywhere,' said the keeper, Richard.

'Well!' Fouquier growled, 'get me that traitor of a warder and try to cheer up.'

The unfaithful messenger was no more to be found than was the girl, but another warder declared that, the night before, someone had stolen his best suit.

After a thorough investigation, the conclusion seemed inescapable: the prisoner had escaped wearing the stolen uniform.

Fouquier, who had had the gates opened to the escapee, became, by that very fact, the principal accomplice of the escape.

However, it was the warder whose uniform had been stolen who was punished – under the pretext that he had not notified the theft immediately.

As for Fouquier, he was eaten up with fury inside, but put on the appearance of a good apostle, saying:

'After all, she was not very guilty, and I would probably have acquitted her.'

Nevertheless, I am convinced that if he had caught her at that moment, he would have sent her without the slightest remorse to the guillotine.[23]

Not all the escapes were as picturesque. The easiest were no doubt those of rich suspects placed under house arrest. There were many such who, taking advantage of a momentary lapse on the part of their guards, escaped abroad: in this way Castellane and his wife sought refuge in Switzerland.

A few detainees died in prison, including some at the Conciergerie. Some succumbed to illness, in which case they were taken to the diocesan hospital; others preferred suicide to despair or the scaffold, which, given the extreme difficulty of escape, remained the ultimate possibility of escaping the Tribunal. It must be stressed that the most enigmatic characters of the Revolution, those who often possessed many compromising secrets, ended their days in prison.

Among those who survived their suicide attempts and were guillotined were the Duc du Châtelet, who swallowed crushed glass and then tried to smash his head against a wall; Chabot, who tried to poison himself; and Osselin, who tried to kill himself with a nail . . . Others were lucky enough to be able to assuage their pain with certain remedies, as one Parisian editor, who had been given a dose of opium by a cell-mate, recounts:

> Up till then, I had been wracked by continual anxiety as to the fate that awaited me: as soon as I saw that my destiny lay in my own hands, I breathed freely and awaited with truly unimaginable calm tyranny's final blow, certain of being able to escape it at the very moment that it struck me. So nothing was more important for me than to conceal that precious treasure. It never left me and even today, when the storms of the revolution seem to have dissipated, I still conceal it most carefully, as much to keep alive within me memories that should not be forgotten as to maintain in all the situations of my life that tranquil, serene attitude with which I then confronted the future . . .[24]

Life in the prisons

Each of the Revolution's prisons had its own peculiarities, its own reputation, its own importance. If one does not count the police stations of the forty-eight sections, known familiarly as the 'violin', there were about fifty such prisons in Paris in 1793 and 1794, fifteen of which were *maisons de santé*, relatively protected from the full rigours of the Terror and intended for the richest prisoners. This does not mean that Fouquier-Tinville did not draw on them from time to time . . . Eleven of them are of special interest: the Abbaye, the Madelonnettes, Port-Libre, La Force, Sainte-Pélagie, the Anglaises, Bicêtre, the Luxembourg, the Plessis, Saint-Lazare, the Carmes (a more complete, more detailed list is provided in an appendix). Different names were used to describe them, in different periods and according to their use: *maison d'arrêt, maison de détention, maison de force, maison de suspicion, maison de santé.*

One of the first to take in the prisoners of 1793 was the Abbaye. By March, it was full – temporarily, at least, for shortly afterwards the first transfers of prisoners began. During the Revolution every Parisian must have seen at some time or other long lines of carts moving towards the *maisons d'arrêt.* By July 1793, the Abbaye contained nearly three hundred prisoners. Even if a year later there remained no more than ten or so, a great many prisoners passed through it, sometimes only for a few days. It is a place worth remembering.

A former seigneurial prison, the Abbaye was as hated as the Bastille on the eve of the Revolution. It was situated at the end of the Rue Sainte-Marguerite, at the point at which it crossed what is now 168 Boulevard Saint-Germain. In 1792, most of the inmates were common-law prisoners, with a sprinkling of officers and soldiers of the royal household, arrested after 10 August. The latter included the Comte de Montmorin, the Abbé Lenfant, the king's confessor, the Abbé de Rastignac, and a number of priests and monks who had refused to take the constitutional oath. On 2 September, as in many other prisons, a large number of prisoners were murdered in front of the gates, in the prison yard, in the gardens and at the intersection of what is now the Rue Bonaparte and the Place Saint-Germain.

The building formed a sort of irregular quadrilateral, recognizable by the two small turrets that flanked the corners of one of its two façades. It was made up of three very tall main buildings, with a small yard in the middle.

The first-class prisoners were allowed to occupy the more salubrious apartments. Thus the Duc d'Orléans, Mme Roland, Vergniaud and a few others were imprisoned there at a time when other, perhaps more comfortable prisons had not yet been equipped to receive them. On the other hand, the poor wretches who had no means were piled into four small, straw-strewn rooms, where the inmates were subject to the smells coming from a sort of cesspit just outside.

The friendships that arose in such conditions were sometimes sincere and deeply felt, as this farewell from one prisoner to those who had shared his room testifies:

To Citizen La Perche, prisoner in the chapel of the prison of the Abbaye Saint-Germain, in Paris.

At the Conciergerie, this 11 November (old style) 21 Brumaire, Year II of the Republic.

Allow me, citizen, despite our differences of opinion, to address myself to you as the longest-standing inmate of our room, to carry out a duty dear to my heart and to express to my former prison comrades my regrets at so sudden a departure, which has not left me time, so to speak, to take my last farewells of them. I hoped to have the pleasure of spending some of my last moments with them and I am deeply grieved to see my hopes frustrated. We have lived in the good company of fellow unfortunates, as prisoners should who are innocent until judgement has been passed on them. I would ask them all, whatever their opinions, to keep a place for me in their memory.

I have not been able to repay to the citizens whose names I do not know, as I had believed I could, the money they forced me to take before my departure. I was led to believe, quite wrongly, that all those found guilty were stripped of their money and forbidden to communicate with anyone. I therefore felt obliged to distribute it among the poor prisoners of the Conciergerie. I am asking my sister to carry out my wishes in this respect. The sum amounts to about seventy *livres* (I have not had time to count it). Indeed I owe that information to them. It may be confirmed by Citizens Viée and Georget, Rue de la Poterie, near the Grève, no. 6, in Paris. I would also ask them to transmit in like fashion, on behalf of my sister, who will no doubt approve it, twenty-five *livres* each to Citizens François and Mougis, porters of the said prison of the Abbaye, and to express to all the warders of that prison in general and to Citizen and Citizeness La Vacquerie in particular my gratitude for all that they have done for me. They have combined the care due to unfortunate prisoners with the rigour of their ministry.

I would beg Citizens Viée and Georget to console my sister, whom I love with all my heart, and my relations and friends.

Kalb[25]

It was at the Abbaye that, on the evening of 13 July 1793, a large, noisy crowd followed a horse-drawn carriage from which emerged a young woman, looking somewhat dishevelled after the rough handling that had preceded her arrest. For murdering Marat, Marie-Anne-Charlotte Corday d'Armont had very nearly been lynched by the crowd.

Charlotte Corday was no doubt one of the more ephemeral characters of the Revolution, but also one of those about whom it would be easy enough to compile an entire library. For, though it did not have a lasting political effect, her gesture aroused great emotion. At the time when writs were out for the arrest of the Girondins, Charlotte was at Caen, where several deputies belonging to that party, including Barbaroux, were trying to get the departmental administration to act against the decisions taken by the National Convention. Affected by the intense propaganda of the Federalists, the young woman thought she saw in Marat the true persecutor of the Girondins. The pretext for her departure for Paris was a classic affair involving an émigré's property. She was in correspondence with a certain Alexandrine Forbin d'Oppède, a former canoness of the Abbaye de Troarn (Calvados) who, from Switzerland, had asked her to intervene with the government on the subject of her property, then under threat of sequestration.

To assist her friend, Charlotte applied to Barbaroux, who, in turn, advised her to see Lauze du Perret, deputy for the Bouches-du-Rhône. According to a denunciation, hitherto unpublished, it would seem that Charlotte Corday took with her to Paris, on 9 July 1793, two manuscripts, General de Wimpfen's *Manifeste* and *Proclamation aux Parisiens,* which had been entrusted to her because she was going to meet Lauze du Perret. These two manuscripts, which were to be printed and distributed throughout Paris, seem to have been handed over by Charlotte, or via Lauze du Perret, to a certain 'Riou' or 'Rivier', the editor of a Paris newspaper.[26]

As we know, Charlotte Corday's mission did not end there: she went on to stab Marat in his bath. Incarcerated for two days at the Abbaye, she came to trial on 17 July 1793 and was condemned to death.

The three notes reproduced below were the last she wrote. The first she addressed to the Committee of General Safety, asking for permission to have her portrait painted; the second was written to her father and the third expresses displeasure with the lawyer who is supposed to defend her, Doulcet de Pontécoulant, who had not turned up. There is nothing surprising about this, since, unknown to her, he had just been arrested himself.

On 15 July 1793, Year II of the Republic.
To the citizens of the Committee of General Safety.

Since I have only a few moments left to live, might I hope, citizens, that you will allow me to have my portrait painted. I would like to leave this token of my memory to my friends.

Indeed, just as one cherishes the image of good citizens, curiosity sometimes seeks out those of great criminals, which serves to perpetuate horror at their crimes. If you deign to attend to my request, I would ask you to send me tomorrow a painter of miniatures. I would also repeat my request to be allowed to sleep alone. Believe, I beg you, in my sincere gratitude.

Marie Corday.

An article published on 27 July in the *Journal de Perlet*, a revolutionary newspaper supporting the moderate tendency, recounts how Citizen Hauër had been seen at the Tribunal by Charlotte Corday, as he was drawing her portrait. She had begged him to accompany her to the criminal chamber while she awaited the result of the judges' deliberations and, finding the portrait 'well executed and a good likeness', had asked him to finish it in her cell. It seems that she continued to pose 'with unimaginable tranquillity and gaiety'.

Another note written after her condemnation expresses forcefully her sense of responsibility for her act and her fear that her family might suffer as a result of it.

To M. Corday d'Armont, Rue du Bègle, at Argentan.

Forgive me, my dear papa, for disposing of my life without your permission. I have avenged many innocent victims. I have prevented many another disaster. The people will one day be disabused and rejoice at being delivered from such a tyrant. I tried to persuade you to let me go to England where I hoped to remain incognito; but I realized how impossible that was. I hope you will not torment yourself on that account. In any case, I think you will have defenders at Caen. I have taken as my counsel Gustave Doulcet de Pontécoulant. Such a crime allows of no defence. It is for form's sake.

Farewell, my dear papa, I beg you to forget me, or rather to rejoice at my fate, its cause is a fine one. I embrace my sister, whom I love with all my heart, and all my relations. Do not forget Corneille's line: 'Le crime fait la honte et non pas l'échafaud.'

Judgement is to be passed on me tomorrow.

This 16 July.

Charlotte Corday's defence was conducted by Chauveau-Lagarde, who pleaded 'fanaticism', which seemed to satisfy the defendant. She still did not know the fate that had befallen the Girondin Doulcet de Pontécoulant when she wrote:

Citizen Doulcet Pontécoulant is a coward for refusing to defend me when it was such an easy matter. The lawyer who did so acquitted himself with all possible dignity and I shall remain grateful to him to the end.

At the Abbaye, the prisoners talked at length and admiringly of Charlotte Corday. Yet her gesture seems to have encouraged a greater degree of repression. From the end of July 1793 new inmates arrived almost daily at the Abbaye. They were mainly Girondins, who suffered particularly at this time. It is said that Vergniaud made the following comment on Charlotte Corday's action: 'She is killing us, but she is teaching us how to die.'[27]

The atmosphere was a little different at the Madelonnettes. A former convent placed under the protection of St Mary Magdalen, it had been turned by the Revolution into a political prison. In the early months of 1793, the establishment had very few inmates, mainly forgers and thieves, but from September on the prison began to fill up. Unfortunately, it could hold only two hundred individuals, so it soon became overcrowded, with a hundred in excess of that number. Some even remember sleeping in the corridors.

The prison keeper, Vaubertrand, was well liked by the prisoners as was his wife, who became the object of a kind of rhyming verse fashionable at the time:

> Dans ton sourire la .... bonté
> Nous peint la plus tendre des ...... mères,
> De ton époux .... l'humanité
> Peint aussi le meilleur des .... pères,
> Chacun de nous serait .... heureux
> Si la loi qui nous fit ses .... frères
> Voulait que ses soins .... généreux
> Pussent adoucir nos .... misères.

A certain Marino, a former porcelain maker and painter by trade, entrusted with the office of police administrator, was also well liked by the prisoners, despite his rather carefree behaviour. One of them, Coittant, remembers seeing him arrive one day ill-dressed and ill-shaven:

> Some of the prisoners tried to present their requests to him. Without even listening to them, Marino went straight up to a rich prisoner he had picked out and, pointing to the poorest ones, said with the utmost gravity:
> 'Look, son, these are the men of my section. You must look after them, you understand?'
> 'Yes, citizen.'
> 'Sit down.'
> 'Yes, citizen.'

'And you'll pay for their food, you understand?' he said, tapping the man's cheek.

'Yes, citizen.'

'Their accommodation, expenses, wine?'

'Yes, citizen.'

'Now, he's the chairman,' he said, pointing to one of them. 'He'll make a note of all the expenses, you understand?'

'Yes, citizen.'

'You're a very rich man – they have nothing. So it's up to you to pay, you understand?'

'Yes, citizen.'

'Don't let me down now!'

'No, citizen.'

'And you'll give them leg of lamb with garlic, potatoes and salad.'

'Yes, citizen.'

After this conversation, Marino gave another little tap on the cheek to his rich prisoner and, apparently in a very good mood, went off whistling.[28]

At the Madelonnettes were imprisoned the royalist writer Chamfort, several councillors from the *Parlement*, the former minister La Tour du Pin, General Lanoue, the administrator Boulainvilliers and a few actors from the Théâtre-Français, including Fleury, who has left us an account of his stay at the Madelonnettes. He tells how, at nightfall, the prisoners organized rather picturesque physical exercises in one of the prison halls.

Thus we took part in that procession, that warlike march. Those darkened corridors, those pale men, those staggering shadows, those will-o'-the-wisps weaving in and out, falling into line, throwing vague reflections on to flower-patterned dressing-gowns, on to white quilted overcoats, on to nightcaps, on to faces that would not have laughed for an empire and all the more comic a sight in that the light, hand-held, coming from below, seemed to smear with bistre all the salient points of the face and bring out only the staring eyes, all that jumble of darkness and light, of movement and repose, vocal outbursts and silences would have been a scene for a skilful painter to catch. The prison keeper's wife sometimes came to see us; she used to say that, once we had got going, we were models worthy of Rembrandt's brush. I think she was flattering us rather, and little Vaubertrand's laugh made me think, more than once, that we were much more like grotesques in the manner of Callot, especially when good Monsieur d'Alleray, holding his candlestick aloft, went and burnt the chin or jabot of

Monsieur the ex-Lieutenant-General de Crosne, who could never understand what it was to start with the left foot.[29]

Late in 1793 the Madelonnettes was evacuated with a view to being reserved for common-law prisoners and a section of the detainees were transferred to Port-Libre.

Port-Libre was the former convent of Port-Royal, from which the nuns had been expelled in 1790 and whose name had been changed, since anything reminiscent of the King was forbidden. Like many other such convents, it had been turned into a prison.

Despite worries about their future, the prisoners were allowed a certain freedom and organized their leisure activities as they wished. Thus a string quartet was improvised. In the chapel, which served as a meeting-hall, the Curé de Marly entranced his listeners on the harp, sometimes accompanying Mlle de Béthisy in her Hymn to the Supreme Being. In the evening, the former chapel became a 'salon'. Everyone brought his own candlestick. In this improvised 'reading-room', a few women embroidered by the fireside. When supper time came round, a large table was set up, and everybody joyfully set about laying the table, forgetting that they were in a prison.

One prisoner has left this account:

Indeed nothing was less like a prison than that house: there were no bars, no locks, the doors were closed by a simple latch. The inmates were well-bred, excellent company, showed consideration for one another, and were most attentive to the women. It was as if we were all members of a single family living in a huge château.

Above the chapel doors was inscribed this optimistic maxim: 'Man cherishes liberty even when he is in prison'.

When necessary, the salon became a refectory. Sometimes two dozen tables of ten places each were laid. At such times, there were two sittings, one at one o'clock, the other at two and as people waited their turn they walked about in the cloisters.

Everybody brought his own plate and spoon – knives and forks were forbidden. The meals were simple, but well-balanced. We still have the menu for 25 and 26 Messidor: soup, skate, artichokes, followed the next day by beef and cabbage, and runner beans.

After washing their hands in the fountain, the stele of which still exists, the prisoners took the air in the garden until nightfall, sitting on a grassy knoll or chatting near an old acacia. It was the hour for the poets . . . three of them were to be found at Port-Royal: Vigée, Florian and Anne-Marie de Beaufort. The last, known as an ardent counter-revolutionary, complained a great deal that she was not allowed to have her young son with her. She had to be content with hearing him declaim:

O vous, dont les sensibles coeurs
Savent aimer avec tendresse,
Venez partager ma tristesse,
Donnez un soupir à mes pleurs;
Et puisse le destin sévère,
Pour vous, hélas! moins rigoureux,
Vous épargner le mal affreux
D'être à la fois captive et mère![30]

Yet she was luckier than another of her companions in captivity, Victor de Broglie,[31] who did not escape death. This is what one witness said of him, just prior to his departure from the Conciergerie:

Although he was informed of his fate two hours before, he was no less tranquil about it. He had just had his portrait painted in miniature; he arranged to have it given to one of his women friends. Vigée was with him and read some of his work; he took out his watch and said: 'The hour approaches; I don't know whether I shall have time to hear you to the end; but no matter, continue until they come to fetch me.'[32]

Next day, shortly before appearing before the Tribunal and knowing that his cause was lost, he wrote this last letter to his wife:

From the Conciergerie, this 9 Messidor
Liberty-Equality

I have been at the Conciergerie since yesterday, my dear Sophie. I go before the Tribunal with an unblemished conscience and the calm that an unshakable patriotism inspires in a courageous man. Whatever the event, he goes to meet it and grasps it firmly. Take care of yourself for the sake of our children, whom I smother with kisses, tears and regrets, as I do your dear self; never forget your poor friend,

Victor de Broglie.[33]

Yet, as Year II advanced, the situation became more threatening, the notions of 'suspect' and 'guilty' tended to merge more and more. The inmates of Port-Libre still did not see things in too tragic a light, however, and a curious mixture of salon-sensitivity and showing-off reigned between the prison walls. These people expressed themselves in pleasing words, little verses, and light-hearted rhymes: 'The Vicomte de Ségur awaited the guillotine surrounded by many, lampooning his gaolers, singing madrigals to the ladies and, under the threat of the blade, maintaining his gaiety and gallant mood.'

But not all laughed. One day it was the departure of Malesherbes and his family for the scaffold, the next, the yelling of Mme de Maleyssie, who was suffering greatly in childbirth. There were the constant complaints of Mme de La Chabaussière, her mother, kept in solitary confinement, or the suicide of the Marquis de Coigny's valet de chambre, found with his throat cut.

Coittant, one of the prisoners in the Luxembourg, has left us a detailed account of all these moments. This is how he describes the scene on 12 Prairial:

> We have just lost the ex-Marquis de La Valette, former guards officer, who has gone before the Revolutionary Tribunal. The cries of his unfortunate wife informed us of the sad event. She hung about her husband's neck, her legs intertwined with his; in that position, she begged the porter to take her off with her husband. This heartrending scene moved everybody except the inexorable porter, who, impatient at the delay, cried out in a harsh voice: 'Come on now, haven't you finished yet?' This wretched porter had already brought despair into the soul of this unfortunate wife. Mme de La Valette's windows looked out on to the garden, where her husband had been playing with a ball.
>   'Call your husband,' the porter had yelled to her.
>   'Why?'
>   'Just call him.'
>   'But, my friend, tell me why?'
>   'To go to the Tribunal.'
>   Hearing this sad news, Mme de La Valette fell stiffly to the floor.

Two weeks later, Coittant had cold sweats:

> I was out walking that morning under the trees of the little cloister when a comrade in misfortune, walking sadly towards me, asked me if I was able to keep steady. I said that I was.
>   'Well, prepare yourself, they've come to fetch you and Gamache for the Tribunal. The policeman is in the records office.'
>   I then went up to my room; I entrusted my watch, my box and the portrait of my Hélène to my friend; I begged him to convey these various objects to her. He promised to do so. He then went down to ascertain what was taking place in the office. He came back, after a quarter of an hour, looking very happy, telling me that a mistake concerning my name had made him tremble for my fate. This news reassured me somewhat, though I was perfectly resigned.[34]

On 7 Floréal a revolutionary general arrived in full uniform, with feathered hat and embroidered collar, a former happy Jacobin, now arrested. A scoffer preceded him through the corridors calling out:

'Roll up, roll up, see the great animal from Africa with sharp teeth, he eats stones, come and see him, gentlemen, come and see him, only two *sols* for a view. This great general of the woods has returned from the deserts of Arabia in a Montgolfier balloon and landed at the Bourbe, roll up, roll up!'

Another former . . . patriot was Citizeness Momoro, who had once represented the goddess Reason, but had been arrested after the condemnation of her husband and Hébert. Did she have in her pocket the last lines that he had addressed to her shortly before mounting the scaffold?

Republican woman, preserve your character, your courage. You know the purity of my patriotism. I shall preserve the same character until death.

Raise my son in Republican principles. You cannot manage the printing-press alone, so dismiss the workers. Hail to the Marat citizenesses! Hail to the Republicans! I'll leave you my memories and my virtues. Marat has taught me to suffer. Your husband, Momoro.[35]

Still at Port-Royal were Fanny de Beauharnais, the old Marquis de Sombreuil, former governor of the Invalides, the writer Richer de Sérizy, Mme de Simiane, La Fayette's mistress and many others. Most of them were lucky enough to be freed after Thermidor.

If Port-Libre seemed like a privileged place, La Force, on the contrary, was one of the most feared of the prisons under the Revolution.

The Hôtel de La Force, which was once situated between the Rue du Roi-de-Sicile and the Rue Pavée, had served as a prison from 1782 and had at first been intended for insolvent debtors. An annex had been built for the use of women, nicknamed the 'Petite-Force', to distinguish it from the Grande-Force, the men's quarters.

Each of the prisons had its own entrance: the first on the Rue Pavée, the second on the Rue du Roi-de-Sicile, but communication was possible between the two buildings on the inside. Moreover, with ingenuity on both sides, a few secret methods of speaking and corresponding had been worked out. A drainpipe served as a speaking tube, the current of a stream brought letters in a clog, which carried the answers back when pulled by a string. It was in this way that Mme de Kolly communicated with her eldest sons during the summer of 1793 (see p. 137).

The façade of the Petite-Force looked rather fearsome. Approach was prevented by stone posts linked by chains. A tall vault sheltered a circular peristyle, in which the carriages could turn round under cover. In 1793, the cell doors shut with a loud crash behind the beautiful Olympe de Gouges, charged with federalism and 'feminism', and on the Duchesse de Bourbon, the sister of Philippe-Égalité.

The façade of the Grande-Force could be seen from the Rue Saint-Antoine through a frightful alleyway bristling with large paving stones and flanked by sordid hovels. Once one had gone through the main gates, one passed successively through two further gates before arriving at the so-called 'records' yard.

The inside of the prison was no more welcoming and the conditions of detention did not help. No communication with the outside world was possible, in principle, but, as one of the prisoners explains, 'our friends and relations were ingenious enough to obtain a few consolations for us . . . in a folded handkerchief, in a pigeon's beak, in the hem of a necktie . . .'[36]

Where food was concerned an improvement appeared with a decree of the Convention of 16 November 1793, compelling the richer prisoners to pay for the meals of the poorer ones, often common-law prisoners.

It was also during 1793 and more particularly 1794 that there flourished in the prisons curious individuals nicknamed '*moutons*', informers who kept the authorities in touch with what was happening inside the prison.

Among those in La Force, the Comte de Ferrières-Sauvebeuf is noteworthy for the sheer quantity of his writings. His reports, which regularly handed over 'infamous villains' to Fouquier-Tinville's mercy, at least have the advantage of providing detailed information as to what took place behind the walls of La Force. Here is his account of the case of one woman, Camille Haller (who belonged to the family of Swiss bankers of the same name), who managed to slip from one prison to the other to be with her lover, the businessman Louis Comte, who was supposed to be in solitary confinement:

In June last, old style, I saw the aforementioned Comte walking in the courtyard of La Force, the police administrators having given the order to the keeper [he was kept in solitary confinement, author's note]. He was with a woman who seemed to me to be hiding her identity under a lace veil. There was a heavy shower and he asked me, when I was close to him, if he could take shelter in my room, which was the first next to the gate. I allowed him to go in and I was not with them.

When he came out, he came up to thank me. Since he was naturally very talkative, he told me that the lady he had been with was the Comtesse Camille, that I had formerly seen her in society and that, since I had a wicked tongue, she had not wished to make her identity known. I then remembered very well her reputation in times gone by, but I said that, after her compliment, she could go and take her frolics elsewhere next time and I told them at the gate that they were not to be allowed in again. I then learnt that Comte was in solitary confinement and that Camille had borrowed a pass from the police administration from another woman, by means of which she had been able to outwit the vigilance of the keeper, who believed that the pass was for the woman who was carrying it.

It was not the practice to give details on the pass and this document had gained her admission. I immediately informed the keeper, who in turn informed the police administration and, next day, if she had turned up again, she would have been arrested.

The first porter in the quarters in which Comte was held had been won over. I learnt this and many other facts from a man who, in the past, had denounced him to Dangé, the administrator, who was subsequently guillotined, and who had overlooked it. This same man had been witness to the fact that Comte wrote to Camille with invisible ink between the lines of newspapers that the porter took to this woman, who, no doubt, was privy to the great plot [the conspiracy abroad, author's note], since she appeared to possess unlimited resources, which I doubt she would have been able to acquire from what remained of her superannuated charms . . .

Ferrières-Sauvebeuf, who spied, listened at doors, observed the comings and goings of prisoners throughout the day, wrote down in the evening the thousand and one everyday facts of prison life. He denounced a certain woman, Joli, purveyor to the prison, who had a monopoly of food supplies. But the food was very bad and Ferrières accused her of selling part of the meat intended for the prisons to her friends. He explained this by the fact that she was the mistress of the Hébertist police adminstrator, Dangé, who was trying to starve the prisoners and provoke a revolt. He tirelessly denounced the stratagem of a certain Delainville, who, abusing his title of *défenseur officieux* gained access to the prisoners and, for a very large sum, arranged their transfer to quiet, less onerous *maisons de santé*:

I can provide the Committee of General Safety with definite evidence concerning the conduct of the aforementioned Delainville, who is well known for his transfers.

I have evidence that Delainville, *défenseur officieux*, obtained permission from the police administration for the transfer of a lottery administrator and a banker to a *maison de santé*. When they turned up at the gate to leave, the keeper found them in such glowing health, that he opposed their departure. But, the next day, despite his insistence, a new, very peremptory order forced him to acquiesce.

Delainville long ago promised to get an old, infirm Englishman called Richard transferred to Belhomme's. This individual thought that he would obtain it more promptly, having handed over to Delainville, through his wife, an advance of fourteen hundred *livres*, as he told me in the courtyard, in the presence of several prisoners . . .

An impenitent scribbler, Ferrières-Sauvebeuf cannot stop himself writing down – he is the only one who does – his slightest observations, his slightest thoughts, beginning with those that concern him directly. Thus he writes to the members of the Committee of General Safety:

I should add, citizens, that in this prison I am regarded by all the prisoners as your spy and that of the Revolutionary Tribunal. I am rewarded with five hundred *livres* a month, though I have been several times to the Revolutionary Tribunal as witness, and yesterday to your committee. If anything consoles me, it is the thought that I am not among those who fear me . . .

And he goes on:

I have given innumerable proofs of my loyalty, but the quality of ex-noble that I have effaced by my revolutionary conduct will no doubt not be enough reason to have me proscribed, since good citizens, born in my former caste, serve the Republic so well as members of the Convention and members of the Committee of Public Safety . . .

Among the many individuals against whom he gave evidence and was to send to the scaffold, one might mention André Chénier, Princess Caroline of Monaco, the Duc and Duchesse du Châtelet, the Comte de Saint-Paul, Louis Comte, Mme d'Éprémesnil, General de Flers, the Prince d'Hénin, the Comtesse d'Ossun, and the police administrators Dangé, Soulès and Froidure.[37] Most of those chosen by Ferrières-Sauvebeuf belonged to the nobility and the haute bourgeoisie, those who possessed large fortunes that fell into the hands of the Republic. His aristocratic origins enabled him to inform the Committee of General Safety most usefully about the fortune and domicile of certain prisoners, or the family connections and whereabouts of the property of others.

On the other side of the Seine, quite close to the Jardin des Plantes, was Sainte-Pélagie. In the seventeenth century, between the Hôtel de la Pitié and the Rue de la Clef, a few buildings were converted into a hospice to house prostitutes. The establishment had been given the name Sainte-Pélagie, in memory of a courtesan of Antioch, who, after scandalizing her contemporaries with her debauchery, became converted and ended her days with a reputation for sanctity. Sainte-Pélagie served as a house of refuge for 'sinful women' up to the Revolution, when it became a political prison. Several well-known prisoners stayed there. One of the first was the Duc de Biron, a general in the Republican army, recalled from Italy for combating the insurrection in Vendée. Suspected of treason, he had rightly been arrested, it seemed, according to the words of his good friend the Duchesse de Fleury, 'such was the inertia of their chief [Biron] that it had acted in a sense as a column of the enemy army'.[38]

The general stayed at Sainte-Pélagie for six months before being guillotined in December 1793. If Mme Roland is to be believed, he was an extremely gallant gentleman and often visited the ladies. In a letter to Montané, a prisoner in La Force, she reassures her correspondent, while making fun of his anxieties regarding his wife, herself a prisoner at Sainte-Pélagie. She tells him that although Biron makes regular visits to the ladies' quarters, he always comes accompanied 'by the best possible protection against any such alarming attempts on her virtue', namely, Mlle Raucourt, a charming actress from the Comédie-Française. Later, from the Conciergerie, Biron was to write this last letter to a certain Citizeness Laurent:

> In a few hours my fate will be sealed; my dear, hapless friend, you are the more to be pitied, for your sufferings will not end so soon and you will weep for me for a long time to come. If I could glimpse some happiness for you in the future, that hope would much mitigate the harshness of my fate. I have every reason to believe that my sex and the only friend that still remains to me in the world will take good care of you. I recommend you to the care of your brother and even of your lady companion. She will carry out that trust so necessary to my tranquillity.
> Farewell, farewell, I embrace you again and for the last time.
>
> Biron.[39]

After a stay of several weeks at the Abbaye, Mme Roland had arrived at Sainte-Pélagie on 25 June 1793, accused of complicity with the Girondins. Her husband, accused of the same crimes, had been able to flee, but took his own life on learning of his wife's execution.

In her Memoirs, she speaks at length of her stay in the convent of Sainte-Pélagie. She describes the dirty, stuffy cell: 'This, then, is the condition in which the worthy companion of so good a man finds herself; if this is the price of virtue on earth, do not be surprised if I despise life!'

After trying to prove her innocence in a letter to Robespierre and contemplating suicide, she wrote down her last thoughts: 'To be or not to be, that is the question! It will be resolved soon enough for me.'

According to the woman who served her, Mme Roland was like many others: 'In front of you, she summoned up all her strength, but in her room she would sometimes stay three hours at a time, looking out of her window, weeping.'

Two days after the queen's execution, on 18 October 1793, she did not seem to entertain many illusions as to her fate when she wrote to her daughter:

> I do not know, my little friend, if it will be given to me to see you or to write to you again. Remember your mother. These few words contain all the best that I can say to you. You have seen me made happy by performing my duties and being useful to those in affliction. This is the only way to be. You have seen me peaceful in misfortune and captivity, because I had no remorse and because I had the memory and joy that good actions leave after them. These are the only ways of bearing the ills of life and the vicissitudes of fate.
>
> Perhaps – and I hope this is so – such trials as mine do not await you: but there are others against which you will have to defend yourself no less. A strict, well-occupied life is the best protection against all these perils and necessity, as well as wisdom, imposes upon you the law of working seriously.
>
> Be worthy of your parents; they leave you fine examples; and if you know how to benefit from them, your life will not have been in vain. Farewell, beloved child, you whom I have nourished with my own milk and whom I would wish to imbue with all my feelings. The time will come when you will be able to judge the effort that I am making at this moment not to be moved to tears at the memory of you. I press you to my heart.
>
> Farewell, my Eudora.

Shortly afterwards, we see her back, much affected by the trial of the Girondins, during which she had had to answer questions that were 'outrageous to her honour'.

On the day of her condemnation, dressed all in white, her long black hair hanging to her waist, she made a gesture to the other prisoners who watched her pass to the effect that her head was about to fall. Riouffe remembers 'her large, dark, expressive, gentle eyes', eyes that, a few hours later, would stare at the colossal statue of Liberty, then meet for a moment those of her executioner.[40]

Among the inmates of Sainte-Pélagie were also Louis XV's ex-favourite, Mme du Barry, who stayed for several weeks in a single cell on the second floor of the prison. While trying to convince herself that her case was going well, she had to face several interrogations. But the poor woman did not know how much Fouquier-Tinville knew about her past counter-revolutionary activities or her skills in hiding in England jewellery that she claimed had been stolen.

She did not know that the Committee of General Safety had received reports denouncing her and possessed a document proving that she was in close relations with the 'Enemies of the Revolution' in England. In fact, during her sojourns in London, she shared a huge house with such former ministers as Bertrand de Molleville, with whom she plotted to get money and valuable objects out of France.

Tracked down and confused, Mme du Barry admitted a great deal and was to prove accommodating. She was condemned as much on account of the image that people had of her – that of a latter-day Messalina – as of the facts – which were extremely damaging to her. The circumstances of her death, transmitted from prison to prison, froze with terror the hardest-hearted listener.[41]

Others were more fortunate. Fifteen actresses from the Théâtre-Français, who, both in town and on stage, had not concealed their hostility to the Revolution, had just been arrested. Imprisoned on 3 September, they owed their celebrity to the fact that the formalities imposed on other prisoners were dispensed in their case. On the register, against each name, appeared the words: 'This citizeness is sufficiently well known not to have her profession specified here.' According to Mme Roland, the actresses took the whole thing extremely lightly:

> Laughter was heard in the room next door. The actresses of the Théâtre-Français, arrested yesterday and brought to Sainte-Pélagie, were today taken to their homes for the removal of the seals and brought back to prison, where the officer of the peace supped and amused himself with them. The meal was merry and noisy: gay words flew back and forth and foreign wines sparkled. The place, the objects, the persons and my occupation formed a very piquant contrast.

The unfortunate women were nevertheless to have some anxious moments, for the Commune did not seem disposed to freeing them.

Fortunately, certain files had been lost and, with them, the way to the scaffold.[42]

Mme de Bonneuil, whose perfect beauty was so appreciated by Mme Vigée-Lebrun, was also lucky. She had conspired actively, transferring money abroad and trying to corrupt certain members of the Convention, especially just prior to the liquidation of the Compagnie des Indes (of which she was a shareholder). On July 1793, a denunciation addressed to the Committee of General Safety brought her to Sainte-Pélagie.[43] Her memory is associated with that of André Chénier, who loved her madly and immortalized her in his writings under the name of 'Camille'.

The prison also had a number of well-known inmates: the journalist Ducray-Duminil, the actress Rose-Claire Lacombe, founder of the Club of Revolutionary Republicans, Gracchus Babeuf, the painter Hubert Robert.[44] All these inmates lived in constant anxiety as to their fate. One of them, Roucher, has left this memory:

> An hour ago I was awoken with a start. There was a loud noise in the corridors and doors were banging: 'Citizen Such-and-Such, Citizen here, Citizen there! Quickly! Quickly! Get up, you're going to Saint-Lazare! Get up! Look, by the gates, there's light!'
>
> I get up. First I put my portfolio in order, my treasury where your letters are, my dear daughter. I pack my books in the small trunk. I write a few lines to Maman to inform her of the event and I am ready to go. The door opens. Three people's magistrates, wearing sashes, preceded by two resinous, smoky torches, come in:
>
> 'What is your name?'
>
> 'Roucher.'
>
> 'Have you been here long?'
>
> 'In nine days, it will be four months.'
>
> They look for my name on three lists.
>
> 'Right! Jean-Antoine Roucher, man-of-letters.'
>
> 'That is I.'
>
> 'You're to be transferred. Get ready.'
>
> 'I am ready.'
>
> They go out, call at the other cells; the door closes and I busy myself pleasantly enough awaiting this general nocturnal translation . . .[45]

The prison of the Anglaises,[46] which owes its name to the former convent of the English Benedictine nuns, is a good example of a community entirely imprisoned within its own buildings. Indeed, on 3 October 1793, some days after the production of the law concerning suspects, all the nuns were denounced for holding secret ceremonies in their convent.

They were imprisoned in their own buildings and, from the following month, the house began to receive its first prisoners from outside. A constant coming and going now began between the Anglaises and the other Paris *maisons d'arrêt*, particularly Sainte-Pélagie, Port-Libre and the Salpêtrière.

One of the detainees, a certain Foignet, who arrived in late January 1794, has left this account of his stay:

> It looks a very fine place: on the garden side, it is surrounded by a double wall: the outer wall has a huge kitchen garden, the second, which was being built when we arrived, solidly enough to with-stand a siege, complete with broken glass on top, encloses an area (formerly a graveyard), which is used by the detainees for exercise.[47]

He describes the prisoners playing backgammon and vingt-et-un and observes that the inmates treated one another in the 'most polite and most considerate manner possible'. He has some picturesque remarks on the way time weighed heavily on them:

> We occupied ourselves with drinking, eating, smoking, going upstairs, coming downstairs and sleeping . . . Valuable time, which might have been employed serving our country, was dissipated in card games or other debaucheries.
>
> Several young men, among whom I was one, with nothing to do from morning till night, tried to forget their misfortunes by indulging in pastimes that left them next day with nothing but regrets . . .[48]

When Foignet arrived, there were already eighty prisoners there. Two-thirds of them were women, including all the Benedictine nuns, later transferred to Vincennes.

Visits, accompanied by searches, took place from time to time, even at night. During one search, Foignet lost his brandy, while others lost their assignats or jewellery.

Among the women held in the Anglaises, some were to see their fate highly compromised by their links with the Baron de Batz, one of the most curious characters of the time, a fervent advocate of the restoration of the monarchy. Still at liberty, he had already made several attempts to free the royal family and bribed a number of parliamentarians, which, he thought, would throw discredit on the Convention. Sought by the police throughout France, he escaped all the traps laid for him, because, no doubt, he was well informed up to the last moment.

In May 1794, the Committee of General Safety appointed one of its agents, Dossonville, to do everything possible to capture the baron. Now, one of his former mistresses, Marie Babin de Grandmaison, had been in the Anglaises for several months, as had another woman, Mme Duval d'Eprémesnil, whose family had sheltered the baron several times in their Château de Maréfosse, near Le Havre.

So Dossonville instructed one of his '*moutons*' to get the detainees to talk: he promised Marie Babin de Grandmaison her liberty in exchange for definite information about Batz. The poor woman, though she had been in prison for six months, thought that he was hiding near Le Havre under the name of Robert . . .[49] Françoise d'Eprémesnil refused to say a word. Both women were implicated in the trial of the 'conspirators abroad', and were decapitated on 29 Prairial Year II, together with fifty-two other persons. Among them, on that day, was another inmate of the Anglaises, though she was not directly concerned in the Batz affair; her strange case is worth recalling.

Mme de Sainte-Amaranthe was under the impression that she could get through the Revolution, while making a fortune out of the gaming-house, which, through her friendships, had become a hotbed of counter-revolution. Denounced for her *salon*, which had become 'infected with the most revolting aristocracy', she was questioned, then arrested after the fall of her Dantonist protectors. Legend has it that Robespierre had her condemned, together with her young son and her very beautiful daughter, who had previously repulsed his advances. The enemies of the Incorruptible, by deliberately exaggerating the repression, had, in fact, found a good way of hastening his fall and besmirching his memory.

The moving departure of the Sainte-Amaranthes threw the detainees into consternation, but life resumed its usual course, everyone trying, in innumerable different ways, to stifle the fears that gripped him.[50]

2

A DIABOLICAL MANOEUVRE: THE PRISON 'PLOTS'

Up to May 1794, the number of those condemned to death seldom exceeded twenty-five persons per day, even if there had already been several 'large batches', including those of the former members of the *Parlement*, the *fermiers généraux* and a group of twenty-five individuals, including several leading figures of the *ancien régime*, notably a few members of the family of Loménie de Brienne and Louis XVI's younger sister, the unfortunate Princess Élisabeth. Suddenly, in June and July, the number of condemnations to death increased. The law of 22 Prairial Year II (10 June 1794), which abolished a defendant's right to any defence, was the cause of this, in addition to what were beginning to be called the 'prison plots'.

Bicêtre

These so-called prison plots were a diabolical invention that made it possible to lump together a large number of prisoners under the same fallacious charge of rebellion. These 'plots' had first been worked out and implemented at Bicêtre before spreading to other places of detention. But why there particularly? In the popular mind, Bicêtre had kept its reputation as a bad place, a sort of sink of iniquity.

It should be said that from the late Middle Ages, and well before it became a prison, it was already a much feared place, housing a population of 'outcasts' of all kinds. Nevertheless its history had begun better when in the mid-thirteenth century, Louis IX, wishing to encourage the development of monastic institutions, brought to Paris a community of Chartreux and gave them a property situated on the plateau of Gentilly. Later, Jean de Pontoise, Bishop of Winchester, acquired the property and turned the charterhouse cloister into a magnificent feudal dungeon. (Perhaps 'Winchester' had been contracted to 'Wincestre', then to 'Bicestre'.) But this good period did not last very long and Bicêtre soon became a place of ill repute. In the seventeenth century, the medieval ruins, which were supposed to be a shelter for brigands and ghosts, were replaced by new hospital buildings; the hospice then became a prison, perhaps one of the most terrible. In it were thrown, pell-mell, madmen, swindlers, syphilitics, murderers, vagabonds, and delinquents of all kinds. The prisoners were regularly beaten: the sinner had to expiate his sin and was therefore subjected to a childish punishment that demeaned a man and deprived him of all dignity. At the time of the massacres of September 1792, the prison contained mainly common-law prisoners and convicts waiting to be transferred to the galleys: it was on them that the fury of the '*Septembriseurs*' fell.[51]

The following year, Bicêtre housed a large number of individuals who had been charged or condemned for trafficking in false assignats. This was a crime that, in principle, should have brought them before the Criminal Tribunal of their *département*, not the Revolutionary Tribunal, but ambiguous legislation kept up a certain confusion between those charged with minor currency offences, which appertained to the common law, and the counter-revolutionaries, who were trying to undermine the national currency. So a great many traffickers in false assignats, who were properly common-law prisoners, were to be found in Bicêtre, without anyone really knowing whether their intentions were in fact political. The idea of the prison plot seems to have been born out of this situation, with the diabolical help of one of the detainees, a certain Valagnos.

Valagnos found himself in Bicêtre among a whole population of common-law prisoners including, towards the end of 1793, as many aristocrats as businessmen charged with financial offences. There were also 'politicals', including Valagnos, who had been condemned by the Revolutionary Tribunal.

It occurred to the members of the Committee of General Safety and to Fouquier-Tinville that Valagnos could be used as a 'straw man' in an attempt to give credence to the existence of a 'plot' to help prisoners escape.

In the hope of getting a remission for himself, Valagnos agreed to denounce a 'plot' fomented by prisoners in Bicêtre. Encouraged by a former jeweller, Dupaumier, now a police administrator, he drew up lists, named witnesses and made statements in Fouquier-Tinville's presence. Meanwhile, the reality and importance of a 'plot' had been raised in the National Convention by Voulland,[52] a member of the Committee of General Safety, on 8 Floréal. Taken in,

the deputies suspended the implementation of the sentence condemning Valagnos to deportation so that an investigation might
proceed.

Thus encouraged, Valagnos confirmed his statements: on 28
Prairial, thirty-seven prisoners in Bicêtre were sent to the scaffold.
On 8 Messidor, thirty-eight appeared before the Tribunal: two were
acquitted, the others guillotined. Among those unfortunates, some
had been condemned by the Criminal Tribunal, but others had not
yet been tried. And when they were brought before the Revolutionary Tribunal on the charge of conspiracy, the law of 22 Prairial had
already abolished the investigation preceding trial and all means of
defence.[53]

The diabolical invention of the prison plots had just been born. It
was now to spread to other prisons, as Louis Blanc wrote in his
Histoire de la Révolution: '. . . To purge the population seemed
necessary to the party that had Barère as its orator, and he, concealing
his thoughts so little, declared aloud in the Convention that the
Committee of Public Safety had taken steps and in two months the
prisons would be evacuated.'[54]

This is indeed what happened from June 1794. Several prisons
were 'evacuated' by this method, beginning with the Luxembourg,
which had the largest number of prisoners.

The Luxembourg

This was the pleasantest, perhaps the most comfortable of the
'political' prisons. The keeper, Benoît, received the cartloads of
suspects that arrived every day in a friendly, polite manner. An
anonymous prisoner, probably one of the very first, has left this
choice account:

> It is a rather entertaining sight to see arriving in some wretched
> carriage two marquises, a duchess, a marchioness, a count, an abbé
> and two countesses who have a headache on getting in and faint on
> getting out. Not long ago I saw the wife of Philippe, who was
> recently guillotined, arrive; her room is next to that of Basire and
> Chabot, who are still in solitary confinement, and are filled with
> gloom whenever they hear the shrill voice of a pedlar crying, 'Old
> Duchesne's great anger against the monk Chabot'.
>
> In the same corridor are M. de la Borde de Méréville, M. le
> Président Nicolai and Mélin, a former civil servant in the Ministry
> of War under Ségur. In the other corridor, on the left, are M. de la

Ferté, M. le Duc de Lévi, M. le Marquis de Fleury, M. le Comte de Mirepoix; every morning, on rising, they get out their telescopes and are delighted to see that their houses are still standing in the Rue de l'Université. At the end of the corridor, in the library, is a bunch of generals who recount their victories to one another.

In a room on the left, living in conjugal peace, are M. le Maréchal and Mme la Maréchale de Mouchy, who declare that the revolutionary committee have no sense locking up people of their quality, who have handed over their horses to the army and given five hundred *livres* for the widows of the section.

The marshal wears a square-cut brown coat, a knee-length jacket, has white hair and always looks like a protestant minister. His wife has adopted the pleasant costume of a female *sans-culotte*, while keeping the shape of the *caraco* of '77, with its two furbelows behind. It is quite common to encounter the aforementioned *maréchale* wearing a bum-freezer, a candle in her left hand, a cane in her right, climbing the stairs with the haste of a shepherdess from Suresnes climbing the Mont Valérien.

The prisoners are ten or twelve to a room; each of them makes whatever arrangements he can, like Robinson Crusoe when he had given up hope of ever seeing a ship enter the bay; everybody has his own trestle bed and little mattress. Some cook and hang the leg of lamb at the window to make it more tender, others have recourse to the perpetual soup pot of the traitor Coste. The rich look after the poor, with good grace and without prompting. Everybody fraternizes . . .[55]

Another detainee, however, does not seem to notice the same class ecumenism:

The nobility usually kept themselves to themselves, having very little to do with the citizens of the sections of Paris. The Rues de l'Université, de Grenoble, Saint-Dominique, which were heavily represented in the Luxembourg, kept up the strictest etiquette; people called one another Monsieur le Prince, Monsieur le Duc, Monsieur le Comte, Monsieur le Marquis, etc.; they held their salons with the utmost gravity and contended for precedence and visits.

All these 'visits' were to serve as a pretext for the '*moutons*' to denounce 'suspect gatherings' of aristocrats among themselves and to provide motives for the imaginary plots of which the prisoners were soon to be accused.

In the Luxembourg men and women could meet during the day: 'Acquaintances were already being struck up and tiny committees being formed in ever narrower circles,' one detainee tells us.

Versifying, card-playing and music, not forgetting backbiting, filled up the days. Love had a particular part to play: a few ladies rallied to the flag of gallantry. The newcomers among the women soon adapted to this amorous libertinage and, in any case, they all knew that a pregnant woman would have her sentence of death postponed. Sometimes love was more than a pastime. Some of the women were passionately making up for years of forced abstinence, while others managed to bribe the gaolers to allow them to spend the night in the arms of a man, to be followed, next day, by eternal night.

In the Luxembourg, the scandal of which Mme d'Ormesson was both author and victim much amused her fellow captives. Desperate for affection, she was discovered behind a screen in the company of a young man belonging to the prison staff. Furious, the lady began to shriek at the top of her voice, pretending that she had been taken by force and, availing herself of the supreme argument, fainted. The young man had just enough time to disappear as discreetly as he had come.

As a result of this little affair, the police administrator, Marino, gathered all the ladies together, including the old dowagers with their lorgnettes, and upbraided them: 'Are you aware of what the public is saying? . . . That the Luxembourg is the first brothel in Paris; that you are a lot of tarts, and that we supply you with pimps!'

The predictable result was that the men and the women were separated definitively. Everybody complained, but the administration would not be moved.[56]

Meanwhile, prisoners continued to roll in regularly.

The Paris prisons were getting crowded with detainees, pouring in from every corner of the country, transferred from prison to prison.

The tribunals were insufficient to judge so many individuals, most of whose files did not exist or had been lost and who appeared on the prison registers under false names. To remedy this overcrowding, the People's Commission had been set up by 23 Ventôse Year II to examine why all these suspects were being held and to suggest to the Committees of Public Safety and of General Safety what should be done with them: freedom for some, imprisonment or deportation for others, appearance before the Revolutionary Tribunal for those considered to be guilty of the most serious crimes. But this procedure was implemented with extraordinary slowness and in fact the Revolutionary Tribunal continued to pass judgement on the basis of the new law of 22 Prairial, which had also been functioning and allowed it to condemn individuals without investigation, defence or witnesses.

These People's Commissions, introduced by Robespierre, might have avoided excessive repression, but, by impeding their setting up, the enemies of the Incorruptible had found the worst way of getting rid of him and discrediting the 'virtuous Revolution'. So many prisoners, who might have expected that a commission would have decided in their favour, found themselves caught up again in the inextricable, invisible network of pseudo-plots.

The first document produced by these odious machinations was a report dated 3 Messidor and signed 'Herman',[57] an individual whom Robespierre was later to learn to mistrust. This report describes the disturbances in the – then overcrowded – prisons, disturbances that gave credence to the existence of conspirators or agitators that had to be eliminated.

It is a demonstrable fact, too notorious to require further proof, that all the factions that have been successively brought down had their connections and spies in the various prisons of Paris. These individuals were acting on behalf of others, outside the prison, who were planning to stain Paris with blood and destroy liberty.

The Commission entrusted with the general supervision of the prisons cannot but see that all those villains who have had a hand in such plans to destroy liberty, in such particular plots, still exist in the prisons and form a separate gang. This makes supervision extremely laborious and a common cause of disorder, a continual source of attempts to escape, a daily gathering of individuals whose whole existence is consumed in oaths against liberty and its defenders.

It would be possible to discover those who, in each prison, served and are likely to serve the various factions, the various plots, those who, at this very moment, cannot contain their fury or prevent themselves from declaring what they are. Perhaps it might be necessary to purge the prisons at one fell swoop and free the ground of Liberty of these filthy rejects of mankind. Justice would thus be done and it would be easier to establish order in the prisons.

The Commission asks to be allowed to carry out such researches and to report back with its results to the Committee of Public Safety. In consequence it suggests that the following order be issued:

'The Committee of Public Safety authorizes the Commission of the Civil, Police and Tribunals administrations to seek out in the prisons of Paris those who had a hand in the various factions and plots that the National Convention has destroyed and whose leaders it has punished, in addition to those who, in the prisons, were the spies and agents of those factions and plots, and must themselves have plotted, on innumerable occasions, the massacre of patriots and the ruin of liberty. The Commission is ordered to report back to the Committee without delay.

'Furthermore, the police, in concert with the police administration, are to take all necessary steps to establish order in the prisons.'

Signed Herman.

The fear that agitation in the prisons might lead the people to massacre all the inmates led the Committee of Public Safety to issue on 17 Messidor an order that a daily account be presented to it of the behaviour of inmates in the various prisons of Paris and that those who had 'attempted revolt or incited unrest' be tried within twenty-four hours by the Revolutionary Tribunal. Wasting no time, Herman, that very night, brought a hundred and fifty-seven persons before the Tribunal on the evidence of a report affirming the existence of a plot in the Luxembourg.

In order to give greater verisimilitude to this 'plot', certain members of the prison staff, together with '*moutons*', did not hesitate to declare that this 'plot' followed another (equally imaginary) one that had taken place some time before and had led to the decapitation of General Dillon and the deputy Simon (they had been accused of trying to escape, to take over the Convention and to free Danton and Camille Desmoulins, whose trial was in progress!). The accusation brought against the victims of the 'great' plot in the Luxembourg was also based on denunciations, produced to order, such as that of the prison warder who testified against several dozen 'accomplices of the Dillon and Simon plot . . .' An unpublished note from another, particularly determined informer, proves beyond doubt Herman's premeditation in the massacre to come:

> Citizen, I would like to have a meeting with the People's Commission concerning the opinion of a number of individuals who pass as good citizens, but are false.
>
> I beg you to allow me to appear before you, and you will know my opinion and know that I have deigned to give information to the Tribunal.
>
> Boyavel, Lieutenant in the Chasseurs,
> this 17 Messidor, Year III.

It was just such individuals as this Boyaval who helped draw up these long lists of detainees, who were then accused of plotting, or of not having denounced the plot.

On 19, 21 and 22 Messidor, the heads of a hundred and forty-six prisoners in the Luxembourg fell on the scaffold. Among them were to be found a former brigadier, Tardieu de Maleyssie, his wife and two daughters, the younger having, it is said, demanded to be allowed to accompany her family to the scaffold. Less than two weeks later, one of the People's Commissions, set up by Robespierre and paralysed by his enemies, condemned Tardieu de Maleyssie's family simply to deportation.[58]

Meanwhile, investigations had been opened simultaneously in the prisons of the Plessis, Saint-Lazare and the Carmes. But the denunciation of imaginary plots was launched. It was still to have an effect on other prisons.

The Plessis

The Plessis owed its name to its founder, Geoffroy du Plessis, a protégé of Philippe IV le Bel. In 1646, the union of this college with the Sorbonne had increased its renown and the Revolution brought very little change to its organization until the abolition of the Sorbonne on 5 April 1792.

The College then survived thanks to a number of laws passed in 1793 by which teaching was allowed to continue on a temporary basis. Between October 1793 and 1796 part of the Plessis, on the Rue Fromontel, was occupied by the Égalité prison, reserved for those accused of counter-revolution. Pupils and masters, who had sought refuge in the older part, facing the Rue Saint-Jacques, continued to study and teach as before.

In 1794, the number of inmates suddenly increased. The reasons for imprisonment were practically always the same: conspiracy against the Republic, statements in favour of the re-establishment of the monarchy, financial support to the external enemies of the Republic, giving asylum to suspects, etc.

Men were separated from women. Inmates held 'as a measure of general safety' were mixed with suspects, who complained about this. Among them were the very aristocratic Duchesse de Duras (daughter of the Maréchal de Mouchy), who had been transferred from Chantilly on 5 April 1794. She remembers having occupied a cell from which she had a good view of Notre-Dame, Saint-Sulpice and the Val-de-Grâce. But her furniture was very sparse: 'Our mattresses were on the floor and the wall served as a pillow. Fortunately, the sheets were freshly laundered, which kept one clean.'

Very soon, the prisoners became aware of what was happening at the Conciergerie: the Dames de Bussy and de Grimaldi, who had been taken there and brought back prior to mounting the scaffold, explained to them how dozens of individuals stopped there before appearing before the Tribunal and how the carts were filled regularly every day. People in the Plessis were now very worried indeed:

The removal of the victims was becoming more and more frequent: usually it happened as we were walking in the courtyard. I thought I saw the unfortunate M. Titon, a councillor at the Paris *Parlement*, under the windows of his wife and daughter, who had not been given permission to take their final sad farewell. It was then five o'clock in the evening and, next day, at noon, he was no more.

Carts arrived at different times and the defendants were packed into them. Fouquier-Tinville's carriage arrived. That man's coachman was certainly worthy of such a master; as the victims got into the cart, he cut capers and his clothes were those of a buffoon. It is almost impossible to describe, especially when such scenes are repeated several times a day, the terror aroused in us when the great gates opened. I can still hear their banging echoing in my ears.

The clerks of the Revolutionary Tribunal preceded the carriages, their hands filled with indictments. For a moment there was a terrifying silence, like death itself. Everyone thought that the fatal summons would be postponed for him; our faces betrayed our anxiety, our heart and minds were in the grip of fear. The clerks went along the corridors, calling out the names of those who were to leave, giving them only a quarter of an hour to get ready. Almost struck dumb with fear, we took leave of one another for ever, not knowing whether we would still be alive at ten o'clock next morning. One's sleep is light when accompanied by such anxieties, and interrupted so often by the arrival of new convoys.

On the eve of the Festival of the Supreme Being, all the detainees were brought down into the courtyard, which we found filled with an enormous quantity of branches and foliage. We were told to make garlands of them, to decorate the gates. I pretended to work at it for a few minutes, then retired to my room; several of our wretched women inmates performed their task with much zeal and wanted to set up a Liberty Tree in the middle of the yard. The keeper, less absurd than they, would not let them do so, saying that such a decoration would not be suitable for a prison. They danced in the yard. The gaolers attended this strange festival [it was Whit Sunday], a day when Robespierre allowed the worship of a God providing he did not bear that name. One of them sang my praises (he was not a bad fellow) and told me that he thought I would behave in a fitting manner when I went to the guillotine.

Convoys arrived every minute from all over the country. One

contained eighty peasant women from the Vivarais, wearing strange costume. We asked them why they had been arrested; from what we could understand of their patois, it was because they had gone to mass.

This crime was regarded as so serious that they had been sent to the Tribunal, which our merrier comrades called 'Fouquier's shop'.

Some ladies from Normandy came by, visibly terror-stricken. They had not brought their costumes, but they spent their time from morning till night writing their memoranda and petitions, a dangerous habit during the Terror, calculated only to hasten the moment of death.[59]

Several of these women inmates were denounced as conspirators with the Duchesse de Duras. It should be said that some of them were under particular threat: the Creole Montréal, mistress of the English banker Walter Boyd; the wife of the Swiss Romey; the wife of Deveaux, secretary to the Baron de Batz; the Comtesse de Linières, friend of the Swiss banker Perrégaux – traces of 'the most odious libertinage' had been found at her home; Mme William, *née* Arabella Mallet, a relation of the bankers of that name; Mme de Turpin, wife of the former director of the Treasury, who was particularly well informed on the theft of the crown jewels. A whole list to which should be added the sister-in-law of the *fermier général* Douet, Mme Blondel, to whom Malesherbes, on the eve of his arrest, had entrusted Louis XVI's secret archives: papers that, according to his nephew, d'Antraigues, 'would make the hair stand on end when they are known'. All these women had been denounced to the Committee of General Safety by one of the inmates, Jeanne Ferniot, Hugues' widow, the only female prisoner to our knowledge to have acted as an informer.[60]

In the men's section, this role was taken by the son of a former councillor to the Besancon *Parlement*, Courlet de Boulot, who claimed wrongly to be the Comte de Vernantois, but who was in fact of noble origin. This was in no way unusual. Indeed among the detainees rightly or wrongly named as informers were a number of nobles or relations of nobles: the Comtes de Ferrières-Sauvebeuf and Baraguey-d'Hilliers, Prince Charles of Hesse, the Marquis de Saint-Hurugue being the best known.

Courlet proved to be an excellent informer in the prison of the Anglaises, only to appear on 28 Prairial before the Revolutionary Tribunal with Batz's 'accomplices'. He had given evidence for the prosecution against the defendants and had naturally been spared.

Transferred to the Plessis, he was given the task of organizing a 'plot'. But he proved a clumsy operator: his manoeuvres met with the disapproval of the prison keeper, Haly, and of another informer called d'Aubigny.

> It was all agreed: the calumny would be set up in such a way that everybody accused in that prison would be sacrificed with the utmost speed. But before judgement was passed, a certain d'Aubigny had second thoughts and consulted a certain Toustin, who convinced him of the full horror of what he was doing . . .

A report addressed by Citizen Drouet, a guard at the Plessis, to Citizen Sanson, a captain in the gendarmerie attending the tribunals, dated 18 Messidor, tells how a 'thick knotted rope' hung from the roof of the prison to the first floor. The same report also tells how the keeper, Haly, removed the rope, declaring that it had been left there by workmen during repairs to the building and had not, therefore, been placed there by prisoners attempting to escape.

At the Tribunal, this paucity of proper evidence meant that the prosecution lost its case. On 28 Messidor, nine of the eighteen defendants were acquitted. One witness tells us:

> For lack of evidence, the proceedings were discontinued, but, after the hearing, Haly, the keeper, was ill treated. It was said that he was the reason why the Tribunal 'made a duck', that if he had given the proper evidence things would have turned out differently . . .

Later, Courlet de Boulot, who had been approached by the mysterious organizers of 'plots', was guillotined on 9 Thermidor, twenty-four hours before Robespierre.

Another document reveals the responsibility of Fouquier-Tinville in this affair and the haste with which Courlet, who possessed so many secrets, was got rid of. One denunciation against him was painfully extracted from an inmate called Jacquemin in the morning of 9 Thermidor:

> Since I was not expecting Courlet to be taken to the Tribunal today, I put off denouncing him until this morning: yesterday, on the subject of the prison plots, he told me that they would all take place, but they did not dare to revive the one in the Plessis, which had already been attempted twice, that in the first he had been charged and that in the second he had been called as a witness, and he added that the Revolutionary Tribunal was nothing less than that of 2 September [1792] in another form . . . His somewhat threatening behaviour would rather have had the effect of preventing the discovery of a plot if any had existed to be discovered . . .

During the trial of Fouquier-Tinville the writer Langeac was to confirm that 'Courlet had been dealt with in such haste to prevent him revealing secrets and exposing the manoeuvres that were then being practised.'[61] In other words, Fouquier-Tinville and the instigators of the prison plots used men like Courlet, whose counter-revolutionary crimes were a guarantee of their devotion and whom they could break at will if their work was not considered to be up to the required standard.

Saint-Lazare

Unlike the prison of the Plessis, that of Saint-Lazare, which we know through the paintings and drawings of the artist Hubert Robert, was to provide the scaffold with an important contingent of victims.

The 'maison Lazare', as it was called in 1793, was situated in northern Paris on the edge of the Faubourg Saint-Denis, almost surrounded by fields. From 29 Nivôse Year II, the date when Saint-Lazare became a prison, to 12 Pluviôse, close on 625 prisoners were held there. They came from La Force, the Madelonnettes, the Plessis, Sainte-Pélagie and Bicêtre.

On one register, the general reasons for imprisonment were listed thus: suspect, highly suspect, related to an émigré, as a measure of general safety, cause unexplained (awaiting new orders).

One prisoner remembers that at the time when Saint-Lazare was opened the police administration of the Commune of Paris had transferred from Bicêtre a large number of common-law prisoners, in general detested by the people, and had mixed them with mere suspects. The Hébertists, who were close to the Commune, felt threatened and thought by this manoeuvre to be able to organize a prison uprising, which would justify a massacre of the prisoners. Such a terrible event would, in turn, assist them in seizing power. This manoeuvre, though carefully planned, failed nevertheless:

> While the sad victims [the prisoners] were thus subjected to unbearable fears by the hypocritical orders that he had had printed in all the newspapers, Henriot[62] alienated public opinion more and more against the *maisons d'arrêt* . . . But, since the first arrest of Ronsin and his clique took place at this time, the massacre was postponed. Then the thieves of Bicêtre were removed and the poor Lazarists began to breathe once more . . .[63]

Throughout this period of great political tension, just prior to the trial of the Hébertists, the prisoners were subjected to strict supervision:

The instructions given to our guards were terrifying: they were forbidden, under pain of death, to speak to us, to answer us, or to make the slightest sign to us: such a terrible impression was made on them by these instructions that most of them went white with fear as soon as they saw us at a window, lest they might be thought to be talking to us. Some of them, whose brains had been thoroughly confused by fear of the guillotine, suddenly pointed guns at us to make us go away; three or four times they opened fire, but fortunately missed their aim. These incidents were a source of great disturbance in our house; we shook with indignation at seeing ourselves treated in this way and it required all the wisdom of the keeper Naudet to restore calm. Those poor guards could be excused for being so afraid: one gendarme had been guillotined for accepting a letter that a woman had written to her husband, an inmate at Sainte-Pélagie . . .[64]

The prison was divided into three floors, each forming three huge corridors, leading to the rooms. The first floor, which housed the women, was called the Prairial corridor; the second, which housed men, Vendémiaire, and the third, also intended for men, Germinal.

All the prisoners had the right to have their food brought in from outside and some could even be served by people from outside. They could furnish their rooms as they wished and were allowed books and newspapers.

A great many letters between detainees and their families have survived. Whether they came from inside or outside the prison, all were seized by the keeper and handed over to Fouquier-Tinville.[65] Reading them does introduce a certain comfort and warmth into that bleak world.

To Citizeness Boilleau, Rue Révolutionnaire,
former Saint-Louis, at Paris, this 4 Floréal.

My dear friend,

I beg you to do your utmost to bring a well-seasoned lettuce salad or rather the materials for making one, we have bowls; but try to make sure that it is fresh and in good condition. If you have no money, try to get hold of some for this advance. As I am writing to you by the small post, I don't want to send it to you, but I shall get it to you later. Don't forget the oil and vinegar. If you cannot get money to do this, take the trouble to come and see me and I shall give you what you need to buy what is necessary. We have salt, but bring a little pepper. Try to do this for us today, if at all possible, I shall be very obliged to you, and bring as much oil as you can. I shall be very obliged to you and embrace you with all my heart.

Your husband Boilleau.

Prisoners' families did their utmost to get a few parcels through to improve the normal standard of prison life. Here is Citizeness Fournier, anxiously awaiting her husband's return:

I am sending you a pigeon, some redcurrants, apricots and a bottle of wine. I'm not sending you any linen because you did not ask for it. I embrace you with all my heart. I wish I didn't have to say so, but I kiss you in good earnest. I don't know when I will have that pleasure, I'm waiting for you with such impatience.

I am your friend and wife, Fournier.

Another touching note, scribbled hastily on a post opposite the prison entrance and given to the porters with a basket of food, declares:

To Citizen Maisonneuve,

A pigeon, an artichoke, a bottle of wine, a handkerchief. If Catherine finds any figs, she'll bring you some. My cousin has gone out for you. She kisses you tenderly and I too.

Your little cousin, if it please you.

Unaware that the mail is intercepted, a detainee expresses anxiety about his wife and writes to her again:

To Citizeness Bourget,
house of the lemonade seller, Rue des Poulies,
no. 179, section of the Gardes Françaises, at Paris.

15 Messidor, Year II of the French Republic

I wrote to you the day before yesterday. I awaited a reply yesterday and today and I have none. Are you confined? If so, let me know and the sex of the child. I asked you for a basket of cherries, my comrades will pay me for them and I will get the money to you. I need a handkerchief, a pair of stockings, and a needle and thread to repair my breeches; I don't have any more tobacco.

Your husband, Bourget.

Since February, the poet Roucher, in the Saint-Lazare prison, had gained permission for his five-year-old son to be able to join him.

The child was a veritable ray of sunshine for everybody, especially for such women prisoners as Mmes de Talleyrand-Périgord, de Saint-Aignan and de Maillé, who competed for his attentions. Then came the day when the prisoners heard talk of the 'prison plots'. One of them remembers:

Although we were not allowed to read newspapers, some news got into the prison nevertheless. We questioned the newcomers – the

Revolutionary Tribunal and the number of guillotined were our main concerns. We trembled with terror at the account of the number of victims whose heads were falling each day. We heard talk of the plots in the Luxembourg and in other *maisons d'arrêt*, and could not imagine how a handful of detainees, without connections, without resources, without weapons, had been able to weave such webs. We judged other *maisons d'arrêt* by ours, in which the greatest order, the greatest submission reigned, and in which we were held back rather by our respect of the law than by locks. We congratulated ourselves that we did not have such men among us capable of formulating escape plans, nor bold enough, nor villainous enough, to plot from the depths of their prison against the representatives of the nation. Alas! we were unaware that thunder was rumbling over our heads, that at that very moment a fictitious plot was being worked out to implicate us, that at the very table where we sat there were monsters with just such designs, ready to point the finger at the wretches chosen to suffer the penalty for just such crimes that existed only in the diabolical imagination of their vile denunciators.

A certain Manini, an Italian, a man known since the Revolution as an informer and a spy, and who had done nothing else in the various *maisons d'arrêt* in which he had been held, was the inventor of the fiction. His accomplice was a watchmaker called Coquery, a fool whom he had won over either by promises or by threats. So, one fine day, this Manini denounced several individuals held at Saint-Lazare for having offered sixteen thousand *livres* to the watchmaker to cut through a bar of the only window on the first floor where there were bars, with a view to escaping and then murdering the members of the Committees of Public Safety and of General Safety, in particular Robespierre, who, it was said, was to have his heart torn out and eaten by a young man named Alain, a fruiterer's son who was always alone and seldom spoke to anyone. This window looked out on to a sort of terrace and the farm garden, but a distance of about twenty-five feet lay between them. Immediately below was a sentry box. Once the bar had been removed, the plan was, according to Manini, to push through a plank of wood that would form a bridge from the window to the terrace. It is to that narrow, fragile bridge that the so-called conspirators would have entrusted their fate. No doubt they would have been able to put the guard below to sleep, as well as the other guards nearby. Had they not done so, the guards would have seen everything, heard everything and, it is reasonable to believe, would not willingly have acceded to the escapees' wishes. This, then, was the masterpiece produced by Manini's imagination, with the help of Coquery.[66]

There were several informers at Saint-Lazare, but the most famous of them was no doubt Pépin-Desgrouettes. A legless cripple and a prolific writer, he joined the brotherly society of the Jacobins in 1791 and became an active member. He was very influential and drew up the most violent motions against the royal person. At the same time, he was suspected of keeping up with England 'a correspondence dangerous to public welfare' and was implicated in the polemics that accompanied the liquidation of the Paris Water Company. Making a great show of his patriotism after 10 August, he had been a member of the Tribunal of 17 August 1792 and had shown himself to be particularly determined in unmasking those implicated in the theft of the crown jewels. In 1793, he had acted as '*défenseur officieux*' and, for large sums of money received from the defendants, claimed to be bringing from the *départements* the necessary defence witnesses and documentary evidence. Out of about forty such 'clients' half were guillotined![67]

Denounced in turn, Pépin-Desgrouettes entered Saint-Lazare on 2 Floréal. His incarceration was strangely like blackmail, for, in order to save his head, he had to become a prison informer, an activity that could not have been unfamiliar to him. At his trial, one witness declared: 'For larger and larger sums, he has eliminated from the list that he drew up the names of those who had given him money. With Manini and others, he argued over which names were to appear on the list and they agreed that they would put first, in order of preference, priests, nobles, rich men and scholars.'[68]

On 6 Thermidor, the group of informers in Saint-Lazare gave evidence before the Revolutionary Tribunal against seventy-four individuals, who were all condemned and executed within three days. Among them was a sixteen-year-old boy, young Maillé, who was accused of throwing a herring 'filled with worms' at the head of his gaoler. His mother, who had considerable wealth in the West Indies, was summoned at the same time as he. At the Tribunal, it was noticed that it was Citizeness Mayet and not the Comtesse de Maillé who had answered the call: this woman was nevertheless condemned to death. As for Mme de Maillé, she appeared next day, 9 Thermidor, in the same court where the day before her young son had been condemned. She broke down and her trial was postponed until the following day. The events of 10 Thermidor saved her life.

On the same list was Baron Trenck, who owed his fame to the forty-two years that he had spent in the prisons of the King of Prussia. A play had even been written about his adventures, which included several escapes. The 'agent of Coburg', that is, of the Duke of Saxe-Coburg-Gotha, he had always pretended to an ardent patriotism, but maintained close relations with members of the 'party abroad', in particular with the Austrian banking family of Frey.[69] He was the lover and protector of a young woman, Louise Desmarets, who had also been arrested and was in the Plessis. Incurring great risks as a result of this affair, she had had to disguise her identity to save her head and had not hesitated to pass herself off as a prostitute. Completely taken in, the Comtesse de Bohm, also a prisoner, has left this portrait of her in her Memoirs: 'She did not blush at being a woman of the streets. Her rather beautiful body served as an envelope for an audacious, ardent, deeply tainted soul . . .'

Louise Desmarets escaped the scaffold, but Baron Trenck did not: condemned to death, he wrote a farewell letter to his wife. Perhaps he also wrote to Louise Desmarets, but if he did, the letter has not survived.

> My worthy, dear wife, I walk towards death with the sole regret that I must leave you. Coburg forced me to return to France. I die innocent. Avenge my death against the villains who are sacrificing me: forget, if you can, dear wife, the unhappiness that, during my deplorable lifetime, I have caused you and our children, whom I commend to share your love always.
>
> Farewell, my worthy wife, farewell, my wife, farewell my dear children; may God be a father to you! I give you my blessing. Honour my remains in the person of the good old man who will bring you this letter; he was my companion in prison in France and the support of my sad old age. Farewell forever, my dear and worthy wife! Farewell! Farewell!
>
> Frederick, Baron Trenck.[70]

The Carmes

The last of the prisons to see these so-called plots, the prison of the Carmes, was a former convent in the Rue de Vaugirard which, in December 1793, had been converted to house a large number of suspects. It was not one of the more comfortable prisons as this inmate, who must have spent some time there, recounts:

> Here the corridors are not lit; one does not always have the pleasure of seeing the garden; for a long time now I have been able to catch no more than a glimpse of the women through their windows – there are some twenty of them and they eat in the refectory after the men. The corridors are varnished; though spacious enough, they

are airless and infected by the noxious fumes from the latrines. The
windows are blocked up to three-quarters of their height, so that
the light enters only from the top and, over the little opening there
is, there are thick bars. One senses at once that this is a proper
prison in all its horror. The inmates do not take care of their persons
as at the Bourbe. They are not properly dressed: they are mostly
without ties, wear nightshirts and dirty pantaloons, their legs bare,
a handkerchief around their heads, their hair uncombed, their
beards unshaven.

The women, our sad companions in misfortune, are a sorry
sight. They wear a short dress or a *pierrot*, sometimes of one colour,
sometimes of another. However, we are fairly well fed; at the only
refectory meal, we have as much bread as we like and a half-bottle
of wine each. But our keeper is harsh and unpleasant . . .[71]

This gloomy picture is complemented by the more picturesque
memories of Mme de Nicolaï, who, as a child, sometimes managed
to slip into the prison to visit her mother, Mme de Lameth:

There was a gaoler called Roblâtre, who wasn't at all fierce. He was
fond of the juice of the grape and, as a result, allowed me
sometimes to go and see my mother and spend part of the day with
her. We were very glad to see one another again. I took care to hide
in my corset a number of letters and newspapers, for the poor
prisoners could not receive any. They would ask me at the gate if I
was taking anything suspect in and I always said no . . .

I went to that prison several times. My mother and Mme
d'Aiguillon were in the same room, with two trestle beds without
curtains. There were no curtains on the windows either. I remember several of the women in prison with them, including Mme de
Custine [who was so well-known for her brave conduct at the trial
of her father-in-law and husband at the Revolutionary Tribunal,
during which time she remained sitting at their feet throughout
their condemnation]. There was M. de Beauharnais – I think his
wife was there for a long time, too, but she left fairly soon – he left
only to be guillotined. He was a good friend of all the prisoners and
an intimate friend of these ladies; by a delicate act of cruelty, on the
day of his execution, a large bunch of flowers was tied in front of
their windows . . .[72]

Most of these women were under no illusions as to their fate. Mme
de Nicolaï continues:

It is remarkable that my mother and Mme d'Aiguillon, though
both still young and so used to the refinements of life, bore this
imprisonment with a calm and a patience that made their youthful-
ness and their behaviour all the more extraordinary. Their resigna-

tion was astonishing. Among the few clothes that they had been allowed to bring with them, they had slipped a *caraco* [the name of a garment worn by women at the time] more elegant than the others, which they refrained from wearing and kept for the day when they would be taken out for execution, since they expected to be guillotined at any moment . . .[73]

On 4 Thermidor, forty-five prisoners in the Carmes were suddenly removed, whereas during the last three weeks of Messidor the cart had not appeared. The departure took place according to the usual scenario, immortalized in Muller's realistic paintings. At the top of some stone steps, an officer bearing orders from the Tribunal appeared, the lists of the dead in hand . . . The roll-call began. The unfortunates whose names had been read out had just enough time to make their last farewells and to disappear: an embrace, a look, a few last words of advice . . .

The 'plot' in the Carmes had been organized by several informers, including a certain Virolle, a former noble, who, it was claimed, committed suicide shortly after the lists of prisoners had been drawn up and who had been presented on the day of the trial as the ringleader of an imaginary plot.

On the list of conspirators was Alexandre de Beauharnais,[74] who, knowing that he was doomed, hastily wrote a letter of farewell to his wife, the future Empress Josephine, who was also in prison:

> 4 Thermidor Year II of the one
> and indivisible Republic.

> It appears from the sort of interrogation to which a fairly large number of detainees was subjected today that I am the victim of villainous calumnies brought against me by several aristocrats, so-called patriots, at present in this house. Presuming that this infernal machination will follow me to the Revolutionary Tribunal, I have no hope of seeing you again, my friend, nor of embracing my dear children.

> I shall not tell you of my regrets; my tender affection for them and the brotherly attachment that binds me to you can leave you in no doubt as to the feelings with which I take leave of life. I also regret leaving a country that I love and for which I would have given my life a thousand times over. Not only shall I not be able to serve her, but she will see me torn from her bosom, supposing me a bad citizen. This frightful idea does not allow me not to urge you to speak well of me in the future: work to rehabilitate my memory, proving that a life entirely devoted to serving one's country and to the triumph of liberty and equality must in the eyes of the people repulse hateful calumniators, who have been drawn above all from

the class of suspect people. This work must be postponed, for in the revolutionary storms, a great people fighting to destroy its chains must surround itself with justified mistrust, and no more fear to forget a guilty man than to strike an innocent.

I shall die with a calm that nevertheless allows me to feel the dearest affections to the last, but with that courage that characterizes a free man, a pure conscience and an honest soul whose most ardent wishes are for the prosperity of the Republic.

Farewell, my friend, console yourself with my children, console them by enlightening them, and above all teaching them that it is on account of virtue and civic duty that they must efface the memory of my execution and recall my services to the nation and my claims to its gratitude. Farewell, you know those whom I love, be their consoler and by your care make me live longer in their hearts.

Farewell, for the last time in my life, I press you and my dear children to my breast.

Alexandre Beauharnais.[75]

With him perished most of the former nobles, including Gouy d'Arsy,[76] the Prince de Salm[77] and the Chevalier de Champcenetz,[78] co-editor with Rivarol of the royalist newspaper *Les Actes des Apôtres*. Accompanying them on the same day was another prisoner condemned to death, Ange de Beauvoir, who was in love with the youngest inmate of the Carmes, then pregnant by him. Before leaving the prison he had time to engrave these few verses on the wall of his cell:

Amour, viens recevoir une dernière prière
Accorde à Désirée un avenir heureux;
Daigne ajouter surtout à sa belle carrière
Les jours que me ravit un destin rigoureux

Si de l'excès des malheurs qu'on essuie
Naît quelquefois notre félicité
Bientôt sera répandu sur ma vie
Le charme heureux qui suit la volupté

Mon coeur brûlant adore Desirée,
Quand Atropos viendra trancher mes jours
Le dernier des soupirs sera pour les amours
Qui lui diront combien elle fut adorée.[79]

There remained the final stages of the calvary: the appearance before the Revolutionary Tribunal, often preceded by a 'stay' in the Conciergerie.

3

FROM THE CONCIERGERIE
TO THE SCAFFOLD

Tolling like a bell in the ears of the detainees of Year II, the word 'Conciergerie' evoked the Revolutionary Tribunal and the guillotine. Like the other prisons, the Conciergerie received suspects directly from outside, but it was also sent detainees from various prisons in Paris and even from the provinces who were on their way to the Revolutionary Tribunal.

Its four towers, three of which have pointed roofs, placed at intervals along the façade of the Palais de Justice on the Quai de l'Horloge, are well known. Inside is a tangle of buildings and gloomy, damp courtyards. Gothic halls stand side by side with dark common rooms, narrow staircases and corridors that never see the sun.

Awaiting trial

On their arrival, the prisoners were taken to the records office, a fairly small room divided in two by a glass partition, in which the records clerk entered their names in the register. One newcomer, the Comte Beugnot, remembered that moment. Two men were lying on a worn mattress, their eyes staring, seeming to see nothing, motionless as if dead. Plates, bottles, bits of bread and meat were littered around the floor. They had both been condemned and were awaiting the cart.[80] According to Bailleul, a deputy also imprisoned in the Conciergerie, the records office was the scene of a great deal of commotion:

> Women and their husbands, mistresses and their lovers sat on rows of benches placed against the walls. Some caressed one another with as much carefree gaiety as if they were in rose arbours. Others

looked very sad and were shedding tears . . . Out of one window, I caught sight of some wretched woman watched over by a gendarme, lying on a sickbed, looking very pale, awaiting the moment of execution.

Gendarmes swarmed around the gates. Some were taking prisoners, whose hands were being untied, to their cells. Others called for those prisoners who were to be transferred, tied their hands and took them off, while a clerk, with wild-looking eyes, yelled out orders in his insolent voice, lost his temper and seemed to think that he was a hero because he insulted with impunity unfortunate people who could not hit back . . .[81]

The staff recruited by the prison administration was not generally noted for its delicacy. Invective was the rule and alcoholism did not improve matters. The keepers Richard and Bault tried to humanize the stay of their inmates, particularly when they were in a position to pay, but, usually, the prisoners, whether rich or poor, spent their first days shut up in the dirtiest and gloomiest cells. The Girondin Riouffe remembers being thrown into one such cell after a journey lasting several days from Bordeaux to Paris. By the light of a lantern, he could just make out a few shapes lying on the straw. Two or three rather unwelcoming faces looked up at him.

Exhausted, he fell asleep. In the morning, still half asleep, from which state he had no desire to emerge, he was surprised to find himself imagining 'pretty shops filled with scent, all the things that fashion offers to the most elegant coquetry, and attractive saleswomen, who, with provoking eyes and seductive lips, attracted the attention of the curious . . .' This idea merely added to his despair.

Next day, the gaoler moved him into a room in which he found a trestle bed, covered with a woollen blanket. The room was large, fairly clean and occupied by seventeen people.[82] The beds were separated by wooden partitions. One of his companions remembers the '*tableau mouvant*' of that little society:

It was among the nobility that I saw the most counter-revolutionaries and advocates of the monarchy, weeping over the tomb of Capet and calling on the *ancien régime* with loud cries. I saw fanatical, ignorant priests and felt sorry for them. I saw counter-revolutionaries, a horrible species. I saw respectable curés, who had performed acts of virtue and charity in their village, reading their breviary as they went to bed: they spoke to me of Christ's miracles and I smiled.

I saw merchants and bankers who had received their indictments and who, before going to bed, went over their accounts, checked their capital and drew up company rules.

I saw Sans-Culottes, excellent patriots, ardent revolutionaries, sacrificed to obscure hatreds; their oaths brought tears of blood to my eyes.

I saw farmers say their morning and night prayers, commend themselves to the good Virgin Mary, make the Sign of the Cross when it thundered, curse the spoliations of their émigré lord and bless the Revolution, but [who] would hear nothing about juring priests [those who had taken the oath of allegiance], regretting the absence of masses, sermons and homilies . . .

I saw empty-headed, brainless young men pirouette gracefully between two gates, sing the praises of our daily fare and write epigrams on the present government . . .[83]

Sometimes, those prisoners who had fewest illusions as to their fate insisted that their portraits be painted, and those who had that talent were much in demand:

> There was a time when each of us regarded his death as certain; with that sad conviction, it was still a pleasure to have locks of our hair cut off, to stick them around medals, portraits and send them to our wives, our mothers, our children, to those dear persons that we would never see again.[84]

Among many others, a young woman, Catherine Laviolette, asked to be represented with her hands on a skull. This charming picture was intended for her husband, whom she regarded as responsible for her death. She had, it is true, left him for her lover, a certain Mandrillon, who had compromised her in some espionage affair. Her stay in the Conciergerie was to be remembered by several witnesses, including this prisoner who relates her last words to him:

> The wellspring of my tears is dried up: I have not shed one since yesterday evening. The most sensitive of women is no longer susceptible of any feeling; the affections that were the happiness of my life have lost all their strength. I regret nothing: I look upon the moment of my death with indifference.[85]

On 8 January 1794, accompanied by Mandrillon and another condemned couple, she mounted the cart. A police observer, who happened to be on the spot, noted in his report:

> While in a café, in the Rue Saint-Honoré, I saw four persons, including two women, in the cart. They were laughing together at the citizen who was driving them to the guillotine and at the public around them. Onlookers were saying: 'They certainly look like

traitors and one-time aristocrats. If we were moved to pity, they would merely scorn us.'

'Look how they mock our justice,' said one citizen. 'They go to the scaffold laughing.'[86]

Sometimes the atmosphere at the Conciergerie was 'somewhat gay', as when the inmates had drunk rather more wine and liqueurs than usual: 'Our heads were then heated and we competed among ourselves as to who could say the most extravagant things.'

One daily drudgery was the roll-call of inmates in the yard. We must imagine three or four porters – often pretty drunk – holding a large dog on a lead in one hand, and a list of badly written names, which they could scarcely make out, in the other. A name was called out, but nobody understood:

> They swore, flew into a rage, threatened us; they called the name out again: they consulted one another and, in the end, we finally understood the name that they were trying to say. They then counted out the rest of the herd; they miscalculated, then, flying into a temper, they ordered everybody back into the yard. We came back, then were marched off one by one. There were more mistakes and it was sometimes only after three or four attempts that their clouded vision allowed them at last to ascertain that we were all there.[87]

Some prisoners, who were unable to distract themselves from the frightful prospect of their condemnation, had thought of simulating their own deaths. In their rooms, they acted out the Revolutionary Tribunal. The roles were distributed according to taste and ability. Some represented the judges and the prosecutor; others the defendants and witnesses; others, again, the executioner and his assistants. The trial invariably ended with the execution of the defendants: their hands were tied behind their backs, they were laid out on a bed, their necks under a plank of wood. The second act took place in hell. Wrapped up in sheets, the more agile of the group mimicked ghosts, and a young lawyer from Bordeaux, Ducorneau, played the Devil, pulling the guillotined man or woman by the feet, all without being able to help laughing. A few days later, the same Ducorneau received his indictment.

The night before he appeared before the Revolutionary Tribunal, he wrote these few verses on a corner of the table after a lively supper organized by his friends:

> Si nous passons l'onde noire,
> Amis, daignez quelquefois
> Ressusciter la mémoire

De deux vrais amis des lois.
Dans ces moments pleins de charmes,
Fêtez-nous parmi les pots,
Et versez, au lieu de larmes,
Quelques flacons de Bordeaux . . .

Adjutant-General Boisguyon, who had also been 'very much amused by the guillotine', saw his last day arrive without losing his sense of humour. As he climbed up into the cart, he declared to Sanson: 'Today's the actual performance: you'll be surprised how well I know my role.'

His sensitivity and delicacy are apparent in the last letter he wrote to a pharmacist friend at Châteaudun.

Citizen,

I was condemned to death yesterday at 4 o'clock in the afternoon and in two hours I shall be no more. I beg you to inform my mother, taking all necessary steps to mitigate the effect of the news upon her. Send someone to be with her, so that she may learn of my fate in gentle circumstances and not receive this information by letter . . . Assure her of my tender feelings for her and of my wish that she find in the virtues the consolation that she will need.

Of the proceeds from my share-cropping at La Haloyère I have only ten thousand *livres* left, which I have placed with my cousin Hardancourt, who also owes me 500 *livres* for the interest accruing from 1794 (old style) and 500 *livres* for the interest from '93, against which I owe him 430 *livres* for providing military equipment when I was in the army. The poor rest of my possessions have been confiscated. Tell my mother this and tell her not to worry about it. Farewell, citizen, greetings and fraternity.

Boisguyon[88]

Again it was to amuse their companions in misfortune that those who had been before the Tribunal, but had been condemned only to imprisonment, amused themselves imitating, in the most comic way, the bombastic voice and gestures of Fouquier-Tinville, or of Liendon and Naulin, his substitutes. They imitated the self-satisfied manner of Dumas or Subleyras. They parodied the *défenseurs officieux* and the care they took not to compromise themselves.

The number of prisoners held at the Conciergerie continued to increase. In four months, from 8 August to 18 December 1793, it had almost doubled, exceeding five hundred persons. Herman, the president of the Tribunal, was worried by this and wrote on the matter to Fouquier-Tinville:

The Conciergerie can only take four hundred detainees and at present six hundred are crammed into it. Many of them are sick: the sewage fumes are so strong that when one goes into a room with a torch, the flame goes out. It is absolutely necessary, Citizen, that you find some large, suitable, safe and airy premises and transfer to it two hundred and fifty of the persons at present in the Conciergerie, including, among others, those sick that can be moved. If this house remains any longer in its present state, it is to be feared that the plague will wreak its havoc there.[89]

In the absence of the plague, one was most likely to catch scabies or putrid fever, a contagion facilitated by the number of transfers from one prison to another.

The Comte Beugnot recounts the detainees' efforts to preserve some semblance of dignity, despite this promiscuity:

In the midst of these gloomy spectacles, which were repeated each day, the Frenchwomen lost none of their usual character; they devoted themselves assiduously to the need to please. The part of the prison in which we lived looked out on to the women's yard. The only place where we could breathe a little more easily was a small hall, measuring twelve feet by seven, formed by two vaulted arches, at the bottom of the staircase and between the women's yard and the gate. This sort of corridor was separated from the yard by iron grilles, but the bars were not so close together that a Frenchman should ever have reason to despair.

The corridor was our favourite spot for walking; we went down there as soon as we were taken out of our cells. The women came out at the same time, but not as quickly as we did, since their toilet demanded its indefeasible rights. They appeared in the morning elegantly attired *en négligé*, the various parts of which were matched with so much freshness and grace that the whole did not in the least suggest that they had spent the night on a litter, usually on fetid straw. Generally the society ladies imprisoned in the Conciergerie maintained to the end the sacred fire of good form and good taste. When they had appeared in the morning *en négligé*, they returned to their rooms. At about noon, we saw them come down again, scrupulously dressed, their hair done in the most elegant manner. They behaved rather differently from the way in which they had behaved in the morning; there was something more reserved, more dignified about them. In the evening, they appeared *en déshabillé*. I noticed that all the women who could do so were faithful to the three costumes of the day; the others added to their elegance by being as well groomed as the locality would allow. The women's courtyard possessed a treasure, a fountain that provided as much water as they wanted; and, each morning, I would watch those poor unfortunates who had brought with them – who perhaps possessed no more than – a single set of clothes, busily engaged around this fountain washing, laundering and drying their clothes with noisy emulation. They devoted the first hour of the day to these activities, from which nothing would have distracted them, not even the arrival of an indictment. Richardson has observed that a concern for clothes and the mania for making parcels are, in a woman's mind, of equal if not greater interest than matters of the utmost import.

I am persuaded that, at that time, no promenade in Paris afforded a view of such elegantly turned out women as the courtyard of the Conciergerie at noon; they were like a flowerbed in full bloom, yet framed in iron. France is most likely the only country and French-women the only women in the world capable of offering such odd combinations and of producing effortlessly all that is most attractive, most seductive in a setting that is the most repulsive, most horrible that the world can offer. I loved to observe the women at noon; but I preferred their conversation in the morning and I took part in the more intimate conversations in the evening, when I ran the risk of disturbing no one's happiness; for in the evening everything was taken advantage of, the growing shadows, the porters' tiredness, the absence of most of the prisoners, the discretion of others and, at that moment of peace, which served as a prelude to night, we blest more than once the thoughtlessness of the artist who designed the railings. Yet the creatures capable of such inexplicable abandon had their death warrants in their pockets.

I was more or less witness to something even more remarkable of this kind. A woman of some forty years, but still fresh and in possession of fine features and an elegant waist, was condemned to death in the first ten days of Frimaire, together with her lover, an army officer from the North, a young man who appeared to combine an elevated mind and a charming face. They came back from the Tribunal at about six o'clock in the evening. They were separated for the night.

The woman knew how to use her powers of seduction. She gained permission to be reunited with her lover. They gave that last night up to their love, draining yet again the cup of voluptuousness, and tore themselves away from each other's arms only at the very last minute to climb into the fatal cart.

I have never ceased to be astonished by such heroism, of which I did not feel myself to be in the least capable. I have yet to ascertain whether it degrades or enhances a people to have provided so many examples of it; but it is true at least that it gives a physiognomy that is like no other. Proximity to women provides us with less serious distractions of which I was more jealous. We were often able to take luncheon with them. Benches, more or less elbow-high, were improvised on either side of the bars; amid all the confusion of the time and place, we laid the table for luncheon and if a place still remained vacant on the women's side, there was no lack of graces to fill it. In truth, they were not of those women who spread themselves with abandon on a *chaise longue* and besport themselves at some elegant tea party; they were less pretentious and much more piquant. There, despatching sweetmeats, which one's appetite seasoned, despite the poor quality of the produce, delicate observations, subtle allusions, brilliant witticisms were exchanged from one side of the bars to the other. We would speak pleasantly of all things while being tedious about nothing. We treated misfortunes as one might a naughty but amusing child and indeed we laughed very openly about the divinity of Marat, the priestliness of Robespierre, the judiciousness of Fouquier. We seemed to be saying to all those flunkeys: you will kill us when you will, but you will not prevent us from being pleasant.[90]

Railings separated the men's quarters from the women's but, as Beugnot makes clear, the bars were not close enough to prevent contact of hands and lips. At night, the task of guarding the railings fell to Ravage, the warder's dog, and it was no easy one. Sometimes he allowed the prisoners to go first into the yard, then into the women's corridor. One morning, he was discovered proudly bearing, attached to his tail, a hundred-*sou* assignat and a note on which was written these words: 'Ravage can be bribed with a hundred-*sou* assignat and a few sheep's feet.' Everybody burst out laughing and Ravage lost face. He was locked up as a punishment.

Among the women were a few prostitutes. The story of one of them, Catherine Halbourg, nicknamed Eglé, is moving on account of its injustice. She had been picked up with one of her women friends in the Rue Fromenteau. Chaumette, an influential member of the Commune, had conceived of the idea of implicating them both in the affair of the queen and to have all three executed together. But the Committees were opposed to it. Condemned for counter-revolutionary statements, she happened, on the day before appearing before the Tribunal, to pass the Duc du Châtelet, who was to be tried that same day. Terror-stricken and half drunk, he was blubbering. Eglé addressed him thus: 'You must learn, Monsieur le Duc, that those who do not have a name acquire one here and those who have one must learn how to bear it.' The police officer Prévost saw Eglé die two days later. Unlike her friend, Claire Sévin, she refused to declare that she was pregnant. On the cart, accompanied by three aristocrats, she alone seems to have preserved her humour and sense of repartee. From the top of the scaffold, she cried out courageously: 'Farewell my friends, long live Louis XVII!' The spectators, Prévost tells us, were 'indignant at such behaviour'.[91]

The most famous detainee of all, Queen Marie-Antoinette, arrived at the Conciergerie on the night of 2 August. Her cell, which was twice as large as the one open to visitors today, was lit by two windows that looked out over the women's yard. Its walls were bare, the floor was brick. Her entire furniture consisted of a trestle bed (with two mattresses, a bolster and a blanket), an ordinary table, two prison chairs, a wash-basin and a small screen. Some attempts were made to soften the severity of the place: the prison-keeper Richard and the servant-woman Rosalie Lamorlière had put fine sheets and a pillow on her bed and a vase of flowers on the table. The newspapers of the time have left us this description of Marie-Antoinette's habits in the Conciergerie:

> Antoinette rises every day at seven o'clock and goes to bed at ten. She calls her two gendarmes 'Messieurs', her servant-woman 'Madame Harel'. The police administrators and those who approach her officially call her 'Madame'. She eats with good appetite; in the morning, chocolate with a breadroll, at dinner, soup and a lot of meat – chicken, veal cutlets and mutton. She drinks only water, like her mother, she says, who never drank wine. She has finished reading *Les Révolutions d'Angleterre* and is at present reading *Le Voyage du jeune Anacharsis*. She does her own toilet, but with the stylishness that a woman does not abandon until her dying breath. Her room looks out on to the women's prison; but the women prisoners seem not to heed the proximity of the former queen.[92]

In September 1793, after the queen's failed attempt to escape, which was known as the '*affaire de l'œillet*' ('the Carnation affair'), Marie-Antoinette was put into the prison pharmacy, which was adapted so that she had no communication with the outside world. But, contrary to what was said, she was very well treated there, until the last moment. At the Tribunal, she appeared in an elegant white dress, 'very clean' in the opinion of one witness . . . (See her farewell letter, p. 126.)

Facing the Revolutionary Tribunal

After a stay of uncertain duration in the Conciergerie, sometimes no more than a single night, the moment came to appear before the Revolutionary Tribunal.

It was on 10 March 1793 that the Convention had decided to set up this Tribunal with the purpose of judging those who had violated the internal or external security of the state or had attempted to re-establish any other form of government than that of the one and indivisible Republic. From 5 April 1793, the public prosecutor at the Tribunal was allowed to have arrested, charged and tried any inmate simply on the denunciation of the authorities, or even on that of a single citizen. Trials could neither be appealed against nor quashed and could take place within twenty-four hours.

Until the late summer, the Tribunal was mainly concerned with cases concerning emigration. The fury of the regime was directed mainly at those émigrés who had returned to France. At a stroke the legislation of 1792 concerning emigration was annulled and replaced by a single, extremely strict decree dated 28 March 1793. Its unexpected promulgation had aggravated the already precarious fate of thousands of émigrés desperately seeking forged residence certificates. Many were arrested at the moment of trying to 'arrange' their business with unscrupulous civil servants.

At first, the Tribunal showed clemency: the number of those condemned to death was lower than that of cases with no grounds for prosecution, acquittals and prison sentences. But after the law of 22 Prairial, which was harder on the defendants, the Tribunal became as expeditious as it was severe, often basing its judgements on the false testimony of prison informers.

The sessions of the Tribunal were held in rooms adjoining the Conciergerie: usually in either the 'Liberté' or 'Égalité' hall. They were generally held in the morning, but attracted a large number of spectators, if this police report is to be believed:

> Abomination and scandal in the great hall leading into the session chamber: this hall is like a backstreet. Everything is for sale here. Water is spilt everywhere, every kind of indecent behaviour is to be found and most of those who spend the day there are idlers, prostitutes and sometimes even people without homes, who spend the night there.

The author of the report finally urges the public 'not to bring with them children below the age of reason or discernment'.

The prosecutor read out the charge prepared the day before, then the presiding judge summed up the case. The witnesses were called. The jurors then withdrew into the jury room and the defendant was taken off into a nearby room.

Meanwhile, the Tribunal remained in session. Behind the barrier that separated them from the floor of the court, the spectators tried to guess the outcome. Eventually a bell announced the return of the jury. When they were seated once more the president called them one after the other and asked them to reply to the usual questions as to the defendant's guilt. The defendant was brought back into the chamber and the presiding judge told him of the jury's decision. The public prosecutor then spoke a few words requesting the application of the law and, after the judge had asked the defendant if he had anything to add in his own defence, sentence was finally passed.

It should be noted that during the first two years of its activity, the Paris Revolutionary Tribunal delivered far fewer death sentences than is often imagined.[93] Thus, from March 1793, when it was set up, to January 1794, 381 death sentences were passed out of 1,046 cases brought before it: 34 were deported, 15 condemned to the *fers*, 6 to the *gêne* (long-term imprisonment) and 66 for the duration of hostilities. 209 were released without charge and 336 acquitted after trial. On the other hand, 1,370 death sentences were passed between 8 June and 30 July 1794, a short period that represents the height of the Terror.[94]

The last moments and the journey in the cart

When the death sentence had been passed, the condemned prisoners were taken to a cell already reserved for them. Often the execution did not take place until the following day; often they were carried out at night. It was the custom to serve the condemned prisoner with an excellent meal, with as much wine as he wanted to drink . . . providing he could pay for it. But this only applied to the better-off prisoners, such as the Duc d'Orléans or the Duc de Biron, who were served with oysters and white wine. For the rest, these last moments were wretched, as the letter of this condemned man shows:

> 12 Nivôse, second and last year of the
> Republic for the sender of this letter.

Public prosecutor,

There is an abuse at the Conciergerie. I denounce it to you and those who commit it: porters, who are as grasping as they are harsh and inhuman, are allowed by Citizen and Citizeness Richard to strip the condemned prisoners of all they have. I am referring not only to various effects that they may possess, but even to their ordinary clothes, such as overcoats, jackets, etc. In my case, they even went so far as to remove a bandage which I have worn as a result of a wound I received at the siege of Namur. I tried in vain to persuade them that having the bandage removed was very painful for me. They replied that the law did not allow me to keep it. This cruelty was pushed so far that I was not even given a blanket. I would beg you, in the name of humanity, not to allow such abuses to continue any longer. I would also demand, on behalf of those who would support me, the abolition of another common abuse, namely the seizure of personal wallets. All these facts will be confirmed by the citizen gendarmes about me. I owe them this justice: to acknowledge their honesty and delicate feelings.

Before ending my letter, I would beg you to remember that the law in accordance with which the jury passed sentence on me is not applicable in my case; that the law of 19 August is the one that I could have been tried under. It carries the words: 'When there is collusion on the part of an agent of the Republic with a contractor, a death sentence will be passed.' Now, in my case, this does not apply since what occurred was between people who did not know one another; therefore there should be no death sentence. But this, no doubt, was an oversight: therefore, without rancour, I forgive you and your dear colleagues for my death. Farewell, greetings and fraternity.

Bonnefoy.[95]

Another prisoner, guillotined on the same day, complains of the conditions of detention in a letter to his 'sister', who, in fact, was his mistress:

Paris, this 3 Nivôse Year II
of the Republic.

I was flattered, my dear sister, that you should send me news every day. You know how dear and precious that has always been to me and, in the cruel position in which I find myself, it is becoming still more so. Yesterday I saw the inspector who is in charge of my case. He thinks the Committee will at last deal with it today.

Send me linen. With the filth and damp here it is difficult to keep clean. This is made worse by the fact that I don't undress, since I am always lying on the campbed.

Send young L'Harmonnier to me this morning. I must speak to her and give her an errand. I would like her to be here as early as

possible. Farewell, my dear sister, whatever sentence awaits me, I
am your inviolate friend and unhappy brother.

                                                    Faverolles.[96]

Like him, the woman whom he loved, Agathe Jolivet, was
brought before the Revolutionary Tribunal the following day. Both
were accused of assisting the counter-revolutionary plans of 'the
infamous Dumouriez and of supporting the internal and external
enemies of liberty'. In particular, Faverolles was accused of being 'an
agent of the federalists of the Midi' and of having 'contributed to the
rebellion of the aforementioned Lyon': a trunk containing his correspondence was seized at Agathe Jolivet's and provided ample
proof. A double condemnation to death was pronounced, to be
carried out the following day.

Removed shortly afterwards to the cell for condemned women,
Agathe Jolivet wrote her last letter to Fouquier-Tinville:

> Citizen, as I left the court after the sentence that you thought fit to
> pass concerning me, one of your members provoked me into
> saying certain things concerning the unhappy inhabitants of the
> French territories.
>
> I have decided to give a great deal of information, but only on
> condition that I can spend the last few moments that remain to me
> with Faverolles.[97]

Did Fouquier-Tinville accede to her last wish? We do not know.
Nevertheless the lovers were reunited on the following day for the
preparations prior to the execution. And their happiness at being
together seemed to make them forget the horror of their situation, as
this police observer remarks:

> When one of the executioner's assistants held out his hand to
> Agathe Jolivet, to help her up into the cart, she grasped it, leapt up
> the few steps at one go and, against all expectations, laughingly
> threw her arms around Sanson's assistant. Faverolles, Bonnefoy
> and another condemned man, Dutremblay, burst out laughing in
> turn, which much displeased the onlookers, who began to shout in
> chorus:
> 'To the guillotine! To the guillotine!'
> Turning to one of them, Faverolles replied:
> 'Go on! It'll be your turn soon enough!'
> And Bonnefoy added:
> 'Perhaps tomorrow!'[98]

Another onlooker, who was following the cart, was surprised by
their confidence and arrogance:

One is no less a villain for looking as sincere as the woman Jolivet. On the cart, she talked to her lover Faverolles, who did his best to laugh and in such a manner that one might have thought that she was going to dine with him at Saint-Cloud. She often brought Bonnefoy and Dutremblay into the conversation and they seemed to take a very active part in it. As they got out of the car, they all four embraced one another and took leave of one another with strangely free and affectionate gestures.[99]

This was no isolated case. That of Jean-Jacques Durand, former mayor of Montpellier, was just as moving. As he walked up the steps to the scaffold, a policeman notes in his report: 'Ready to bear the penalty for his crimes, he began to laugh, repeating over and over, "Farewell, my brothers!" The onlookers replied: "To the guillotine!" And he went on laughing.'

He had just written this letter of farewell to his wife:

> To Citizeness Durand, Hôtel de l'Union,
> Rue Saint-Thomas-du-Louvre, no. 26, at Paris.

My beloved,

Be not too much afflicted, I assure you that I die content; the severity of men assures me of God's mercy; it expiates the sins that I have committed and prevents those that I might have committed. You know my weakness, my extreme sensitivity: it may have misled me; God is good enough to prevent it; come now, let us not be separated! I shall always be with you, with our children, watching over you. When you think of me, know that I am there and that I still love you.

I forgive my enemies; do likewise. What they did they thought they were doing for the best and I have only myself to blame. Accuse them of nothing. What can one accuse men of when God alone does all? It is he who is separating us for a moment, so that we may the more surely be reunited, reunited forever, so you see that it was necessary! Farewell, my beloved; console yourself for life with the image of eternity. It is that which we shall pass together: only my misdeeds might have prevented it. Thanks to God, that danger is past. Farewell, my beloved; no, I do not say farewell, I say good night, for I am about to sleep for a time, a little time! When I wake, I shall see my beloved again and nothing will separate us more. I embrace our children, our parents, our friends: console them for my death. I leave them my life. I leave them also my example. May they learn through my sins to overcome their characters, to moderate their passions and not to follow at all times the devices of their hearts, which may lead them astray. May they love their country as I have loved it, and serve it the more happily.

My children, love your mother and obey her as you would us both. All my rights over you I convey to her; she has her own and mine. My dear parents, I am angry at the pain that I have caused you; your suffering is the only suffering that I feel at this moment. Farewell, I go to the place to which the master calls me, he is releasing me from my labours in the middle of the day. I shall rest until evening; then all shall be well among us. Farewell my beloved, farewell.

Durand.[100]

A certain Blanchet was also remarkable for his behaviour during his last moments. His final farewell was to his wife:

Farewell, my wife and children, for ever and ever. Love my children, I beg you, tell them often what I was, love them for us both. Farewell my wife and children. I go to draw the curtain of life.

You, my friends, console my wife and children, that I beg you. Farewell, Maître, my friend, farewell Galeau and all those who took part in my misfortunes. Embrace my little children.

I end my days today.

Blanchet, judged a criminal this 23 Ventôse, 1794.

I embrace my wife and my children.

Blanchet.

He continues his farewells on the envelope: 'Tripotin, friend, farewell. My wife, my children, farewell for life.'[101]

Then he died with courage, in the company of an architect and a nun:

He made jokes up to the moment when he told all the onlookers that he wished them a happier lot; that, as far as he was concerned, he was dying for a matter of very little importance. He then took his leave of all the citizens, laughing the while.[102]

Not all the executions proceeded so smoothly. They were more usually surrounded by sobbings, tears, sometimes even shouts, unlike the few who found the courage to talk quietly together, or laugh, or sing. The executioners arrived: an involuntary shudder, nature's rebellion against destruction, ran through the assembly, even among the most courageous.

When the assistants made the finishing touches to the '*toilette*' of the condemned (the opening of shirt collars, the exposure of the nape of the neck), some suddenly demanded the '*griache*' (prison slang for close-stool), others asked for an extra glass of brandy.

The real torture was the journey from the Conciergerie to the place of execution. It could take an hour to get to the Place de la Révolution. Later, when the guillotine was installed in the Place du Trône-Renversé (the present Place de la Nation), it took longer still.

The spectacle was never identical and, according to the police reports, there were always a lot of people present.

One such report relates a conversation between apprentice printers as the condemned went by:

'Good lord, when will we have had enough of shedding blood?'
'When we've no longer any guilty left.'
Another:
'A man's death doesn't cost much.'
'If they guillotined for thinking,' another replied, 'how many people would have to die?' Then the last speaker added:
'Don't let's talk so loud, we might be overheard and caught. . .'

Next day, in the afternoon, another policeman, attending a multiple execution, heard a woman call out nearby: '*Quelle horreur!*'

Several citizens wanted to seek a quarrel with this citizeness over the word that she had just used:

'What do you mean by that? Are you angry that the conspirators should be punished?'

'No,' she said, 'I meant that it is surprising that, with so many sent to the guillotine, it has not stopped the others in their evil ways.'

Citizen Pourvoyeur notes again:

Like the Place de la Révolution, the Palace is always full of folk. They aren't surprised by the apparent self-control of the guilty. They say that they would be quite happy to see the last one die and even complain that we are proceeding too slowly.

From the cart, Citizen Tunduti de la Balmondière addressed the same gawpers in these terms: 'Cowards and fools that you are! You want the Republic and you have no bread. But, I tell you, before six weeks are out you will have a king – and we need one!'

It is true that the crowd was sometimes heard to murmur as the carts went by: 'They are the lucky ones, they won't have to waste their time any more waiting at the doors of butchers and other shops for their daily food supplies . . .'[103]

On 4 Thermidor, Year II, five carts proceeded on their way to the Faubourg Saint-Antoine. A priest was walking discreetly beside them, trying to catch the eye of several women in one of them.

A storm was raging and the wind came in sudden, powerful gusts. The ladies in the first carriage were most incommoded by it, especially the Maréchale de Noailles. Her broad hat was blown back, revealing a few grey hairs. The women stood unsteadily on their wretched planks, their hands tied behind their backs. Suddenly a lot of people who happened to be in the street, despite the downpour, recognized her and turned all their attention to her, tormenting her still more with their insulting shouts, which she bore with patience:

'There she is,' they cried. 'There's the marshal's wife who used to go about so grandly in her fine coach, there she is in the cart like all the others!'[104]

Sometimes there were incidents. A few over-excited onlookers threw mud at the condemned men and women. Sometimes insults rained down on the wretched victims crammed into the so-called 'bier of the living' or the 'coach with thirty-six doors', especially if the prisoners seemed imperturbably calm. On other occasions, the crowd remained silent, surprised, for example, by Mme du Barry's 'Save me, friends . . . I beg you!'

The police reports are almost unanimous in stressing the extraordinary courage of those condemned. On 2 January 1794, Pourvoyeur notes:

We have guillotined several private individuals . . . among them was a young lady who struck the onlookers by the carefree air she maintained to the very end. All along the way she cried: 'Long live the Empire! Long live the Emperor!' People had to acknowledge that they had never seen such courage, or rather such audacity. That young lady was only twenty-two years of age. When sentence had been passed on her, she turned to the people and the judges and declared that her father and brother would avenge her blood after her death.[105]

The onlookers could not always stand such a sight. Some fainted:

One can no longer go out, some said, without seeing the guillotine or those being taken to it; our children are getting cruel and it is to be feared that pregnant women will bring forth children with marks on their necks or still as statues because of the distressing sights they are subjected to in our streets . . .[106]

Many Parisians avoided the routes taken by the carts. Even the press of the time showed great reticence in this respect. The police reports, on the other hand, give us abundant evidence concerning the last moments of the condemned men and women. On 31 October 1793, twenty-one Girondins were led off to execution:

We noticed that the villains in the first carriage were all laughing, especially Fonfrède, who was laughing fit to burst; the others were talking among themselves. In the other carriage, the occupants were behaving in like manner, almost without knowing it . . . Sillery was executed first. Those who followed him displayed a villainous courage; the people grew angry with them. They were all expedited in twenty-six minutes. The execution proceeded at such a vigorous pace that several heads rolled down to the bottom of the scaffold at once. Brissot was executed last. I noticed that when it came to the sixth to be executed, many of the onlookers began to walk away, with sad expressions and in the greatest consternation.[107]

Those who went along the routes taken by the carts were often there simply out of curiosity, trying to put a name to a well-known face. The same week saw Adam Lux, who had fallen in love with the image of the dead Charlotte Corday, walking enthusiastically towards the scaffold; Olympe de Gouges, who, standing in her cart, harangued the crowd; the Duc d'Orléans, phlegmatic and taciturn; Mme Roland, white as marble; Bailly, first mayor of Paris, for whom the scaffold was erected on the Champ-de-Mars in memory of a fusillade against the people, for which he was held responsible. Then fell the heads of the former members of the Constituent Assembly, soldiers and ministers, individuals about whom innumerable anecdotes, true or false, circulated.

A special episode: the departure from the Oiseaux

A few days prior to Robespierre's fall, the attention of the Revolutionary Tribunal was drawn to a little known *maison de détention* in the Rue de Sèvres, not far from the present-day Boulevard des Invalides.[108] An agent of the Tribunal, a certain Ducret, who had just visited the château and park of the Princesse de Chimay, at Issy, had learnt that the princess was being held in a *'maison de suspicion'*, in the Rue de Sèvres, known as the Maison des Oiseaux. When Fouquier-Tinville learnt of this, he exclaimed: 'In the Oiseaux? I've been looking for her for the past three months!'[109]

Citizen Ducret's visit no doubt aroused the public prosecutor's interest in this establishment, with its special regime. The detainees, who were mainly either aristocrats or extremely rich, paid a rather high *pension*, which, in some cases, allowed them to keep their children and servants with them or to have their food fetched in from outside. The standards of hygiene there were very acceptable and the inmates were allowed to move freely through the house and adjoining garden. Most of them were afraid not so much for themselves, as for their relations being held in the Carmes or at Saint-Lazare.

In fact, in six months, only three individuals had been taken to the Conciergerie and condemned. Until the morning of 7 Thermidor, the greatest names in the French nobility were to be found there. This is how d'Hornoy, a leading judge, also an inmate, recounts the departure from the Oiseaux:

The bell rang. This unexpected signal, which announced something new – and any novelty was to be feared – filled our hearts with terrible foreboding. I dashed to the gate and found under the vault a tall man with a hateful face, wearing a medal in his buttonhole, a bundle of papers in his hands and several gendarmes around him. I learnt that he was a clerk from the Revolutionary Tribunal, that a carriage and four was there, that some twenty or twenty-five of us might be taken away and that we were all to assemble in the courtyard.

I went back and found that Mme d'Ossun and Mme de Maillé were no longer there and that Mme de Cuvilly was highly alarmed. I comforted her as best I could, took her by the hand, led her to the courtyard and set her down there. With terror, I looked for those closest to me and my heart trembled on account of the strength of the ties that bound me to them. I found that almost everybody was putting a good face on it and seemed more surprised than frightened. The keeper had begun a general roll-call. The clerk interrupted him, moved to the middle of the circle and himself called out 'Grammont d'Orsan'. This mangled name echoed in all our hearts and tore at mine. He called out the name a second time. 'We have nobody here of that name,' someone replied. He called it out a third time. The wretched Mme d'Ossun, whom none of us dared to look at, rose to her feet: 'It might be I,' she said, moving forward with a firm step. The clerk directed her to take her place there. The horrible minister of death called out one name after another: 'Darmentières, Chimay, Narbonne-Pelet, Cécile Quévrain, Quérhoënt, Maulévrier, Raymond de Narbonne.' All these women took their places, without betraying any trace of weakness. As each name was called out, the wretched victims moved so promptly that there was no occasion to repeat it. 'Forward march!' yelled our ferocious gaolers with all the barbarous delight of an insult.

The clerk then called three men, the Duc de Clermont-Tonnerre, the Marquis de Crussol d'Amboise and M. de Saint-Simon, the Bishop of Agde. This last individual replied, from his window, that he was coming down. Leclerc, with the ferocity of a tiger, took delight in repeating his name and the quality that was to take him to the scaffold several times. At last we were told that the list was complete for that day.

This was the most painful moment. Fear for oneself and for those dearest to one could now be transferred unalloyed to our eleven unfortunate martyrs, arrayed on the fatal bench. A gutter that ran across the courtyard was pointed out as the boundary that was not to be crossed. This trickle of water now became for us the Styx, which our comrades had just passed.

The Marquis de Crussol, whose name alone, of course, and the fate that had brought him to the Constituent Assembly were crime enough, walked up and down this boundary in surprise and suddenly stepped over it. 'I forbade you to cross that gutter,' yelled the clerk and the victim resumed his place on the bench.

The wretched Mme de Quérhoënt, an elderly, infirm valetudinarian, constantly tormented by her fears, which we found foolish, had tormented us all with them. We kept up a running battle with her. She walked with the same firm tread as her companions and, when she passed near me, I heard her say: 'Well, gentlemen, were my fears so foolish?' All the reproaches that I had allowed myself to make of her I now turned back upon myself, causing me unbearable remorse. The victims were sent in turn back to their rooms, accompanied by a warder, who would not let them speak to anybody, to fetch a few necessaries to take with them.

Mme de Narbonne-Pelet, who was old and sick, returned, leaning on Cécile Quévrain, her chambermaid, condemned with her. She asked for a bag. 'You won't need one,' Antoine, who had accompanied her to her room, yelled back. 'Forward march.'

The Duc de Clermont-Tonnerre, an old man of seventy-four, a respected soldier, asked, as he crossed the courtyard, where M. de la Ferté, his cousin, intimate friend and chamber companion, was to be found. Somebody tried to reply. 'Don't speak to him,' yelled Leclerc. 'Forward march!' and the poor wretch could not embrace his friend, who was deeply upset at hearing his name called out.

The most courageous, most moving of all, perhaps, was the Comtesse Raymond de Narbonne. Still young, as lovable and fascinating as ever, she was separated by force from her ten-year-old daughter who was there. She was given permission to rise for a moment and to cross the fatal gutter. With great dignity, she walked up to the Duchesse de Choiseul: 'Madame,' she said, embracing her, 'I place my unhappy daughter in your hands. I beg you to be a mother to her for a little time.'

And she turned back, calmly, and returned to her funereal post. When the horrible official had gathered all his victims together, when he had counted them several times over, he sent them out one after another. They all disappeared from our sight for ever and the gates shut upon them like a stone sealing their grave.[110]

Before taking the road to the Conciergerie, the convoy stopped at Sainte-Pélagie, to collect the former Princess of Monaco.

Next day, 8 Thermidor, just before appearing before the Revolutionary Tribunal, Mme du Quérhoënt, her indictment in her hand, wrote to Fouquier, bathing her letters with tears:

> I was ignorant until this moment, citizen, of what I could be accused. I see that I am accused of emigration, though I have never left the territory of France for one moment of my life.
>
> I beg you, citizen, to allow me to send for my certificates of residence, which are with my agent, Rue de l'Université, at a baker's shop, no 492, I believe, but definitely at the corner of the Rue Bellechasse, in the house of Citizen Du Motel. Greetings and fraternity.
>
> Donge-Quérhoënt.[111]
> This 8 Thermidor.

Cécile Quévrain, Mme de Narbonne's servant, who was also found guilty, claimed to be pregnant by a merchant by the name of Bouchot. The Princess of Monaco also claimed to be pregnant. Both were taken to the hospice of the Revolutionary Tribunal, while their companions were led off to the scaffold.

Cécile Quévrain, 'Mme de Narbonne's third chambermaid', was accused of following her mistress into emigration and, on their return, of assisting and sheltering numerous émigrés.

At the Tribunal hospice, she wrote a 'memorandum' intended for the Convention in which she tried to prove her innocence.

> Citizens,
>
> Citizeness Cécile Quévrain requests your clemency once again, in the name of the Supreme Being, of justice, of humanity and of a wretched ninety-year-old father, whom, in dying, I leave without resources, since I am all that he has left, and, lastly, of a brother, who lost a leg in the battle of Jemmapes, for whom I have spent my last *sou* during those terrible five months that he was in the hospital at Valenciennes.
>
> You heard yesterday of my death sentence, you know the extent of my innocence, you also know that it is on account of the title 'confidante', which I resolutely reject, that I am brought to this pass: what, a woman who has belonged to Citizeness Narbonne eleven years and who, of course, enjoyed her benevolence far more than I, is left in peace, while I, because my good heart led me to provide her with the cares that age required, am lost. Believe me

when I say that it is not my life that I regret, but my unhappy father.

Yesterday, when I heard the woman who has been arrested called before the Tribunal, I thought I was saved. I admit that I appeared there with all the calm and tranquillity of the purest innocence; I was fully persuaded that justice would be done me when I saw Citizens D'Aine *(sic)* and Poincelot arrive. I seemed to see my guardian angels: I did not doubt that they had come to save me. I do not know by what fatality they were not listened to. Would you not dare, citizens, to say a word of truth to save a poor victim? No, I dare to hope that the reign of justice and humanity is not past.

It is on this that I base my case and I beg you, on bended knee, whichever citizen of you reads this paper, to go at once to the Convention and submit a small memorandum that I am addressing to it, demanding the justice that any good Republican will always be ready to give. I dare to hope that it will be given me, it cannot be otherwise. I ask you only for one word of truth, which is that I have never been the confidante of Citizeness Narbonne, no never. I did not fear that I would be put to death for joining Citizeness Narbonne six months after the others, who have been left unmolested: there is nothing but an unfortunate misunderstanding with the woman who is at Picpus. I beg you, citizens, [illegible word], it would be sweet to owe you my life.

Greetings and fraternity.

Horror of death made me declare that I was pregnant. This is not so. I have been transferred to the hospice. Time is running out. Do not abandon me, I beg you.[112]

As Cécile Quévrain, in the depths of anguish, was writing her letter, the Princess of Monaco was writing this note to Fouquier-Tinville:

Citizen,

I wish to inform you that I am not pregnant. I wanted to tell you. Though I can no longer hope that you will come, I beg you to do so nonetheless. I did not soil my mouth with this lie out of fear of death, nor to avoid it, but to give me one day more, so that I might cut my own hair, and not have it done at the hands of the executioner. It is the only legacy that I can leave to my children; at least it must be pure.

Choiseul-Stainville-Joseph-Grimaldi-Monaco, foreign princess, and dying from the injustice of French judges.

Indeed the case of this princess was an unlucky one.

The principality of Monaco had signed a treaty of alliance with France on 21 September 1791. But, on 14 February 1793, following a report presented by Carnot, the Convention had decreed the annexation of Monaco to France.

Since the princess was regarded as a foreigner before that date, the laws on emigration did not apply to her.

Unconcerned about her considerable fortune, she had undertaken a journey to Rome, during which she had been noticed among many of those opposing the Revolution: Lord and Lady Hamilton, the Duchesse de Fleury and Mme Vigée-Lebrun, who admired her 'charming face'.

Having become a French citizen in the spring of 1793, she immediately returned to her country so as not to appear on the list of émigrés and to avoid the sequestration of her property.

Arrested in Paris when she was trying to regularize her situation, she presented forged residence certificates and was freed on bail. Unfortunately for her, her husband had joined the insurrection in the Vendée – and the couple had not taken the precaution of divorcing. With the law concerning suspects of 17 September 1793 the princess's situation became precarious. A new warrant was issued for her arrest.

She sought refuge with her friend Rollet d'Avaux, then, so as not to compromise her, hid in the former Benedictine convent of Panthémont in the Rue de Grenelle.

She was arrested in the winter of 1793–4 and sent to the Petite-Force, where the regime was particularly harsh. She no doubt negotiated her transfer to another prison. Some such manoeuvres were carried out if this unpublished note, signed by a certain Ferré, and addressed to the princess, is to be believed.

> Do you know if the unknown person has been transferred? She must be: let me know how you are. My feelings accompany you everywhere. Receive my homage.

We do not know the identity of the 'unknown person', but the princess was taken to the prison of the Anglaises and, on 27 Germinal, transferred with eleven other women to Sainte-Pélagie. Denounced during the first days of Thermidor by Ferrières-Sauvebeuf, one of the informers in La Force, she was condemned to death together with her business adviser, Citizen Viotte, and the inmates of the Oiseaux.

After plaiting and cutting her own hair with a piece of glass, she wrote this note to her children:

> My children, here is my hair. I have postponed my death one day, not out of fear, but because I wanted myself to cut off these sad remains of me that you might have them: I did not want it to be left

to the hands of the executioner and these were my only means. I have spent one more day in this agony, but I [words crossed out, author's note] do not complain.

I ask that my hair be placed under glass, covered with black crêpe, put away for most of the year and brought out only three or four times a year in your bedchamber so that you may have before you the remains of your unfortunate mother who died loving you and who regrets her life only because she can no longer be useful to you.

I commend you to your grandfather: if you see him, tell him that my thoughts are with him and that he stands in place of everything for you, and you, my children, take care of him in his old age and make him forget his misfortunes.

To her children's governess, Citizeness Chevenoy, she wrote:

I have already written to you and I am writing to you again to commend my children to you. When you receive this note, I shall be no more, but let my memory make you take pity on my unhappy children. That is the only feeling that they can now inspire.

I leave you, as a souvenir, the ring in which my children's names were inscribed and which you should have received by now – it is the only thing at my disposal to give. Let Louise know the reason why I postponed my death, that she may not suspect me of weakness.[113]

Paris de l'Épinard, a detainee at the hospice, saw the princess leave on the morning of 9 Thermidor 'among a line of inmates from the women's quarters, without betraying any other emotion than that of legitimate indignation against her murderers'.

Addressing the other detainees, she said: 'Citizens, I go to my death with all the tranquillity that comes of innocence, I wish you all a better fate . . .' She then handed her hair and her letters to the porter, who led her out to the cart. As she entered it, she turned to him and said: 'Swear to me, in the presence of these honest men, whom the same fate awaits, that you will carry out for me this last service, which I expect of a human being.'

Turning to a woman (no doubt Cécile Quévrain), whose 'despondency' was painful to see, she said: 'Courage, my dear friend! Courage! Only crime can show weakness.'

Two of the 'conspirators' of Saint-Lazare, Mme de Butler, a native of the West Indies, and the Comtesse de Périgord, who also claimed to be pregnant, accompanied them. The four women, the oldest of whom was only thirty-two, joined the group of condemned men and women for that day. It was 9 Thermidor and as the line of carts moved slowly towards the Rue du Faubourg-Saint-Antoine, the tocsin rang in the distance. A rumour announcing the fall of Robespierre and his friends was already spreading through Paris.

The convoy, it seems, was stopped by the people. There was talk of suspending the execution. General Hanriot, commander of the Garde Parisienne, having previously been warned, galloped on to the scene, cleared the way and ordered the carts to move more quickly.

Twenty minutes later, they were in front of the scaffold. The carts stopped, surrounded by guards, and the condemned were put into two rows facing the Faubourg Saint-Antoine. Pale, tense, shivering despite the time of year, several of them lowered their heads or shut their eyes.

The first was called. In the next thirty seconds, three dull sounds followed one another; the plank swivelling, the lunette banging, the blade cutting . . . A second victim was ready. The third was called. It was the Princess of Monaco. She climbed the steps in her turn. On the platform, her youthful beauty shone in the dazzling July light.

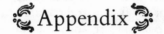

Appendix

MONEY IN THE PRISONS OF THE TERROR

A thoroughgoing study of the prisons of the Terror reveals quite clearly, in the background, the importance that financial transactions had in those places. It was a constant game of hide-and-seek between the possessors of large fortunes, who were trying to preserve their property, and the Republic, which needed it to finance the state. To this should be added the more political intentions of the counter-revolutionaries, who tried to ruin the Republic by worsening the serious economic and financial difficulties that faced it.

Indeed, for the counter-revolutionaries, it was a question of putting an end to the Revolution and the man who represented it: Robespierre. What better way than to do everything possible, in secret, to encourage the Terror? Robespierre would fall all the sooner. And, on 10 Thermidor Year II, it was Robespierre who was handed over to the crowd, to its hate. He is held up to public execration, which survived long after his death, in innumerable writings. Take, for example, these few lines written a hundred years later:

> The effect was produced long ago and, even supposing that it is regrettable, which I do not believe, it would be in nobody's power to destroy or weaken it. Hatred of Robespierre is as popular a phenomenon as Napoleon's glory.

An extraordinary process of disinformation and travesty of the facts was set in train simultaneously by former instigators of the Terror, businessmen and royalists: precisely those against whom Robespierre was fulminating only a few weeks before his death, those for whom 'the Revolution was a commercial matter, the people a tool, the nation a prey' and those who, 'lustful for gold and domination, insolently preached equality, thundered against speculation, yet shared out the public fortune with those who practised it . . .'[114]

Few contemporaries were honest on the subject of Robespierre. However, let us quote the very royalist Aimée de Coigny, Duchesse de Fleury, an active agent of the British secret service:

> It was under his domination that I was imprisoned, nearly lost my head and saw many of my friends and relations of both sexes go to the scaffold. If I am so lacking in rancour against his memory, it is because it seems to me that all the horrors perpetrated by those who preceded him, surrounded him, betrayed him, and destroyed him, have been piled upon his name . . . His most fawning courtiers were his most vehement murderers, piling upon his memory the full weight of the blood shared by the Terror, which he might have ended with their heads.
>
> In decapitating Robespierre, those wretches had decapitated their own Jacobin revolution and the system on which they were counting in order to be able to succeed him; they did not have time to fall into step with the legend that they were perpetrating. In men's memories, the defeated always have a bad place. At least I am willing to allow M. de Robespierre the fine name of Incorruptible . . .[115]

Among those 'artisans of the Terror' who purposely exaggerated the repression and encouraged dubious financial practices, one ought to stress the role played by several members of the Committee of General Safety, members who, despite the denunciations that were often made of them, never had to ascend the steps of the scaffold and were sometimes covered with glory and honours under the Directoire and Empire. A deputy for Versailles, Lecointre, had denounced them in the Convention, but the prosecutions got bogged down in the rivalries between them, on the one hand, and Tallien and other Thermidorians, on the other.[116]

Yet it was they who had had arrested hundreds of individuals without applying article 9 of the law of 17 September 1793, according to which the Committee was to be informed of the identity of all persons arrested and the grounds for their arrest. On this point, Foignet, who was held in the Anglaises, has this to say:

> No, it will never be forgotten that the Committee signed and delivered, without examination, thousands of arrest warrants, that it did not carry out the laws that might have proved favourable to the detainees, that it is the prime cause of the murders of a large number of victims. Similar crimes make their authors criminals towards the entire nation. The greater the courage needed to bear the ills inseparable from a great revolution, the more severely must one deal with those who profit from times of confusion and abuse their power to enslave a section of the very people whose represen-

tatives they are only in order to work for the people's good. They may claim that they have imprisoned only enemies of the public good. It would be easy enough to confound them, by showing them the warrants for the release of prisoners issued since 10 Thermidor, after examination of the documents that they themselves had in their possession.[117]

There can be little doubt that nobles and rich bourgeois were arrested, not so much on account of their titles and qualities, as of the use to which their fortunes were put in assisting the counter-revolution.

However, carried away by its own zeal, the Committee of General Safety saw suspects everywhere, except in its own offices. Indeed we know that many spies and agents in the pay of foreign powers or of émigré princes sat in the Revolutionary Committees, urging them to extremism and violence. Their aim was not only to sink the Revolution in a bloodbath, but also, by encouraging corruption, to discredit parliamentary and governmental institutions.

It is now accepted that this corruption involved many of those close to Danton, including Chabot, Basire, Alquier, Rovère and Guffroy. On the other hand, their sympathy for the counter-revolutionaries is well less known, because of the great efforts made to erase all trace of it.[118] Later, only Julien de Toulouse had difficulty in clearing himself of his long-standing relations with one of the leaders of the emigration, the Comte de Lachâtre, with whom he was in contact through the Comtesse de Beaufort.

Two cases seem to give credence to these sympathies and this corruption. An unpublished letter, written from the prison of the Anglaises, tends to prove that certain of Danton's supporters often helped émigrés to carry a little of the national heritage away with them. This letter came from Mme de Laubespin, who had been imprisoned since September 1793 with her father-in-law, who was later to be guillotined. Closely linked with the great counter-revolutionary plots, Élisabeth-Charlotte de Scorailles, Marquise Mouchet de Laubespin, had also taken an active part in attempts to salvage the immense fortune of her relation, the Duc du Châtelet.

Arrested, and fearing that she would be called before the Revolutionary Tribunal at any moment, she refers in her letter to her friendship for the deputies Rovère and Guffroy, begging to be freed. By error, the letter happened to reach the Committee of Surveillance for Paris.[119]

The second case, which is not entirely clear, is interesting because it involves Amar, one of the best-known members of the Committee of General Safety. An émigré, d'Aligre, a former presiding judge at the *Parlement*, and one of the very wealthiest men of the time, had entrusted a number of his possessions to a certain Mme de Crussol, who was herself extremely rich. She had been arrested as a suspect in September 1793 and everybody believed her to be in prison. In fact, she had been living peacefully at home for several months. When this anomaly was discovered the two citizens entrusted with her surveillance were immediately put into solitary confinement and executed soon afterwards.[120] Mme de Crussol was in turn brought to the Conciergerie, then guillotined, without being subjected to any interrogation concerning her relations with Amar, whose name and private address were found in her notebook. It is likely that she owed the fact that she had been able to stay in her own home to him. At what cost?

Similarly, corruption appears to have reached certain members of the Revolutionary Tribunal. Coffinhal-Dubail, one of the vice-presidents of the Tribunal, used his influence to have his compatriot, Mesnil-Simon, who had involved him two years earlier in some inglorious business concerning the misappropriation of an inheritance, executed.[121] Dumas, another vice-president, ordered the arrest of Citizeness Pottier de Lille, whose husband, a well-known royalist, had just been guillotined. She had reproached him for not intervening in her favour and had threatened to reveal publicly the bribes that he had accepted. 9 Thermidor saved his life.[122]

And what of Fouquier-Tinville? It has been claimed that two women from Auteuil, the Dames de Boufflers, had escaped certain death thanks to him. It seems that it was the private tutor of the Boufflers' children, a friend of Fouquier, who pleaded on their behalf.[123] Yet, despite the efforts of his many enemies, no one has ever been able to prove that the public prosecutor was corrupt. On the other hand, we know that he 'covered' for the weaknesses of Committee members and he has been held responsible for the disappearance of several documents and for literally emptying certain case files.

In her memoirs, Mme Roland claimed that Dillon and Castellane, accused of complicity with General Dumouriez, were able to leave prison after paying 30,000 *livres* to the deputy of Chabot.[124] An unpublished note, written at the time when Fouquier-Tinville was in power, also implicates him in this mysterious affair.[125]

It would seem that it was thanks to Chabot that the two men were freed. Shortly afterwards, Dillon was arrested once again; implicated in a conspiracy affair, he died on the guillotine.

In her somewhat prolix way, Mme Roland cites another case of corruption in the summer of 1793:

At the time, 22 August, I was keeping an eye on a certain Mlle Briant, living at Cloître Saint-Benoît, no 207, a kept woman, whose lover is a forger of assignats. Denounced, it seemed that he would be prosecuted, but the gold flowed into the hands of the administrators; he who organized his search and seizure knew where he was hidden; his mistress was arrested for form's sake; the administrators who appeared to have come to question her gave her news of her lover; and they were soon to be at liberty together, since they had money enough to pay.[126]

If she is to be believed, Fouquier-Tinville set the example:

Fouquier-Tinville, public prosecutor at the Revolutionary Tribunal, known for his evil life, his impudence in issuing indictments for no reason, regularly received money from those charged. Mme de Rochechouart paid him 80,000 *livres* for Mony, the émigré. Fouquier-Tinville took the money. Mony was executed and Mme de Rochechouart was warned that, if she opened her mouth, she would be locked up and never see the light of day again.[127]

This evidence, though partly based on fact, is apocryphal. At the time when the Lyonnais notary, Mony, suspected of complicity with Mme du Barry, was being investigated, Mme Roland had already been dead for three months. But it was, in fact, the Comtesse de Rochechouart who intervened in his favour in high places and saved him from the scaffold. She knew a number of Montagnards, seemed to be very close to Hébert and spent considerable sums buying the freedom of detainees.

In another affair, it was one of the jurors of the Revolutionary Tribunal who was named as implicated in such corrupt practices. The Marquise de Peysac, a rich widow accused of sending money into Holland, was certain to be executed. One of her friends, Lord Massereene, had set about buying certain of the jurors. One of them, Garnier-Launay, seems to have been compromised, as the accusation made by the poor woman a few moments before leaving for the scaffold seems to testify:

Citizens,

I have no reason to reject the jurors appointed to try me – unless Citizen Garnier is one of my Lord Massereene's creditors. Because they have accused me of preventing them from paying, when I alone could have decided to accept an arrangement, namely, to give two hundred thousand francs in cash, and, for the rest, as much per year, most of the creditors refused this arrangement.

I can offer proof of everything I am saying: it was the bank of my

Lord Massereene which was to provide the money. If Citizen Garnier is not a creditor of my Lord Massereene, I do not reject him. Greetings and fraternity.

19 Pluviôse.

                                                    Chapt-Peysac.[128]

Corruption played a none too inconsiderable role during this period and a number of other practices concerning property were to be found in the prison. These practices facilitated the transfer of property to mysterious destinations and involved, of course, the richer detainees. In various roles, the participants in such practices were invariably: the members of the Committee of General Safety, their agents and informers, Fouquier-Tinville, the judges or juries of the Revolutionary Tribunal, the Hébertist members of the police administration and the agents in Paris of émigrés or bankers.

What is to be said of the aims pursued by all these people? On the one hand, some hoped to save their lives or property, while, on the other, those who received compensation did not agree as to its destination. How many portfolios, after being the object of bitter negotiation, eluded national ownership after discreet manoeuvres had enabled them to find their way into the coffers of a Belgian or Swiss bank? One can guess the complicities that might have been involved in these last-minute transactions, sometimes in the highest circles of government. When the former director of the Mint, Emmanuel Roettiers (see p. 157), was arrested for embezzling public funds, he was found to be the depositor of property belonging to émigrés, property that had been entrusted to him in the form of donations or false debts. A week before his all too expected condemnation to death, his notary, Denis de Villières, visited him at the Conciergerie.[129] In this way, by a deed signed on 12 Ventôse, Roettiers was able to obtain power of attorney on his behalf for his wife, thus giving her full authority over the administration of his entire property, present and to come. At the same time, Roettiers' wife was able to arrange matters in such a way that within forty-eight hours her husband no longer owned anything at all. It is quite possible that the chairman of the Finances Commission at the Convention, Cambon,[130] advised his friend Roettiers what steps should be taken once he realized that he could no longer save him.

In another affair, which also involved several hundred thousand *livres*, it was again Cambon who was implicated. In January 1794, he was entrusted with the task of examining the accounts of the Swiss banker Perrégaux, who was known to have sent funds to various émigrés. According to Lafitte, the future governor of the Bank of France, then one of Perrégaux's employees, Cambon did not prove very demanding in his search for proofs of Perrégaux's complicity with the émigrés and counter-revolutionaries.[131] And yet the Swiss banker, whose mission was officially to serve the French government in its commercial affairs abroad, had the closest possible relations with the Anglophile financiers, Necker and his family. He was a partner of Gumpelsheimer, a Frankfurt banker, who was in contact with the British government and who had given him the task of paying men to maintain a state of disorder in France and to push through ultra-revolutionary measures intended to weaken the country. Indeed a letter has been found among Danton's papers showing that the Foreign Office had specifically given him just such a task.[132] Arrested in December, imprisoned at La Force, he had all the time in the world to advise the rich detainees of their financial affairs. He was freed by a decree of the Convention three weeks later.

One has only to read the Duchesse de Fleury to grasp the role played by international business circles in the counter-revolution.

Such men as Barère, Hébert, Momoro, Merlin de Thionville and Vadier were small fry compared with the great corsairs who manipulated wars and frontiers. At the time of Dumouriez, the Belgian brothers Simon were in charge of supplies to the army. They were succeeded by d'Espagnac, who had been a priest, but who was an indomitable rogue, and by Guzman, who was certainly an agent, but of what? And then there were the bankers, very much at ease under the Terror, except Proly, an Austrian agent, MM. Boyd and Ker and a Swiss, and therefore serious, M. Perrégaux . . .[133]

The men of the Revolutionary committees were highly skilled at tracking down or, on the contrary, collaborating with the agents of international financial circles. They entrusted plans, directives, and missions to junior agents who had a long past in politics – or prison. But why did they recruit them? It must be remembered that before 10 August 1792, several aristocrats had taken an active part in the policy of corrupting the Revolution introduced originally in the Tuileries by Mirabeau, and taken over on his death by Louis XVI's secret advisers, in particular Talon, Sainte-Foix and Bertrand de Molleville. What they were trying to do was to stop the Revolution by means of money, by corrupting the Paris police, the Jacobin deputies, popular ringleaders and journalists. The Court had not hesitated to spend vast sums in the hope of winning over 'left-wing' circles and the senior officers of the National Guard.

Now several of those we find in 1793–4 acting as the informers, spies or secret agents of the Committee of General Safety had already pocketed the money paid to them through the civil list, but had not yet rendered the services expected of them. Furthermore, disturbed by the accusations of corruption that were beginning to threaten them, they now saw their salvation only in a radical shift of position after 10 August, thus turning against their earlier seducers, who had now become embarrassing witnesses.

One of the most famous of those who changed camp in this way was Jean-Baptiste Dossonville.[134] Arrested and tried after 10 August, he was mysteriously acquitted just prior to the September massacres. Recruited by the first Committee of Surveillance, he had been entrusted with various espionage missions in the troubled waters of the world of forgers, on the boundary between common law and political crime.

Very soon, he was suspected of connivance with the counter-revolutionaries whom he was supposed to be pursuing. He was finally arrested after a fantastic blackmail affair, in which he had been implicated together with one of his acolytes, the Comte de Pigace. Held for three months at Sainte-Pélagie, he suddenly reappeared as the principal agent of the Committee of General Safety, entrusted with possibly the most secret, in any case the oddest, most delicate of missions. Thus he was officially given the task of pursuing, with the utmost thoroughness, the famous royalist conspirator de Batz, while others had given him the unofficial task of never catching him. Dossonville, an astonishing character, was also associated with other shadier affairs, both inside and outside the prisons. Yet his name was never to appear on any of the committee's registers, a fact that he himself acknowledged under the Restoration when applying for a pension from Louis XVIII:

> My name doubtless does not appear on the accounts, for I had my own register, which was numbered on each page and initialled by one of the members [Amar].[135]

No less curious a character and one whom Dossonville knew very well was the Abbé d'Espagnac, a detainee in La Force. This former priest and one of the pillars of the counter-revolution had made a huge fortune in speculation. A confidential report, dated 1793 and hitherto unpublished, sums up in a few words the kind of activities that he indulged in when, as manager of a company dealing with military transport, he was under contract with the Ministry of War:

> It has been noticed at the Treasury that whenever an order has been sent out for d'Espagnac, the value of money rose by two or three percent, because those deals were calculated in specie and paid in cash. The huge losses that the assignats have undergone at different

times may be attributed mainly to these successive rises. Such speculation has cost the nation over one hundred and seventy million in stock and, on his own account, he has stolen over thirty.[136]

Arrested, freed, arrested again in the company of André Chénier's mistress, the beautiful Lucrèce d'Estat, he was in La Force during the winter of 1793-4.[137] At this time he was the object of particular solicitude on the part of Dossonville, who, invested with new powers, appears to have visited him in his cell.

The deal proposed for the anticipated freedom of the Abbé consisted of transferring to the policeman an enormous sum, nine million *livres*, to be drawn on the Pérregaux bank in Lausanne. Did Dossonville accept? We do not know. In any case, the Abbé d'Espagnac was then transferred to a *maison de santé* on the outskirts of Paris (Rue Saint-Maur, no 22), from which escape was much easier. The walls of this establishment, which sheltered a number of mysterious transactions usually involving colossal sums of money, belonged to a Swiss, Jean-Baptiste Romey, with whom the Abbé d'Espagnac had once been a business partner.[138]

The Abbé d'Espagnac managed to escape, but was immediately caught again. Dossonville in his *Memoirs* and the barrister Lavaud, a former *défenseur officieux*, in his *Campagnes d'un avocat*, unfortunately give only one, somewhat watered-down version of this affair. According to a recent thesis, this attempted escape was all part of a politico-financial strategy, for the Abbé, who was well acquainted with capitalist circles, would have been more useful in prison than outside it. The refuge of the Rue Saint-Maur enabled him to act, through agents, against Hébert, the supposed agent of the Baron de Batz, his business enemy. A. de Lestapis writes:

> For a long time, very little importance was attached to the struggles between the capitalists that took place between 1789 and 18 Brumaire. Thanks to some very fine studies on the subject, this is no longer the case today. But perhaps it is not yet realized how ruthless this long partisan war between the high financiers was. 'Sharks', like Batz and d'Espagnac, for example, carried on a strange duel through their respective clientèles, a merciless duel that ended in blood, that of the former priest.[139]

Marie-Thérèse Vielle, who was living with the Abbé d'Espagnac, disappeared shortly before the police arrived to arrest her. It was to her that the Abbé wrote this final letter:

> I commend to you the only person who has had the courage to come and see me and to obtain for me every possible comfort from

the moment of my confinement. This person, who is as commend-
able for her wit as for her face and heart, will bring you this letter,
herself I hope, for I do not believe that she will ever dwell in a place
soiled with my blood. She intends to join you. Receive her, I pray
you, as another myself, her and her lovable child . . . Alone for six
months, she is like a family to me. No doubt justice will be done me
one day; so I charge you and my friend to avenge my memory.[140]

One month after the execution of the enormously rich Abbé,
François Louis Honoré Sahuguet d'Espagnac, his cousin, who had
also been held in La Force, was included in the arrest warrant issued
by the Committee of General Safety that brought the former
parliamentarians to the Revolutionary Tribunal. It was by a 'miracle
of Divine Providence', to use his own words, that he alone escaped
the scaffold. He does not say very much about the nature of the
intervention, or the name of this Providence.[141]

Citizen Romey, the owner of the strange *maison de santé* in the Rue
Saint-Maur, was a key figure in the counter-revolution or rather, a
two-faced figure. On the one hand, he was regarded as an unofficial
agent of the Committee of General Safety: 'No sooner did he hear of
a plot fomented by perverse men to undermine the assignat and to
raise the price of specie than he denounced it at once to Citizen Amar,
member of the Committee of General Safety.'[142] But, on the other
hand, his principal and secret role was to get his hands on the
property of suspects who were in danger of being guillotined, in
order to convey it abroad, often to Switzerland. Romey had been
initiated into business by the banker Perroteau and was an intimate
friend of Francois-Elie Ducoster, Necker's agent in Paris in 1794, and
principal financial backer of such counter-revolutionary leaders as
Boulogne, Caumont-La Force or La Trémoille.[143]

He was in contact with all the leading circles of the counter-
revolution, both inside and outside the prison. Among them were
Citizen La Plaigne, a financial backer of Mme Robineau de
Beaunoir's gambling house, Louis Comte, agent of the Swiss banker
Emmanuel Haller, Bonnard, agent of the Duc des Deux-Ponts,
Mme de Billens, ex-wife of a Swiss citizen and mistress of the banker
Ker, agent of the British government, etc. Through Romey, the
whole of European banking was thus represented in the prisons of
the Terror.[144] His mistress, also of Swiss origin, the Comtesse de
Linières, owned a gambling house at the Palais-Royal, financed by a
certain Cappot de Feuillide. We know that most of those gaming
houses in Year II were intended as an outlet for false assignats and a
means of 'laundering' large sums of money of uncertain provenance.
Now this is what Cappot de Feuillide had done for large sums

coming from the Marquise de Marbeuf, a fabulously rich woman who was to appear before the Revolutionary Tribunal.[145]

Convicted of wanting to corrupt Citizen Morel, secretary to the Committee of General Safety, with a view to destroying papers seized at the house of Mme de Marbeuf, Cappot de Feuillide was condemned and executed a few days after her.

Meanwhile, Romey had managed to 'inherit', as Ferrières-Sauvebeuf put it, large sums of money from Cappot de Feuillide's funds: 'He had submitted no accounts to the agents of the Republic,' Ferrières-Sauvebeuf tells us, 'but he owned gaming houses . . .'[146]

Under the Terror the *maisons de santé* that sheltered the richest suspects seemed to have another purpose than that of allowing their inmates to lead a more agreeable life than in ordinary prisons. They also gave the impression that they had been set up in order to allow their inmates to manage their affairs in a convenient manner. Among the visitors who regularly turned up, there was a procession of notaries, financial agents, stock-exchange brokers, auctioneers, but also, occasionally, blackmailers. Thus the two financiers, both natives of Saint-Malo, Magon de la Balue and Magon de la Belinaye, were able to be visited by an individual who offered them passports for Switzerland, passports apparently signed by Robespierre, all for the sum of 300,000 *livres* – a low sum for those multimillionaires. According to the author of this account, Berryer, a financial adviser to the Magons, they were guillotined because they refused this proposition.[147] Berryer's hatred for Robespierre and the existence under the Revolution of a traffic in false signatures remove any suspicion from the Incorruptible, but this was certainly a genuine case of blackmail.

One of these houses, one belonging to Citizen Belhomme, was honoured to count the wealthiest people among its inmates. Thus Maximilien Radix de Sainte-Foix, former manager of the Comte d'Artois's estates, secret adviser to Louis XVI in the Tuileries, speculator in national property, financial backer to General Dumouriez's conspiracy, was transferred there from the Conciergerie on 7 Pluviôse Year II on the orders of Fouquier-Tinville. He escaped the scaffold and spent his days peacefully at Belhomme's until he was freed, thus proving that a conspirator could be treated with great leniency.[148]

A whole slice of the history of the Terror is written on the walls of the Paris prisons of Year II, silent witnesses of the last moments of the condemned, but also of transactions of every kind involving enormous sums of money – especially prior to the decrees of Ventôse, when most of the detainees hoped to save their property from sequestration by entrusting it on paper to 'friendly hands'. The condition for the success of such operations was secrecy. Today their existence is a matter of suspicion rather than proof and the documents concerning them are rare, difficult to assemble and interpret. Nevertheless, it may be said that these operations, on the whole, represented a considerable loss to the Republic. Indeed they do not seem to be unconnected with the wave of repression that struck the *maisons d'arrêt* in June and July 1794.

PART TWO

LAST LETTERS

Most of the letters collected here were written before 9 Thermidor Year II, which marks the fall of Robespierre and the end of the Terror. Why? Partly because the death sentences passed after this date by the Revolutionary Tribunal were fewer in number and partly because the farewell notes and letters were now intercepted less often and therefore reached the families to which they were addressed and are no longer traceable.

Each of these letters is very moving. Some were written by the light of a night-light in a cell in the Conciergerie, others on a knee or post, a few moments before the hands of their signatories were bound forever. In those last moments the reactions of the condemned are sometimes surprising, always very varied. A certain Géant writes to his wife:

> My dear Anne-Lise, human nature is nothing, man appears for an instant and his soul must fly off to the bosom of his creator. Mine will prepare your place there. Live for our dear children, I go to join my ancestors and yours . . .[149]

Condemned the same day, the Comte Poutet remains pragmatic in the directives he gives his wife:

> Respect the laws, as you have always seen me do. Good behaviour always comes more easily to a woman than to a man. Home life, which has always suited you most, is more fitting than ever. I do not commend our children to the best of mothers and to the most loving of wives . . .[150]

A very religious man, Citizen Collignon, of Metz, urges his wife 'to leave this earth of presumption as soon as possible'. He adds: 'I hope to merit the martyr's crown by my resignation.'[151]

Morisset urges his wife to set up house in the provinces: 'Flee this accursed land, look after yourself for our children's sake, I die in the unshakeable confidence that you will keep the word that you have so often given me . . .'[152]

Courtonnel, a Norman innkeeper, assures his wife of his innocence and exhorts her to be brave:

> Farewell, for ever. I am overcome with regret at leaving you, but I shall bear my fate steadfastly to the end. Embrace my children for me and remember their father. Love his memory, but do not be unreasonably affected by his death.[153]

Mme de Grassin commends her mother and three children to her sister-in-law and concludes with these words: 'Do not be anxious on my behalf, follow my steadfastness, you will have no difficulty imagining it.'[154]

The shaky, almost illegible handwriting of this letter betrays the signatory's intense emotion.

The repetitions, the mistakes in construction and above all the traces of tears often belie the declarations of serenity and resignation. The words themselves betray fear: Collin hopes to be able to mount the scaffold as 'a free man' and promises 'to die fasting', without drinking alcohol.[155] Many admit to weeping as they write their letters, others seem indifferent to their imminent death, like this unknown man:

> To the Citizens of La Chapelle and Bel-Air: Farewell, all my friends.
>
> Farewell, my friends, I already cherish the other life. I am about to draw the curtain on this one. I am not just going there, I am flying there. Tomorrow, you will see me in the public newspapers: there I shall be a conspirator.
>
> Farewell for ever, the judgement that you have passed upon me is more sound.[156]

In all these letters it is not so much a question of the prospects opening up after death as what is being left behind: memories, 'examples', a beloved family, but also debts. As a leitmotif there recurs, in every possible form, the painful 'do not forget me'. Those condemned to death are comforted by the idea that their memory may survive them, so it is important that it be pure: all proclaim their innocence and declare that they have not merited the supreme punishment, that befitting murderers.

If 'the example of a father may be a fitting enough memorial', certain objects (locks of hair, epaulettes, handkerchiefs, etc.) often accompany the last letters. Sourdille-Lavalette was alone in swallowing his wedding ring. Very often the prisoners, especially the women, insist on cutting their own hair so that it may not be sullied by the executioner's hands. Thus the Princess of Monaco asks her daughters to lift, each year, the crêpe veil that would cover the glass jar in which her hair would be kept. Portraits of prisoners, including those condemned to death, were executed in large numbers, including those of Victor de Broglie, Catherine Laviolette,[157] Citizen Harelle[158] and Citizeness Paisac, *née* Antoinette Albisson, who probably wrote this unsigned farewell note to Fouquier-Tinville:

> To Citizen Fouquier-Tinville,
> public prosecutor of the Revolutionary Tribunal.
>
> I beg you, citizen public prosecutor, to be so kind as to send to my son, a child of ten, staying in the Rue de Berry, my portrait,

which you will find on a portfolio in my red morocco writing-set, which must have been handed over to you. You are taking from him a mother whose picture, at least, must remain with him.[159]

Again, Gueau de Reverseaux urges his family to find comfort in the cult of his memory:

The first moments are painful but then the memory of those who have been dear to us leaves a sweet sensation in the soul that is not unpleasurable. I hope my wife and children will soon find themselves in that situation.

But even Gueau de Reverseaux urges his family to abandon any desire for revenge and sincerely forgives the man, a notable in the city of Rouen, who has brought about his death:

I write to you, citizen, at the point of death, to assure you that I shall take with me into the grave no resentment against you or against any of those who – I believe unwittingly – have brought me to where I am . . . I forgive with all my heart those who may have been my enemies.[160]

Not everybody reacted like that, of course. Dufresne (see p. 143) wishes upon his denunciator the same fate as his own.

Many letters speak of debts to be settled, a few of debts to be recovered. Citizen Bottagne, who belongs to the second category, writes: 'Descharmes owes me six hundred *livres* from St John's Day last, ask him for them on my behalf before he learns of my death.'[161]

On both sides of a closely filled sheet,[162] the Comte Paillot describes in detail to his son the situation of his business affairs: debts owing and owed, inheritances, various contracts, etc.

Even if they amount to no more than a few *livres*, debts are truly sacred and all those condemned insist that they be settled. The acknowledgement of debts is also a means for some to make disguised legacies and to protect property from confiscation under the law. In the second case, the final letter serves as acknowledgement (see the letters of Beaulieu and the Marquise de Charras, pp. 92 and 158).

Others have final secrets to reveal. The journalist Duplain, a British agent, addressed Fouquier-Tinville thus:

I am writing to you, citizen, from the Conciergerie, on rag, since I have no paper. I have something to reveal to you that will be of great use to the Republic, to your Tribunal and to yourself. Send a gendarme to fetch me and I shall share my secret with you. Greetings and fraternity.[163]

Josset de Saint-Laurent, an agent of the Prince de Condé, addresses Robespierre in similar fashion. His letter was intercepted by Fouquier and he went to the scaffold without saying a word.[164]

Lastly, some of those condemned write to the Convention for pardon. Two women, Catherine Laviolette and Cécile Quévrain, write to the president of the Assembly. Catherine Laviolette asks her children to intercede on her behalf: 'Go, go to the Assembly. Go and see Danton, tell him how innocent your mother is!'

Justice followed its course.

Were all these letters actually written by the hand of their signatories? It is unlikely, but it is difficult to be certain without knowing each individual's handwriting. In some cases, it is obvious that the letters were dictated. That of Coquet La Grande Barbe ends with these words: 'I cannot sign'. It is surprising to observe that among those who were supposed to be educated (aristocrats, grand bourgeois) many have a handwriting that is difficult to read. The explanation that they were in the grip of uncontrollable emotion is not entirely satisfactory. It is more likely that many of them were not used to writing, having always had secretaries at their disposal to carry out this task for them, while other, more elderly prisoners were simply weak-sighted. In the absence of a secretary, the condemned prisoners appealed to their companions in misfortune or to one of the juring priests who attended their last moments.

❦

BEAULIEU DE SURVILLE,[165]
Louis-Alexandre (1757–93)

Beaulieu was one of the very first to appear before the Revolutionary Tribunal. He was accused of a particularly serious offence in time of war: that of secretly transferring funds to the enemy.

On 15 September 1792, a law was passed forbidding 'the exportation of gold and silver, whether or not in the form of coinage, gold and silver vessels and gold or silver jugs used in religious services'. For, since 10 August 1792, the aristocracy had been trying to protect most of its jewellery and silver from the investigations of the Revolutionary authorities. In order to do this, aristocrats made use of such 'merchants' as Beaulieu. Like most of his colleagues involved in this kind of operation, Beaulieu had passed himself off as a merchant, which allowed him to travel abroad and return to France quite freely: indeed article 6 of the law of 8 April 1792 and article 8 of the decree of 28 March 1793 on emigration made an exception of this offence for 'merchants, their agents and employees, so that they may undertake journeys abroad, for the purposes of their trade or profession, providing they are known to practise this activity and possess valid certificates . . .'

Very soon a large number of rich landowners, émigrés who had returned in secret or their financial agents, took advantage of these provisions and a whole class of 'merchants' in pictures, lace or cereals suddenly appeared in France in 1792.

Beaulieu, officially a wine merchant, bought specie and precious objects for Republican assignats (which, indeed, had lost half their value since 1791).

He was in close contact with a former captain of the dragoons and medical officer of the Comte d'Artois's Swiss guards, Sieur Riviers de Mauny, who had commissioned him to buy various quantities of old red wine, new wine or white wine. The 'wine' in question was

actually old *louis d'or*, new *louis* and silver respectively, as the police
realized from their correspondence.

Mauny was arrested and his papers seized on 4 March 1793 as he
was transporting six thousand *louis d'or* without being able to explain
how he came by them. Indeed he was suspected of having gone
abroad illegally several times. Suspected of being his 'agent', charged
with effecting for him 'purchases of specie and transmitting on his
orders funds to various émigrés', Beaulieu was arrested in turn. At
the Revolutionary Tribunal, the charges laid against the two men
were overwhelming. Mauny was even accused of trafficking in arms
under cover of importing exotic plants.

Accused by Fouquier-Tinville of obtaining 'by the most shameful
speculations the means needed by our enemies to overthrow liberty
and to re-establish despotism and slavery', they were both condemned to death.

One witness, who saw them walking towards the scaffold,
remarked on Mauny's 'extremely strong character': 'without him,'
he says, 'Beaulieu would not have found the strength to continue to
the Place de la Révolution.' A few hours before his death, the
unfortunate man asked one of his friends, Citizen Decagny, to thank
his defenders:

My dear, good friend, I embrace you for the last time: accept all my
thanks for the trouble and pain that I have caused you and forgive
me for it. I am sorry to have deprived you of the two thousand *livres*
you gave me recently and for which you have no written receipt. I
hope this letter may serve. I also owe you a sum by current account
that may amount to four or five hundred *livres*.

I hereby acknowledge that I owe you these sums.

Would you be so kind as to convey my thanks to MM. Collot,
Julienne and Alexandre. I have too little time to say much more,
since I only began writing at 8 o'clock in the morning.

I embrace you a thousand times and am, to my last moment,
your very sincere friend.

L.A. Beaulieu.

To his wife he wrote:

Be consoled, my very good lady and dear friend. Be consoled, I beg
you. I have a calm and steadfastness of soul that are a great help to
me at this moment. My greatest pain is that which is being caused
you. So I would beg you with all my heart to be consoled; look
after yourself well, you owe it to Them, you owe it to their
upbringing. Share farewells with good, dear Adelaide. I might
have been taken from you by some disease or accident.

Farewell, I embrace you all from the bottom of my heart. I thought that I would have more time to write to you.

Farewell once more, your friend.

L. A. Beaulieu.

Farewell, I have always loved you with all my heart.

THE 'LA ROUËRIE' PLOT[166]

The so-called 'La Rouërie' plot in Brittany, revealed to the public in the spring of 1793, was one of those many counter-revolutionary undertakings conceived, worked out and financed by émigré princes and foreign bankers. With the exception of the one in the Vendée, many of the 'foreign conspiracies' aimed at inciting a whole region to revolt did not begin to achieve their aims.

This was certainly the case of a Breton plot led by a former officer of the French guards, Armand Tuffin de la Rouërie, who had been given full powers by Louis XVI's brothers to defend the royalist cause.

The king's former minister, Calonne, then a refugee in England, closely followed La Rouërie's activities and had instructed him by a letter dated 4 October 1791 to suggest the most favourable places for a landing of troops in Brittany. These soldiers, made up of French émigrés and mercenaries, were billeted in the Channel Islands. For strategic reasons, Calonne was opposed to the emigration of all those monarchists who might serve the cause more usefully by remaining in France.

The number of those involved in the plot amounted to several hundred. In such circumstances, how could a few traitors not be infiltrated among them? Indeed the Committee of Surveillance learnt of the existence of a Counter-Revolutionary Association of the West through a physician friend of La Rouërie's called Chévetel-Latouche, a member of an eminent Breton family, whose father was physician to the Châteaubriands.

This Chévetel-Latouche exposed the whole affair to Danton, who, in September 1792, ordered the executive council to organize the infiltration and dismantling of the association. In order not to arouse suspicion, Citizen Lalligant-Morillon acted as intermediary between Chévetel-Latouche and the Committee of General Safety.

Chévetel-Latouche, who enjoyed the confidence of the Bretons, followed all their activities while on missions to Koblenz, London or Paris. He then wrote a faithful report of what he had seen. He related how, in Paris, he had taken part in the selling of false discount-bank bonds sent to La Rouërie by Calonne, which had been rejected by a banker, but accepted at a lower price by the speculators at the Palais-Royal. It should be explained that, at this time, Calonne, a sworn enemy of the Revolution, had had forged the considerable sum of one and a half thousand million *livres*. According to Chévetel-Latouche, 'he intended using them as much to pay agitators as in the hope that, if this forged money circulated, it would lead to a fall in the value of the state's real money'. He had these assignats manufactured in London and had already conveyed over three million in one-hundred-*livre* notes to Louis XVI's brother, the Comte d'Artois, who was then to introduce them through Switzerland.

The Breton conspirators also possessed a fortune in forged notes and, it seems, distributed them profusely.

A considerable stock-pile of forged money had been hidden at the house of the Comtesse de Trojoliff, a friend and cousin of La Rouërie.

This money was intended to buy new contacts, especially in the administration, and to aid certain members of the higher clergy in their counter-revolutionary undertakings.

Many priests followed their instructions, refusing to take the constitutional oath and fleeing the towns, taking the now fanatic populations with them to the depths of the countryside. There was a proliferation of miracles to confound the persecutors and to manifest God's intentions. The Virgin had appeared on a raised altar, in a secret place, far from the impious gaze of the Republicans. The son of God himself had attended a blessing of flags, handed out by the ringleaders to credulous peasants. Angels, covered with celestial flames, had appeared, promising a speedy victory to the defenders of altar and throne. Such rumours circulated in the countryside of Brittany, Poitou or Vendée, giving added force to the peasants' cries of 'Long live the King! Long live religion!' But although the revolt took off in the Vendée, the attempts by La Rouërie and his accomplices failed in Brittany.

In October 1792, the French governor was informed of plans for an enemy landing. Originally expected in the Côtes-du-Nord, in October, it had then been postponed to March 1793, in order to coincide with simultaneous uprisings in several French regions and with the march of the Duke of Brunswick's army on Paris. As far as Brittany, where the activities of the plot were well known, was

concerned, there was time to put an end to it. A search was made for
La Rouërie, who had taken refuge in the manor house of his friends,
the La Guyomarais, who were convinced royalists. However, he fell
seriously ill and died of a fever in January 1793. The Committee of
General Safety seized its opportunity. Before his successor had been
appointed, it ordered the arrest of the principal conspirators – several
hundred of them – whose meeting-places were known. The unexplained slowness with which Beuronville, the Minister of War,
signed the order for the movement into Brittany of the troop of
seven thousand men demanded by Lalligant-Morillon gave them
time to escape to the Vendée or into the nearby islands of Jersey and
Guernsey.

Beuronville was criticized personally by two deputies in a report
that blamed the failure of the ambush on the lack of immediate
mobilization. The two deputies, Sevestre and Billaud-Varenne,
wrote to the Convention:

> The minister, Beuronville, constantly refused to give his signature
> to that urgent operation and to send the necessary troops. It was
> only on 15 March (1793) that he finally made up his mind.

However, Lalligant-Morillon had had twenty-six individuals
arrested and seized documents buried in the grounds of the Château
de La Fosse-Hingant, where meetings of the plotters had taken place.
The reading of these documents and the observation of certain facts
led Basire, a Dantonist deputy, to remark in a report to the
Convention:

> I wonder why the executive council was informed of this con-
> spiracy only in September last year, when, as we know, it had
> existed since 1790 and one could hardly have been ignorant of the
> fact? Why has so much information been provided about things
> and so little about people? By what fatality have we been able to
> bring to justice in this great trial only twenty-six individuals, of
> which the Revolutionary Tribunal has condemned only twelve,
> including several women and so few people of consequence in this
> matter? Time may one day raise the veil that still covers part of this
> affair . . .

Basire, executed six months later, had implicitly raised the
hypothesis of complicity on the part of certain members of the
government. It is probable that they included Beuronville, the
Minister of War, whom Dumouriez saved from certain death on the
scaffold by 'handing him over' to the Austrians. The principal actor
and witness, Lalligant-Morillon, was condemned to death in Messidor Year II, for refusing to answer questions.

The La Rouërie affair ended in June 1793. At the end of the fifteen-day trial, death sentences were passed on thirteen of the conspirators. These included the five principal agents: Picot de Limoëlan, Fontevieux, Pontavice, Moëllien and Vincent. Then came La Guyomarais and his wife and a certain Thébaut de La Chauvinerie, found guilty of harbouring La Rouërie. Lastly, there were five financial backers accused of taking part in and financing the plots, whose names appeared on receipts found in the grounds of the Château de La Fosse-Hingant.

On 18 June 1793, in the early afternoon, two carts left the Conciergerie. A large crowd was there, observing the prisoners and, in particular, two women: Thérèse de Moëllien, a great beauty, and Angélique de la Fonchais, who looked resigned and seemed very young to die. At the foot of the scaffold, the condemned men and women embraced one another. According to one witness, Dutard, three or four men were called in turn. The women followed. Pontavice was called last. In all, the execution took only thirteen minutes.

Of all those condemned, ten wrote one or several farewell letters to their families. All are previously unpublished.

GROULT de La MOTTE,[167] Nicolas-Bernard
(1730–93)

He had abandoned his post of ship's captain when it became obligatory for former officers of the royal forces to take the oath of allegiance to the Republic. Born at Saint-Malo, he lived at Saint-Coulomb, the La Motte family seat, an estate situated at about a quarter of a league from La Fosse-Hingant, La Rouërie's headquarters. He was condemned for taking part in the financing of the counter-revolutionary association.

Before dying, he wrote to a tradesman, asking him to convey his farewells to his brother:

To Citizen Conquedo, grocer, at Saint-Malo.
Paris, 18 June 1793.
My dear Conquedo, when you receive this letter, I shall probably be no more: I have been condemned to lose my head on the scaffold. I beg you to tell my brother that I died loving him and all

his family. I am not writing to him, I am not writing to my mother, I am not writing to my sister, I know how sensitive they are. Take care to choose the right moment to tell them and dear Joachim of my fate; they give me much cause for regret. I am worthy of their friendship and of the esteem of all those who know me.

My innocence is as clear as the day, but what care I for what most men will think of me? My friends know me, they will regret my passing. I beg you to give my eternal farewells to your dear wife and to all those who have loved me. Do not forget to tell all the good inhabitants of the Deux-Mottes that I die loving them. Poor T [illegible] must regret my death. I commend him to dear [illegible word]. Remember me to all the inhabitants of Saint-Coulomb, they will shed a tear on my grave. I loved them.

Farewell, dear Conquedo, I am going to die. Tell my father that innocence has an easy conscience, even at the foot of the scaffold.

> Groult de La Motte.

His second letter was addressed to a friend in Brest:

To Citizen Jean-Marie Le Cam, second-hand dealer,
Rue du Val-d'Or, no. 11, at Brest.

> This 18 June 1793.

My dear Jean-Marie, when you get this letter, your friend, your former master, will be no more, his head will have fallen on the scaffold. Remember that he deserves your regrets and esteem, he was always faithful to his friends and to the Republic. He has been condemned on mere suspicion, but let us forgive, all is up with me, and I appear before the Eternal with a pure heart and one never sullied by a desire for revenge.

Tell your wife to remember me and tell your sweet little Catto to give a thought sometimes to her Uncle Motte; tell Ivon that I am always his friend, tell Agnès that I love her, tell the [illegible word] never to lose their esteem for me, I merit it.

Farewell, for the last time, my dear Jean-Marie, I am about to die. I am consoled at the thought that I take with me the regrets of all those who have known me. Farewell. Farewell.

I forget none of my friends, you know them, tell them all that I die wishing them every happiness.

> Groult de La Motte.

TROJOLIFF,[168] Thérèse de Moëllien, Comtesse de (1762–93)

Daughter of Sébastien-Hyacinthe de Moëllien, Seigneur of Trojoliff, former councillor at the *Parlement* of Brittany, she was born at Fougères. Her mother was La Rouërie's sister. She was a great beauty and Châteaubriand leaves this memory of her in *Mémoires d'outre-tombe*: 'I saw that Comtesse Trojoliff, who, a cousin and intimate of the Marquis de La Rouërie, was implicated in his conspiracy. I had as yet only seen beauty in my own family: I stood dumbfounded seeing it on the face of a strange woman.'

According to Chévetel-Latouche, she accompanied La Rouërie to Koblenz and brought back with her, hidden in her belt, full powers from the king's brothers. It was she, too, who unsuspectingly announced the marquis's death and revealed his burial place to the same Chévetel, who lost no time in passing the information on. Lastly, it was she who, on the eve of her arrest, destroyed the list of the association's members that she had held, a list containing several hundred names.

She received her death sentence with no trace of surprise, addressed her last thoughts to a woman friend who, as she had done, lived at Fougères, then died courageously.

To Citizeness Vendel,
at the Maison de la Trinité, at Fougères.

This 18 June.

I shall be close to the Eternal, my friend, when you receive this letter. I hope that my forgiveness of my enemies will obtain for me that of my own sins, my crimes against Him, for the frequent forgetting of His benefits is no doubt one that could not be redeemed too much. And the sacrifice of a few years is no great matter to whosoever can appreciate life at its true value; the sentence of death passed on me aroused no feelings in me, all the tribulations to which I have been subject since my arrest have given me a sufficient disgust for life, and the continual spectacle of poor wretches certainly has this effect.

Farewell, my poor friend, do not regret me, I die with trust and almost with joy. At what a fine banquet I shall be this evening, my friend, I shall await you there; your virtues call you there. I have nothing with which to reproach myself in my conduct towards mankind, I have never had any but feelings of humanity, I sincerely wish the happiness of those who have brought me to the grave; but towards God, my friend, I was not so innocent; I loved Him, but served Him ill. I hope that He will forgive me; so let my friends not weep over my happiness, we shall all be together again ere long, be the interpreter of all my feelings for them.

Farewell, my unhappy friend, I have taken every possible precaution to return to you the rest of the assignats that you lent me.

FONTEVIEUX,[169] Jean-Baptiste-Georges Camasse de (1759–93)

After embarking on a military career as a very young man, he had taken part in the American campaign and had joined the legion commanded by La Rouërie. Close on fourteen years later, in 1791, he saw La Rouërie again in England and, rallying to the cause of the nobles, joined him in Brittany. He was not only the marquis's aide-de-camp, but also that of the Duke of Brunswick, a general in the Prussian army, 'according to whose movements La Rouërie made his own plans'. He went several times to Koblenz, travelling without difficulty under cover of a mission from the Duc des Deux-Ponts to the United States, a mission that he had taken trouble to have pre-dated: 'Koblenz, 15 September 1788'.

It was when passing through Paris, returning from one of his trips, that he unsuspectingly communicated various details of the Breton plot to Chévetel-Latouche. He also told him that he had brought into France forty thousand *livres* in notes issued by the discount bank, which he now had to change for metal currency.

For several months, Chévetel-Latouche faithfully reported to the Committee of General Safety the information that he had received concerning La Rouërie's activities and he accompanied Fontevieux to La Guyomarais's manor house, where the marquis, now sick, was hiding.

Perhaps suspecting Chévetel-Latouche's betrayal, Fontevieux returned to Paris. In March 1793, he learnt of the imminent arrest of the Breton conspirators and planned to emigrate definitively.

He was arrested, in turn, and sent to the Abbaye, suspected of emigration and desertion.

Documents found in a glass jar buried in the grounds of the

Château de La Fosse-Hingant proved Fontevieux's guilt in the La Rouërie affair. One of his last two letters, addressed to the National Convention, refers to it, not without a touch of irony:

> To the Citizen President of the National Convention.
>
> Citizen,
>
> The Revolutionary Tribunal has just condemned to death twelve individuals accused of the conspiracy of what was formerly Brittany, discovered in a glass jar, five feet under ground. I shall permit myself no reflection on that judgement, which was no doubt considered by those that passed it as no more than justice, but I take the liberty to observe that, in a Tribunal without appeal, men not being infallible, because their intelligence is limited, I observe, I say, that sometimes when one thinks one is condemning the guilty the innocent are struck down and this is what happened today.
>
> Secondly, I would observe that although the dangers to the Fatherland may sometimes force a Nation to severe measures, it is also the proper dignity of a great people to exercise clemency; this, it seems to me, would be the case here, for this conspiracy exists only in the imagination, and the great conspirator is a glass jar.
>
> Furthermore, the only favour that I may allow myself to ask the National Convention is to urge it to grant me a postponement so that I may enlighten the minds of my judges by bringing documents that would reveal my innocence to all. The National Convention is too thoroughly imbued with the sage maxim that it is better to allow ten guilty men to escape than to take the life of one innocent man: it will not reject my request.
>
> I am, Citizen President, the unhappy Fontevieux.
>
> At the Palais de Justice, 18 June 1793, Year IV of the Republic.

The same day, he wrote to his mistress, Citizeness Cauchy, who lived at 28 Rue de la Révolution, not far from what is today the Place de la Concorde:

> I am approaching, my friend, the terrible moment when I must appear before the Supreme Being, I approach it without terror. I would say, with Essex: 'It is the crime that is shameful, not the scaffold.'
>
> You know the purity of the feelings that have at all times guided my actions. I have always done, I can say this with no affront to modesty, all the good that was in my power; I have done ill to no one. I shall miss my friends and particularly you. I was attached to the earth only through the feelings that I had for my friends. I feel a sense of misfortune only on their account.
>
> I thank you here for all the testimonies of friendship, all the consolation that you have brought my soul, the touching cares that

you have lavished on me during my detention. I would like to be able to show my lively and loving gratitude to you.

We shall meet again one day: sooner or later, the scythe of time crops all heads, levels all. I pity my judges, I pardon them with all my heart, I urge you to be consoled, I conjure you, in the name of the most loving friendship, to preserve your days. If sometimes you think of me, remember that I must necessarily be happy because I died innocent. I have not shed a single tear on my fate. I have wept over the painful situation of my friends, it is they who are to be pitied.

Farewell, my good and sensitive friend, I embrace you with all my heart; if you see my uncle, raise his spirits, help him to bear the mishaps attendant on men's lives, tell him that I loved him, that I love him now, that I shall love him beyond the grave.

Fontevieux.

MORIN de LAUNAY,[170] *Guillaume-Maurice (1736–93)*
Lieutenant-General of the Admiralty at Saint-Malo

Like most of the conspirators, he was a member of one of those families of arms manufacturers in Saint-Malo who had made their fortunes in the mid-eighteenth century. He was related to various families of financiers, to La Rouërie and to the Convention member Hérault de Séchelles.

On the eve of the Revolution, he had been presiding judge of the Tribunal des Traits (a court dealing with financial and commercial matters) at Saint-Malo and was living there when he was arrested at his home in the Rue de la Vicairerie. He wrote his last letter to his sister, Thérèse Guillaudens des Bassablons.

To Madame des Bassablons, Rue de la Charité, at Saint-Malo.

My respectable and incomparable sister, I beg you to continue to show tenderness to an unfortunate wife and beloved children, and to console a mother who, by this event, is to find herself at the mercy of someone who might appear to have feelings contrary to ours. Her virtue is no doubt steadfast and unshakeable, but her advanced age occasions her weaknesses that are inseparable from it.

We have just come from the Tribunal, which has pronounced

sentences of death on twelve individuals, including, apart from myself, Grandville, Limoëlan, the Dame La Fonchais, Lamotte-Groult and Vincent; after that, I have nothing to say except to beg you not to forget me before the Lord.

I must tell you that my property has been confiscated; my dear wife has many claims on it, most of which have already been obtained by my father-in-law. There is the inheritance of Mlle de Lamotte, about which I know little, except the sale of the share-croppings at La Villé and the other one whose name I forget, which brought in 4,500 *livres*. The Houssayes will be able to give you information concerning the surplus.

You should call my son from Paris, staying here could be fatal to him, he is a good boy. It will be company that may be useful in his upbringing. As I am going to recollect myself before God, prior to appearing before him in a few hours, I present my respects to my dear mother, our relations and friends, and embrace for the last time my worthy wife and my children.

VINCENT,[171] *Georges-Julien-Jean (1760–93)*

'Broker and interpreter of languages', Vincent was accused of being in continuous correspondence with the principal leaders of La Rouërie's association, of helping several of its members to escape to Jersey and of giving them assistance 'in money and goods'. His last thoughts were for his wife and children:

To Citizeness Binel Vincent,
Rue de Toulouse, at Saint-Malo

18 June 1793.

My dear, good and loving friend, we must worship the Decrees of Divine Providence, however terrible they may be to bear, and accept them without complaint. You know better than I, dear, good friend, and I have no need to remind you, all that religion commands you and all the consolations that it can offer you. Alas! what a terrible blow I am going to deliver to your loving, generous heart, how very sad my dear, poor children are to be! But, my dear, good friends, summon up all your strength, I beg you, do not allow yourselves to be downcast by your misfortunes, my inno-cence and honour must help you bear it. God united us together, I had a loving, virtuous wife, I had lovable children, who were my consolation. Perhaps, alas, I was too puffed up with pride at my happiness and God wishes to take it from me.

My worthy, loving wife, if I have ever done ill by you, I beg you to forgive me, I shall die ever worthy of your friendship; and if, after this unhappy life, we are allowed a few memories of those who have been dear to us in this world I shall take with me beyond the grave the most loving friendship that I have had for you and my dear children. My loving and beloved friend, if ever I have been dear to you I conjure you by all our friendship to preserve your days, days of which our loving children have so much need. Embrace them very lovingly for me, tell them the love I have always had for them, tell them that, although my death deprives them not only of the most loving of fathers, but of the property that might have been theirs, I die innocent. I leave them my honour, which is the most precious of all possessions; not only will they always be able to hold their heads high, they may even glory in the death of a father who bore his head to the scaffold as an innocent victim of the Revolution.

Take care, my good friend, that the pain of my death does not make them ungrateful towards their Country. She is not to blame for the misfortunes that have befallen us: men are subject to error and, in a world in which passions blind us, innocence is often punished in the place of guilt; but, as good, faithful Christians, we must learn to bear the blows that strike us and to worship the Divine hand that delivers such blows.

My dear children, console your loving, respectable mother, be, by the assiduity with which you follow her counsels and fulfil the duties of your religion, her consolation and support. I embrace you, my dear, good friends, remember me often and pray to God for me. And you, dear, loving wife, receive my last kisses and farewells, when you remember me do not fail to pray to God that He may pardon me my sins and have pity on my soul. I cannot say more, the words fail me in this sad, cruel moment, but I regret life only because of the pain that my death will bring to your heart.

But, my dear, good friend, do not I beg you abandon yourself to pain, respect the Decrees of Divine Providence. We are not to remain forever on this miserable earth and certainly we knew, at the moment we were united, that death was to separate us. God has fixed the moment and the nature of that death, so let us submit to His wishes without complaint.

Farewell, dear, worthy wife, farewell, loving, dear children, receive my loving kisses from each other and pray heaven you will be happier than your unhappy father, who dies innocent and has nothing with which to reproach himself.

LAMOTTE-LA GUYOMARAIS,[172]
Marie-Jeanne Micault, Comtesse (1743–93)

Wife of a Breton gentleman, she was arrested with her husband and two of her young children, Amaury and Casimir, a few days after burying La Rouërie in the grounds of the manor of La Guyomarais. She had taken a 'very active part' in the royalist plot, as this clear-sighted letter, addressed to one of her daughters, shows:

> In spite of the two hundred thousand men announced by the letters from Brussels, it is still rather difficult to believe in a counter-revolution by force; but, when one examines the state of the public purse, one is convinced that the Revolution or the Constitution could fall at any moment. The decree relating to the colonies has succeeded in alienating the class of rich merchants. Our legislators have been sustained so far by speculators and capitalists, who were jealous of the nobility and who expected to benefit from church property; but now that there is no longer any good speculation to be made on the Constitution, our august governors are to be abandoned by the men of money, and they will learn that when one loses the protection of the bankers, one does not live for long off assignats and loose change . . .

At the Tribunal, she acknowledged her correspondence with people abroad, especially with her oldest sons, who had emigrated, and, as she left the Palais de Justice, she cried out: 'Long live the King!' The letter that she wrote a few minutes earlier to her daughters is difficult to decipher and betrays strong emotion:

> To Citizeness Guyomarais, c/o Citizen Micault,
> Rue Basse, at Lamballe.
>
> Well! My dear sister and my dear daughters, your worthy and virtuous father and your loving and best friend are condemned to die tomorrow night for a crime of conspiracy, of which neither he nor I had the slightest knowledge or intimation. The steadfast humanity of an imprudence dictated by the unfortunate L. [La Guyomarais, author's note] has brought our innocent heads to the scaffold. No doubt, my dear friends, the last judge who awaits us will receive us in his paternal arms and allow that our judges, if they are themselves absolved at the Eternal Tribunal, will sincerely repent of the sentence that they have just pronounced. We – I think I can also speak for your worthy father – forgive them with all our hearts.
>
> We have arranged a safe means of arriving in heaven, our desired

fatherland. Without this event, perhaps, which is the glory of martyrdom, my lack of devotion and my attachment to the chimeras of this world below might have forbidden me entrance.

Ah! my friends, how happy I shall be in a few hours. I am left with only one regret and that is to leave you and your brothers in poverty; but console yourselves through resignation: the sovereign dispenser of good and evil will mitigate your sufferings. The generous cares of my brother [condemned to imprisonment, author's note], which he has promised me for the whole family, will support you against adversity.

Lastly, your submission to the eternal decrees, together with a life of suffering and the continual practice of the love of God and of your neighbour, will give us the hope of receiving you in our blessed home. Only allow yourself the regrets you simply cannot help feeling.

Our happiness must console you. Convey to our dear friends our most loving friendship and our farewells to our dear servants.

At the Feast of St Michael next, three years' wages will be due to my chambermaid La Tartet. I owe only one year's wages to all the others. Seventy-five *livres* is owing to the gardener, François Perrin, money that he gave me to keep at the Tour de Batz, where I had paid his wages. We also owe to Joannin, merchant of Saint-Brieux, two hundred and forty *livres*, that is all I remember owing. La Tartet has thirteen *livres* in wages, David the same, La Jeunesse twenty-eight, Fanchon thirteen.

I must now end, my dear friends, my heart and my hands are frozen, in spite of myself: shall I recover from this weakness? But you know how sensitive I am: my great joy at this moment is to end my days at the same time as my worthy husband. His resignation delights me and sustains my weakness. I embrace you for the last time and pray the Sovereign Being to be your protection and support.

Your unfortunate mother and father,

                                        Micault de La Guyomarais.

Don't forget the advice and the good examples of your unhappy brothers. Their hearts are filled with bitterness, but I hope their conduct, like your own, will never belie the honest, virtuous precepts that we have given you.

Mlle Joachim of Rennes has sent us the eighteen hundred *livres* that she was holding for our lawyers. Find the note and send it with our thanks to the doctor, her cousin.

PONTAVICE,[173] *Louis-Anne du*
(1768–93)

Cousin of the Marquis de La Rouërie, he had accompanied Fontevieux on various missions abroad. Associated with the counter-
revolutionary activities of the La Trémoilles, Boisguy, Kératry, du
Buat, and other Breton or Vendéen conspirators, he was arrested on
the same day as Fontevieux, 15 March 1793, but the administrators
of the police department of Paris were unable to prove his emigration
and he was freed on bail.

He was again arrested a few days later on the orders of the
Committee of General Safety and imprisoned in the Abbaye 'until
his uninterrupted residence in France since the decrees on emigration
has been proved and until he produces the security card of his section
and his certificates of civic spirit'. Accused of conspiracy with La
Rouërie on the basis of bills for travelling expenses abroad found at
La Fosse-Hingant, he was implicated in the affair of the Breton
plotters and condemned with them.

He had married Élisabeth-Louise Person, daughter of the late
Nicolas-Joseph Person, Chevalier de Saint-Louis, master of the hunt
to the Duc d'Orléans, who died on 14 July 1789 defending the
Bastille.

In a short note, he requests a trusted friend to take an interest in his
wife's affairs, before writing his last letter to his father, also commending him to look after his young wife:

To Citizen Balsac, at the Hôtel de La Providence, at Paris.

Receive all my thanks, my worthy friend, for the care and
attention that you have expended in trying to save me. Fate has
decided otherwise, my regrets are inexpressible. You know the
object that is the cause of them, be so kind as to mitigate hers, she
has a child; let her preserve her health for the unfortunate being
who has need of her. As soon as you can, go and see M. Jouanne,
the lawyer, and put him in entire charge of my unfortunate friend's
affairs. I have no property of my own. I hope people will not
trouble her on that account, everything is in the names of my wife
and my mother-in-law. Be my interpreter, I beg you, with all those
persons who have been so kind as to take an interest in me. Here I
am giving you a very painful task, given your sensitivity, for which
I ask your pardon. I am, with the utmost gratitude, your friend.

Du Pontavice.

To Citizen Pontavice, living at La Branche,
at Saint-Brice, near Fougères,
département of the Isle-et-Vilaine.

I have just been condemned to death, my dear, loving father, after having gone through four months of imprisonment. I spared you until now the pain that learning of my detention would have caused you, but it was my duty to inform you of this terrible event the moment it could no longer be hidden from you.

I wish to spare my unhappy wife this sorrow. I would ask you, for her sake, as my last wish, to assist her in whatever she may need. I know nothing in the world as estimable as her, she has a right to all your most tender feelings. On 26 March she brought into the world a daughter who will be some consolation to her. Your care and good heart are for me pledges that you will do the rest; do not pity me, I die not guilty and without reproach. In a few hours I shall be perfectly happy, the approach of death is not horrible to me, what follows cannot be.

I embrace my mother, my sister, my aunt. I remain worthy of their esteem and friendship.

Be so kind as to tear up the note of the money that you were good enough to lend me and do not demand payment for it from my poor wife. I do not think that what I ask is unjust. Farewell, my worthy friend, my loving friend, whose fine soul will learn of this event with all the heroism of which it is capable. I am with respect,

Your son, Louis-Anne Pontavice.

This 18 May 1793

LOCQUET de GRANDVILLE,[174] Félix-Victor
(1759–93)

This Breton gentleman had, for only a short while, owned an estate near Nantes and he was accused of trying to lead the citizens of the region into the coalition. In his defence, he claimed that he had never set foot there since 1790. During the court proceedings he thought good to explain his wife's death by the great sorrow she had felt on the death of their daughter. At this, one of the judges retorted harshly: 'Did your wife not rather die of aristocracy?'

It was proved that he had supplied funds intended 'to facilitate' the formation of the counter-revolutionary association, for which he was sentenced to death. He left an infirm mother, who was in his charge, and two young children. He wrote first to Fouquier-Tinville:

Citizen,

I beg you to be so kind as to allow my ring and a casket decorated with portraits of my late wife and daughter to be returned to the two young children that I leave here. It is not much to ask of you, and it will be a portion of my inheritance that would be of no use to the Nation. These young children are at Saint-Malo: Citizen Magon de La Balue, who is my friend, will take charge of the two objects if you send them to me. Farewell, citizen, I am Loquet de Grandville.

Would you also allow my linen to be given to the citizen gendarme.

Before dying, he took his last farewell of his father-in-law, entrusting the care of his children to him:

To Citizen Gouyou de Beaufort, at Saint-Malo,
département of Isle-et-Vilaine:
18 June 1793, second year of the French Republic.

My dear father, do not afflict yourself, who better than you can appreciate how lightly I must take life; I die innocent; I die with the sweet satisfaction of knowing that I have never done ill to anyone; I die forgiving my judges. Your virtuous daughter, who has preceded me, and with whom I shall soon be reunited, was outraged; a vile denunciator tried to besmirch her memory. Tronçon de Coudray, my *défenseur*, has avenged it; the God of eloquence has depicted that dear wife, dissipated the clouds of calumny that obscured virtue itself. Motherly love has remained pure and I am satisfied.

I leave in your care those two pledges of my love, the reward for my victory, those dear children, who may still be happy if Heaven preserve you, and cannot yet feel their father's death: you will speak to them of me sometimes, you will look after them with all my love, you will tell them that my last wish was for my creator and the preceding one for them and for you.

I know that you have several children, but I know that these two are also yours, so you will feed them since my death robs them of their own means: Achille and Aristide represent for you the image of your charming daughter, may they be happy with you, may they long receive the lessons of virtue!

Farewell my second father, farewell my children, farewell my unhappy mother, farewell my dear sister, I also commend those children to you – I know you will love them for love of your brother.

I have requested that my ring, once a pledge of my happiness, be sent to you and that my casket, decorated with the portrait of your daughter and mine, be also sent to you: this is the only inheritance I leave you, my dear Aristide, my dear Achille.

Take care of Marie, their governess.

> Your son, Locquet de Grandville

LA FONCHAIS,[175] *Angélique-Françoise Des Isles,*
wife of Desclos de (1769–93)

Belonging to a Norman family that had settled at Saint-Malo and set up in business, Angélique de La Fonchais was the daughter of the arms manufacturer, Marc-Pierre Des Isles, Seigneur of Cambernon.

In 1787, she had married Jean-Roland Desclos, Chevalier de La Fonchais, lieutenant in the king's navy, who had followed his senior officers and gone over to England in 1791.

Mme de La Fonchais, who had remained in Brittany with her two children, was arrested at the family seat, the Château de la Fosse-Hingant, together with her uncle, Picot de Limoëlan, and her two sisters, wives of émigrés.

During the investigation, it transpired that her name appeared on the receipt for an advance to La Rouërie's organization. She was condemned to death, even though the fatal document concerned, it was later claimed, one of her sisters-in-law, who was older than she and for whom she had sacrificed herself. In a letter to her friend the Girondin Buzot, Mme Roland, writing from the Abbaye, says of Mme de La Fonchais: '. . . I am in the same room and bed as she occupied before me; I caught a glimpse of her when she left . . . Her *défenseur officieux* is beside himself and swears that she was innocent, that her gentle, beautiful face reflected the beautiful soul within . . .'

To her two sisters, who had been condemned to imprisonment, Mme de La Fonchais sent this note, which reached them:

> Dry your tears, my good friends or, at least, shed them without bitterness; all my ills are about to end and I am happier than you. I have just written to my sister-in-law to commend my children to

her; you will wish, I hope, to join with her and become the mothers of these poor orphans. May that precious title help you bear life! I leave you in order to come nearer the divinity. Receive, my very dear sisters, the most loving and affectionate farewell. I would like to concern myself with you longer, but the very idea weakens me and I want to save all my strength.

Farewell yet again and assuage your pain; we will be together again one day! I embrace you with all my heart. Farewell, my friends!

She wrote another letter, to one of her sisters-in-law:

This 18 June 1793

My fate is sealed, my good heart, do not afflict yourself and view this event with as much tranquillity as I. It is not without regret that I leave an existence that might have promised me happy days. I have a favour to ask you, you know the fate of my unhappy children: be a mother to them, my dear friend. May they find a loving, beloved mother in you; this will bring you a mother's cares.

I beg you to fetch them from Limoëlan. Keep them with you. My sisters are in no position to take care of them. I have no other commendations to make to you. I am convinced of the zeal that you will show for the interest of these unhappy little creatures. I have no anxiety, since they will be close to you, you will be their mother.

Farewell, my friend, I do not wish to prolong further the time I am spending conversing with you; I must go to the Supreme Being at whose feet I throw myself. The resignation that I have gives me the sweet conviction that he will pardon me. Think sometimes of me, my friend, speak to my children about me, but banish all bitterness. My ills are about to end, but yours will continue still.

Farewell, my friend, cherish a memory, but do not pity me.

Your sister, Des Isles de La Fonchais.

I beg you, my friend, to work together with my sisters as far as the upbringing of my children is concerned. Their only resource is to be found in you three and it is to the three of you that I entrust them.

PICOT de LIMOËLAN,[176] Michel-Alain
(1734–93)

The eldest of four children of an old Saint-Malo family, Picot de Limoëlan had inherited most of the family wealth. To this was added the fortune of his wife, who came from a bourgeois family in Nantes. Some time after their marriage, he was able to acquire the Château de Limoëlan, near Sévignac, whose name he then took.

He was condemned to death as the treasurer of La Rouërie's association. His last letter was addressed to his daughters, living in Brittany:

> To Mesdemoiselles de Limoëlan, at Limoëlan, near Broons.
>
> I embrace you, my dear children, tell your brothers and especially our traveller, when he comes home, that I loved them to the last moment of my life. I shall not ask you to pray for me, for soon I shall be happier than you. If my prayers are granted, you will be happy, both in this world and in the next. Console your mother, be always obedient to her, and think never of me except to rejoice in the favour that God granted me in making me suffer death for Him. Your father who loves you tenderly.
>
> Picot de Limoëlan
>
> From the Conciergerie, 18 June at 9 o'clock in the morning, in the year 1793; thank, on my behalf, Mlle [illegible word] and all my people.

BERGER,[177] Claude-François
(1728–93)

An ex-Jesuit priest, who became a landowner at La Charité-sur-Loire, Berger had remained very attached to the values of the *ancien régime*. Authoritarian in character, as the passage in his letter concerning his children shows, he did not conceal the most 'anticivic' feelings.

He was denounced to the municipality of Pouilly-sur-Loire in March 1793, then arrested and his house searched. The authorities found receipts there for a subscription to *L'Ami du Roi*, a well-known royalist newspaper, a satire against the constitutional priests and the draft of a letter on the death of Louis XVI, in which Berger expressed all his indignation: 'How could it be that those villains were able to carry out their infernal regicide undisturbed and even without protest? Ah, Paris! What exemplary punishment you deserve!'

On a graver tone, after the proscription of the Girondins and the repression of the regional insurrectional movements, Berger, in another letter, rejoices in the signs of the coming, 'yearned-for counter-revolution'; 'It is simmering gently in that province [the Nièvre] and we await the right moment to come out into the open and, thanks be to God, we are the greater number; here is the good regeneration that will have been obtained for us; it is true that the ordinary, simple rabble, the property-less populace, will pay nothing or little.'

Transferred to Paris, he appeared in October before the Revolutionary Tribunal. After four hours' deliberation, the jurors confirmed his responsibility in the federalist plots of the Nièvre – plots that were aimed at 'disturbing the state in a civil war, by arming citizens against one another'.

On 13 September 1793, at about seven in the evening, the condemned man was taken to the Place de la Révolution.

His last letter was addressed to one of his daughters:

To Citizeness Berger, c/o Citizens Guai and Gide, booksellers, Rue d'Enfer, no 731, at Paris.

Farewell, my dear daughter, farewell for ever. I am condemned, for having, it is said, fomented counter-revolution: I never gave it a thought, but, the fact is, I am a Catholic and have shown too much attachment to the religion of our fathers. God be blessed and praised for everything! I would solicit your prayers and those of all our friends whom I shall not see again until Eternity. I shall appear there in a few hours, may God be pleased to show me mercy and forgive my innumerable sins as I forgive with all my heart my judges, who are clearly in error in declaring me convicted of a crime to which I never gave a thought. Similarly, I forgive my enemies who are the cause of my arrest and death.

My dear child, console your poor mother: support her in her old age and in the terrible affliction in which she will find herself; may she lay her unhappiness at the foot of the cross and give herself up to the decrees of Holy Providence, which are always just and worshipful however terrible they may be. I urge you once again, my daughter, to care for your mother in her old age and to urge your brothers and sisters to console her as best they can. She may claim her marriage rights, her brother will be able to help her in this; in any case, your elder brother, whom I especially entrust with the task, will do well to go and console her or even to take her with him.

I demand forgiveness of my poor wife, for the pain and trouble that I may have caused her, may she forgive me and think of me every day in her prayers. I forgive your elder brother the pain that he has caused me, especially by his marriage; may God pardon him. I also forgive your elder sister and Cadet for the pains that they have caused me by their acts of disobedience, their contempt for your mother's wishes and mine, may God pardon them if they sincerely repent, and make reparation for their sins by redoubling their affection, respect and submission to their poor mother, my loving, bereft wife, whom I embrace with all my heart for the last time. I embrace Nanette, my dear daughter, may she continue to care for her poor mother: God will reward her, I pray and shall pray in Heaven that he may do so, if he has pity on my poor soul, as I beg him so to do and hope in his infinite mercy, through the precious blood of his son Our Lord. I die on a Friday, a day dedicated to his passion and his death. My children, never forget your father in your prayers and urge all your friends to pray for him. Never forget your duties to your mother, to God and to your country.

Farewell, my dear friend, I embrace you once again. I am now going to prepare for death by yielding to God's wishes. Wish no ill to those who have caused my death and never seek to avenge it. The death of Jesus Christ is still not avenged; furthermore, as innocent of what is imputed to me and thoroughly convinced that I did not deserve this fate for unsigned writings that were never sent; but no matter, my good friend, I die resigned to the will of the Most High, who has thus permitted it that I may expiate my horrible sins here below, for which I hope for mercy.

Farewell, my dear daughter, farewell, may Heaven bless you! And, above all, may it shower its favours, the only true ones, upon you.

From the Conciergerie, this Friday 13 September 1793, at a quarter past three.

Berger.

I wrote to you this morning. I do not know if you received my letter and the linen, books and small effects that I sent you in three parcels.

I owe Citizen Saussier, who is in the room where I was, seven *livres*, ten *sols*, for which I am truly grateful: pay them to him, or get Citizen Pottier, whom I greet, to pay him that sum at once.

I also remember that I may owe six *livres* to Charanson's widow, formerly our vine-grower, her son married La Robineau's daughter, make sure she is paid and whatever else I may owe a few vine-growers or labourers. I entrust it to your consciences. Farewell, once again, my dear daughter.

RUTANT,[178] Jeanne-Charlotte de (1771-93)

A native of Saulxures-lès-Nancy (Meurthe-et-Moselle), the daughter of a Lorraine gentleman, Charlotte de Rutant displayed the aristocratic sensibilities of her family in the correspondence for which she was condemned.

A letter written by her in April 1793 and addressed to 'the mistress of Mlle Henriette' at Aix-la-Chapelle was intercepted by the Committee of Surveillance of the *département*. The recto, written in ordinary ink, concerned only matters of everyday family interest. The verso, on the other hand, contained almost illegible sentences written in invisible ink.

When the paper was brought close to a heat source, the young woman's true feelings and preoccupations were discovered. She questioned her correspondent – a female 'relation' – concerning the émigrés and the movements of the enemy armies and informed her that 'Monsieur le Régent', the future Louis XVIII, was writing a manifesto that 'would not be made public'.

Since she seemed very well-informed, the authorities at Nancy went to the château where she had been living with her family, inspected her personal papers and took her off for questioning. Part of an undated letter, signed 'J.C.R.', slipped to them by one of the servants, was to reinforce the charges laid against her. It concerned efforts being made in Luxembourg, 'for the dismantling of France', and it was stated 'as certain that Lorraine, the Bishoprics and Alsace would be for the emperor'.

After due deliberation the Committee decided that 'the girl Rutant' would be transferred at once to Paris. Her father, arrested with her and held at the *maison de force* of the Prêcheurs at Nancy, expected the worst and tried in a moving memorandum to save his daughter from certain death:

It is not enough that my daughter be taken away from her judges at home: if I am to believe certain vague rumours that have reached me, she is to be taken out of my loving care: this blow comes harder to my heart. It is an affront not only to political rights, but to those of humanity. Citizens, either I am suspect of complicity in the crime imputed to my daughter (as my detention would seem to confirm), in which case the order of the law and the very rules of procedure require that I continue to share her captivity, or my interrogation removes all suspicion from me, in which case I must be free and allowed to go wherever the urgings of my affections may call me. What, then, is the purpose of extending my detention? Would it be to deprive my daughter, in the springtime of her age, still so close to childhood, of the help, consolation and counsel of paternal solicitude?

It was all to no avail and Fouquier himself issued a warrant for the girl's arrest. She appeared before the Revolutionary Tribunal on 4 October 1793 and was condemned for corresponding with and spying for the enemies of the Republic.

She was executed the next day about midday with the Norman twins Bellanger, 'drovers', who, according to one witness, 'when on the fatal plank were still crying "Long live the Republic!" '

Three hours earlier, she had taken her last farewell of her brother André, who had accompanied her to Paris and had no doubt attended her trial.

To Citizen André Rutant, Rue Richelieu.

> Sunday at 9 o'clock.

Courage, my friend! And give courage to our unhappy parents. Be consoled, all of you, but do not forget me. You, my friend, even more than my other relations whom I have offended less, forgive me, I beg you, whatever in my conduct may have harmed you. Until this moment, I have expiated those wrongs, if anything could expiate them. I hope they will allow you to have my hair, which will not have been touched by the executioner. I would never have dreamt that a man like the public prosecutor could exist! He alone is responsible for my death. But since God, that all-powerful God, whose forgiveness I beg for me and for all my friends, will judge him one day, I pardon him, at least I hope so.

I hope my excellent friend, my all too loving sister, will not remain longer in this city. I am counting on her presence to mitigate and diminish the sorrow of my incomparable father. You, too, my dear friend, will be necessary to him at this cruel time. I think constantly of the moment when he will learn of my fate. But whatever pain is caused me by what I leave in this world, the

Supreme Being sustains my courage, I hope he will not abandon me. I pray to him for all of you, my friends.

Share my hair between you, my beloved, and do not forget me though your hearts ache when you remember me, farewell!

I urgently beg you, my friend, to express my gratitude to Citizen Chauveau and to those of my fellow-citizens who were present at my trial and seemed to take an interest in the unfortunate defendant. I do not think that it will be taken ill that you embraced the defence of an unfortunate woman, who is deeply moved by the interest shown in her lot.

> Hélas! Hélas! pour vouloir vivre,
> La vie est-elle un bien si doux!
> Quand nous l'aimons tant, songeons-nous
> De combien de chagrins sa perte nous délivre?
> Elle n'est qu'un amas de craintes, de malheurs,
> De travaux, de soucis, de peines,
> Pour qui connaît les misères humaines,
> Mourir n'est pas le plus grand des malheurs!

Since I found and copied out these verses, I have tried to absorb the ideas that they express so well. I believe they have helped me to achieve the calm I now enjoy.

Farewell, for ever, farewell!

GORSAS,[179] Antoine-Joseph
(1775–93)

Son of a master cobbler who had intended him for the priesthood, he had been sent to the Collège du Plessis, in Paris. There he met Vergniaud, who had been given a scholarship, and the two men remained friends for the rest of their lives. A few years later, Gorsas found a part-civil, part-military institution intended for young men who wanted to enter the guards regiments. Later, in *Le Père Duchesne*, Hébert was to question the disinterestedness of this initiative.

Brilliant and caustic, Gorsas had proved his courage and independence of spirit in 1786 by publishing several pamphlets, one in particular against Loménie de Brienne, which landed him in the prison of Bicêtre for a time. During this period he was closely connected with Carra, Brissot and Mirabeau.

In 1780, he successfully launched the *Courrier de Versailles*, an organ of the Third Estate that soon became the target of hack writers on both sides, royalists and democrats. When the king's aunts emigrated in 1791, he was teased for a long time on his advice to them not to take with them anything that belonged to them, even so much as a nightdress, and for a long time to come people spoke of the '*chemise de Gorsas*'.

After 10 August, an event of which he approved, he benefited from the decision of the Commune to hand over to the patriotic journalists the presses, type and machinery of the 'public poisoners' and took over the printing works of Durozoy, the royalist editor of the *Gazette de Paris*.

Elected deputy for the Seine-et-Oise in the Convention, he supported the views of the Girondins on the advisability of the trial of Louis XVI and, in January 1793, voted for his detention and 'banishment until the end of the war'. In his newspaper he launched constant attacks on Marat, while, in *Le Père Duchesne*, he was himself accused of accepting English subsidies.

On 9 March, his printing-works in the Rue Tiquetonne was ransacked. Accused with the Girondins, he fled with others of the same party to Évreux, then to Caen, where he learnt that the Convention had passed a measure proposed by Saint-Just to declare him an outlaw. He went on to Rennes, then returned to Paris on 2 October under a false identity, no doubt with the intention of reaching Limoges, where he had friends and relations. Denounced, he was arrested at the Palais-Royal in a reading-room run by his friend Brigitte Mathey.

At the Revolutionary Tribunal, he was found guilty. All that remained was to hand him over to the executioner. Gorsas demanded the right to speak, which was refused. He turned round and addressed the public galleries: 'People, it is from you I demand the right to speak!' He was jeered at and only had time to shout: 'I commend my wife and children to those who are listening! I am innocent, my memory will be avenged.'

Before being taken off by the guards, he asked one of the judges to accept a list of debts that he had not yet paid. He was told to send his letter to Fouquier-Tinville, who received it and in whose papers it still lies.

Gorsas died at three o'clock in the afternoon. Since he behaved in such a stoical manner, Hébert claimed that he was drunk.

To Citizen Fouquet de Tainville, public prosecutor.

Confronted by my death and wishing not to let any of my creditors lose the money that I have been unable to repay, I declare that I owe:

Citizen Berthaut, paper merchant, Rue Saint-Jacques, about fifteen hundred *livres* for printing paper, which he supplied me with and for which I promised to pay in cash.

I still owe Citizen Egasse and Co money, but I do not know the exact amount.

I owe Citizen Rousseau, banker, eighteen hundred *livres*, for which he must have the note and in addition, two hundred *livres*, which he gave me by hand.

I owe Citizen Guérin, merchant at Mamers, in the *département* of the Sarthe, the sum of three thousand *livres*, which he drew, I believe, on the account of his brother and partner in Paris or of his banker. The said letter or agreement bears my signature on the back.

I commend this note to the citizen public prosecutor. I beg him in the name of justice to settle these sums. The hope that he will be so kind as to do so will be a token of gratitude that I shall take with me.

My unfortunate family is being persecuted. If I committed the crimes that are imputed to me they are not guilty. Is the revenge of the public not sufficiently satisfied even though I declare that I do not deserve it. Is it not satisfied, I say, with my own death?

Finally, I would declare that I have never betrayed my country and that my last wishes are that it be happy, and that after all too many upheavals, it may enjoy calm and happiness.

A. J. Gorsas.

7 October, second year of the one and indivisible Republic.
P.S. I may have other debts that I am unaware of. I commend them also to your attention.

BARBOT,[180] Jean-Jacques

'Barbot, very ill taught, taught still worse. To his title of puny man of letters, he could have added that of specialist in suspect correspondence . . .' It was in these words that a journalist described the schoolmaster Barbot the day after his execution.

The condemned man had welcomed the Revolution with open arms and had been one of the sixty pupils in the final year of the École Nationale des Travaux Publics, who, in 1789, had raised four hundred *livres* of patriotic gifts and laid them on the desk of the President of the National Assembly.

At the height of his enthusiasm, Barbot had written a play, *La Prise de la Bastille*, a 'patriotico-politico-Jacobite' drama, according to the *Almanach général des spectacles*, which was performed at the Théâtre Français, in the Rue de Richelieu, on 25 August 1791 and which, it seems, enjoyed very little success: 'The author of this platitude, whose subject is so overworked and has been much better treated elsewhere, requested in vain, by a printed circular, all the Jacobites to come and applaud his play.'

In fact, as a member of the Society of Jacobites, Barbot had been able to have his play run a few days longer. However, on the occasion of the public festival of 18 September 1791 organized to celebrate the completion of the Constitution, nobody thought of performing it on the actual site of the Bastille, where a temporary theatre had been set up (a fact that was stressed by the *Moniteur universel*).

Barbot, who earned his living as a tutor to the children of families that were little disposed to the Revolution, felt a certain bitterness at the lack of success met with by his patriotic activities. It was then that he began to feel some nostalgia for the *ancien régime*, which he expressed in particular in a series of letters written to friends living in his home town of Blois. Unfortunately for him, they were seized by the Committee of Surveillance of the Loir-et-Cher.

He was arrested and imprisoned first at the Abbaye, then at La Force. On 12 October, he appeared before the Revolutionary Tribunal. On account of his correspondence, his attachment to one of his pupils, who was regarded as suspect, and above all his Girondin loyalties, he was condemned to death.

Shaking with indignation, the editor of *Le Glaive vengeur* wrote:

> Possessed of the demon of counter-revolution, Barbot cried out, 'Long live the King!' on the scaffold itself. And, as his hands were being tied, the indignant onlookers poured abuse upon him and demanded with loud cries that they be shown his head.

Before dying, he asked Fouquier-Tinville to send a letter to the person with whom he had entrusted his last wishes. He tried to persuade him that the few objects that he possessed were not actually his and therefore should not go to the Republic:

> To the Citizen Public Prosecutor
> at the Revolutionary Tribunal at Paris.
>
> Citizen Public Prosecutor,
>
> I enclose a letter, which you will no doubt not delay in sending on to the address indicated once you have read it. I wish, if it is at all possible, that it be sent via the citizen who has kept me company in my last moments. I commend to my pupil and to his parents, two sisters who may lack the necessities of life, being already of a certain age, and having to live solely from the work of their hands. They, too, will certainly have paid some of the debts that I have been unable to pay myself for I am convinced that they will have regard to my last wishes.
>
> J.-J. Barbot.
>
> Please turn the page.
>
> Citizen, there are in my room, Rue Bailly, no 22, various objects that belong to the parents of my pupil, Citizen Lemercier, Rue J.-J. Rousseau. I hope they will be returned to him, since they were only on loan to me. Those objects are firedogs, shovel and tongs, a clock that is on the mantelpiece, three red armchairs and a print that is over the chest-of-drawers, presenting: Clairon d'ange Amédée. There is also a chair belonging to Citizen Lemercier, with a collection of the newspaper, *Le Moniteur*, part of which is bound, and the rest in sheets. This is to be found in a cupboard beside the chimney: it seems to me only just that these various objects should be returned to Citizen Lemercier, to whom they belong.
>
> Citizen, I have left the sum of seventy-five *livres*, I wish them to be given to Citizeness Maviatte for the care that she has lavished upon me in several illnesses and which I have not so far rewarded

pecuniarily. It is a sacred debt that I must pay before all else. My pupil's parents will no doubt discharge my other small debts. Citizeness Maviatte lives in the Rue de Verneuil, near the Rue du Bac, no 420, I think; if that is not the number of the house, one may enquire it from Citizen Lemercier.

J.-J. Barbot.

P.S. If Citizeness Maviatte is absent, sick or otherwise, her sisters and her children will be at home: the money may be left with them; it amounts to the same thing; her children will profit from it. It is the fruit of their mother's labour, they are young and needy.

MARIE-ANTOINETTE
of Lorraine and Austria,[181]
Queen of France (1755–93)

Reading some of the innumerable pamphlets written by revolutionaries on the subject of Marie-Antoinette, the picture emerges not so
much of the Dauphin's mother, as that of the Austrian woman who
thoroughly deserved the treatment that was meted out to her.
Having been for so long cut off from reality, she became a human,
moving figure after the imprisonment of the royal family in the
Temple.

Her character achieves true greatness when she is separated from
her children. When the time comes for her appearance before the
Revolutionary Tribunal, the procedure begins to look like a bad
theatrical production. When a jolting cart brings her closer to death,
she is, at last, a pathetic figure, with her starched bonnet, her red
cheeks and shaven nape.

I did not think it right to omit the reproduction of her last letter,
however well known it may be. It was addressed to Louis XVI's
sister, Mme Élisabeth, who had shared the captivity of the royal
family.

Reading Louis XVI's testament and Marie-Antoinette's last letter,
one notices that they commend their children neither to the Comte
de Provence, the future Louis XVIII, nor to the Comte d'Artois, the
future Charles X, but to Mme Élisabeth.

Like the queen, Mme Élisabeth knew that 'the émigrés repeated
like parrots that the sacrifice of the king had been judged necessary,
that the queen was not wanted as regent, nor her son as king; that the
princes agreed on this with the princes of the blood and the upper
nobility.'

All this was known at the court of Vienna, and it was said that was
why the Emperor, Marie-Antoinette's brother, never received either
the Comte de Provence or the Comte d'Artois during their exile.

In her letter, the ex-queen of France refers to a painful circumstance in the trial during which she had to reply to certain insinuations as to the incestuous nature of her relations with her young son. Then eight years old, the child repeated by heart, without understanding them, the calumnies that had been spread concerning his mother and aunt.

This 16 October, half-past four in the morning.

It is to you, my sister, that I write for the last time. I have just been condemned not to a shameful death, it is such only for criminals, but to go and join your brother. Innocent like him, I hope to show the same steadfastness as he in these last moments. I am calm, as one is when one's conscience reproaches one with nothing; I deeply regret leaving my poor children; you know that I lived only for them, and you, my good, loving sister, you who have by your friendship sacrificed everything to be with us, what a position I leave you in!

I learnt during the proceedings of the trial that my daughter has been separated from you. Alas! the poor child. I dare not write to her, my letter would not reach her, and I do not even know whether this will reach you, receive for them both my blessing here. I hope that one day, when they are older, they will be able to join you and enjoy all your loving care. May they both think of those notions that I have always tried to instill in them: that principles and the exact execution of their duties are the very basis of life; that their friendship and mutual trust will bring them happiness. May my daughter realize that, given her age, she must always assist her brother with the good counsel that her [this word has been erased in the original] her greater experience and her friendship may inspire in him; may my son, in turn, give his sister all the care and service that friendship may inspire; lastly, may they both feel that, in whatever position they find themselves, they will be truly happy only by being united. May they follow our example: how often, in our misfortunes, our friendship has given us consolation, while, in better times, we have been able to enjoy our happiness twofold by sharing it with a friend; and where can one find dearer, more loving care than in one's own family?

May my son never forget his father's last words, which I repeat to him now: let him never seek to avenge our death. I have to say one thing that is very painful to my heart. I know how much that child must have caused you pain; forgive him, my dear sister; think of his age and how easy it is to make a child say whatever one wishes, and even things that he does not understand; the day will come, I hope, when he will feel all the more the value of your care and your kindness to us both.

It remains to me to entrust my last thoughts to you. I would like to have written them down at the beginning of the trial, but, apart from the fact that I was not allowed to write, everything moved with such rapidity, that I really did not have the time. I die in the Roman, Catholic, apostolic religion in which I was brought up and which I have always professed, expecting no spiritual consolation, not knowing whether there are still priests of that religion here, but, given where I am, it would no doubt expose them too much if they tried to come here. I sincerely ask forgiveness of God for all the sins that I may have committed in my life. I hope that, in his goodness, he will accept my last wishes, together with those that I made long since, that he may receive my soul in his mercy and goodness. I ask pardon of all those I have known and of you, my sister, in particular, for all the trouble that, without wishing it, I may have caused you. I pardon all my enemies the ill that they have done me. I say farewell to my aunts and [a word is erased] and to all my brothers and sisters. The idea of being separated from my friends for ever and the sorrow this will cause them are a source of bitter regret that I take with me as I die. May they know at least that, up to my last moment, I thought of them.

Farewell, my good and loving sister; may this letter reach you safely! Think always of me, I embrace you with all my heart, as well as my poor, dear children: my God! How dreadful it is to leave them for ever! Farewell! Farewell! I have now only my spiritual duties to concern myself with. Since I am not free in my actions, I may not be allowed a priest, but I declare here that I will not say a word to him and shall treat him as a perfect stranger.

Marie-Antoinette.

WORMESELLE,[182] Gabriel Rochon de
(1750–93)

❦

LEMOINE,[183] Guillaume-Antoine
(1768–93)

On 9 June 1793, a week before the Convention passed a decree for the arrest of twenty-nine Girondins, the General Council of the *département* of the Gironde met in emergency session and reacted vigorously, declaring that it was forming itself immediately into a People's Commission of Public Safety for the *département* of the Gironde:

> Since the National Convention has fallen into the hands of factionists bribed to dissolve it and to substitute for it a power destructive of liberty, the general council of the *département* has summoned all the constituted authorities. The Committee proposes that from this moment you constitute yourselves as a People's Commission of Public Safety and that you do not dissolve until liberty is reestablished at the heart of the National Convention.

All the notables of the Bordeaux region, including Wormeselle, Lacombe-Puyrégaux and Lemoine, supported this proposition and five days later the new Commission passed an order demanding that the Tribunal that might be set up to try the Girondin deputies should not sit in Paris.

The reaction was hardly to be expected: on 6 August 1793, the Convention annulled by decree 'the decisions made by the so-called People's Commission of Public Safety for Bordeaux. Its members are hereby declared to be traitors to the Fatherland and outlaws; their property will be confiscated to the benefit of the Republic.'

On 1 October of the following year, two representatives on a mission in Bordeaux, Tallien and Ysabeau, sent several of these 'outlaws' to Paris. On 2 November, simply on confirmation of their identity, they were handed over to the executioner. Both Lemoine and Wormeselle left farewell letters:

To Citizen Lafon, Hôtel de Versailles, Rue de Valois.
Courage, my friend, courage.

My dear Duhayet, I am condemned and in a moment I shall be walking to the scaffold; take care of my father – I have been unable to write to him, be his consolation, do not leave him for a moment and both of you hasten to Bordeaux to console my sisters and to give them my farewell. Tell my father of my gratitude for all his acts of kindness to me; tell him that, proud of my innocence, I die calm, with the courage that has never deserted me. I hope my execution will appease the All Powerful, who has no doubt wanted to punish me in the world for my sins and, one day, may we see one another again in Blessed Eternity. Once more, look after my dear father, try to sweeten the bitterness that my execution will bring to his last days; his goodness and kindness are sufficient guarantee that he will never forget a son who loves and respects him. Also take care of my sisters, you know how very dear to me you all are. Farewell, my friend, do not forget me; all my best wishes, your good friend and brother.

Lemoine.

This Saturday.

To Citizeness Wormeselle, rue du Temple, no. 1

12 Brumaire.

These are the last letters that my hand will trace. In a few hours I shall be no more. I am condemned to death.

My wife, whom I have always lovingly cherished, I die full of love for you. I do not ask you to forget me; I know your fine soul, your loving heart, no, you will never forget me. But go on living for our poor children. Remember me to them. May I serve as an example to them, may they be better than I. Raise them in the practice of the virtues. My property has been confiscated; there was so little that it will be no great loss to them.

Raise them in the love of work. Lavish upon them all the love that you had for me.

Farewell, a thousand times farewell. Wipe away your tears and concern yourself only with our children.

Wormeselle.

GOUGES,[184] *Marie Gouze, known as Olympe de (1748–93)*

Olympe de Gouges was one of the very few women to play an active part in the defence of the democratic ideal of 1789. But, unlike Mme Roland, she had no fortune and, unlike Théroigne de Méricourt, the sincerity of her principles was firmly based.

She is known as the ancestor of modern feminism by virtue of her *Déclaration des droits de la femme*, a reply to a *Déclaration des droits de l'homme* that excluded 'the weaker sex' from civil and political responsibilities, but maintained their penal responsibilities: 'Woman has the right to mount the scaffold; she must also have the right to mount the tribune.'

A radical – in 1789 she put on a play against slavery at the Comédie-Française – Olympe de Gouges was also an apostle of non-violence: 'The very blood of the guilty sullies revolution for all eternity.'

At the time of the trial of Louis XVI, her offer to the Convention to act as the king's *défenseur officieux* caused a scandal.

She was refused permission to speak, so she turned to her pen and wrote a great many articles, patriotic plays, political pamphlets and even notices, which she had posted up all over Paris.

Though practically without money, she retained her lucidity and refused to put her pen at the service of the counter-revolution, as Laporte, the intendant of the civil list, suggested. She followed events closely and critically, preaching union and concord between all the parties against foreign intervention. In the end, she joined Vergniaud and his Girondist friends in 1793. After their eviction from the Assembly and the arrest of several of them, she supported their cause first in a letter to the Convention, which was censored, then in her *Testament politique*. Her words went unheeded. She persisted and, despite the danger, wrote *Les Trois Urnes*, a federalist tract in which she proposed that the French could choose their form of government by referendum.

She was about to publish her tract when a warrant for her arrest was issued (20 July): the law punished with death anyone tending, by his writings, to re-establish a form of government other than that of the one and indivisible Republic.

From the *mairie* where she was taken first, she was moved to the Abbaye. There she persisted in launching new attacks on Robespierre and Fouquier-Tinville in a new notice (*Olympe de Gouges to the Revolutionary Tribunal*), which her friends posted up in the city.

In September she was taken to the Petite-Force, then, in the following month, she was transferred to a *maison de santé*, from which she could have escaped. She made no attempt to do so.

Condemned to death on 2 November, Olympe postponed her execution for twenty-four hours, in order to write a last letter to her son. On 3 November 1793, she was executed. An observer noted her 'steadiness' on the scaffold and in the large gathering that crowded into the Place de la Révolution, someone remarked that, on that day, 'they were killing intelligence'.

To Citizen Degouges, general officer in the army of the Rhine.

I die, my dear son, a victim of my idolatry for the fatherland and for the people. Under the specious mask of republicanism, her enemies have brought me remorselessly to the scaffold.

After five months of captivity, I was transferred to a *maison de santé* in which I was as free as I would have been at home. I could have escaped, as both my enemies and executioners know full well, but, convinced that all malevolence combining to ensnare me could not make me take a single step against the Revolution, I myself demanded to go to trial. Could I have believed that unmuzzled tigers would themselves be judges against the laws, against even that assembled public that will soon reproach them with my death?

I was presented with my indictment three days before my death; from the moment this indictment was signed the law gave me the right to see my defenders and whomsoever else I chose to assist my case. All were prevented from seeing me. I was kept as if in solitary confinement, unable to speak even to the gaoler. The law also gave me the right to choose my jurats; I was given the list at midnight and, the following day at 7 o'clock, I was taken to the Tribunal, weak and sick, and lacking the art of speaking to the public; like Jean-Jacques and also on account of his virtues, I was all too aware of my inadequacy. I asked for the *défenseur officieux* that I had chosen. I was told that there wasn't one or that he did not wish to take on my cause; I asked for another to take his place, I was told that I had enough wit to defend myself.

Yes, no doubt I had enough to spare to defend my innocence, which was evident to the eyes of all there present. I do not deny that a *défenseur officieux* could have done much more for me in pointing out all the services and benefits that I have brought the people.

Twenty times I made my executioners pale and not knowing how to reply to each sentence that betrayed my innocence and their bad faith, they sentenced me to death, lest the people be led to consider my fate as the greatest example of iniquity the world has ever seen.

Farewell, my son, I shall be no more when you receive this letter. But leave your post, the injustice done to your mother and the crime committed against her are reason enough.

I die, my son, my dear son; I die innocent. All laws have been violated for the most virtuous woman of her century, [two illegible words] the law, always remember the good advice that I have given you.

I leave your wife's watch as well as the receipt for her jewellery at the pawnbrokers, the jar and the keys to the trunk that I sent to Tours.

De Gouges.

COUTELET,[185] Marie-Madeleine
(1761–93)

On Sunday 6 October 1793 Citizen Lambin turned up at the Beaurepaire section to denounce a woman, the manageress of the Jacobins' hemp-spinning mill, the widow Neuvéglise, suspected of corresponding with émigrés. This woman lived in the mill itself, the buildings of which formed an islet between the Rue Saint-Jacques and what is now the Rue Soufflot.

That same evening, the police inspectors arrived to search the property. However, they mistook one floor for another and were received by Citizeness Neuvéglise's younger sister, Marie-Madeleine Coutelet, an unmarried woman, who worked at the mill. She suggested that the police search her apartment and papers. Three suspect letters were seized and the Coutelet sisters were taken off to their section committee.

Marie-Madeleine in particular had to explain how she had in her possession a copy of a letter addressed to an aunt residing in Rheims in which there was a reference to Parisians 'who celebrate constantly, but lack the talent to get bread . . . They pay very dear for everything, but with the "Carmagnole" their complaints are silenced.' She expressed her sorrow at the fate of Marie-Antoinette, 'taken to the Conciergerie, where she still is, until such time perhaps as she is taken to prison and we see her unhappily murdered'. Lastly, she says how unwilling she is to keep for much longer in assignats the money obtained from selling a house, for she wrote, 'everybody is afraid that they [the assignats] will not last for long. People dare not buy shares [. . .] because there are several banks with contacts abroad that will have nothing to do with our bills. So you see what wonderful things the Revolution is doing for us all.'

The young woman denied having the feelings of an 'enraged aristocrat' and explained how she had written her letter in a 'joking spirit, just for the sheer pleasure of it'. At three o'clock in the morning she was taken to the Conciergerie, her file passed on to Fouquier-Tinville and her sister sent home. The charge rested entirely on the incriminating letter: 'This tissue of invective against the patriots and friends of the Revolution is a masterpiece of aristocracy and could only have been written with treacherous counter-revolutionary intent.'

Marie-Madeleine Coutelet was condemned to death. When the verdict was pronounced, she turned to the presiding judge and said: 'If it is the law that orders it, then I submit to it. You may learn of my innocence afterwards, but too late.'

Shortly before her execution, she wrote a final letter to her family, with a thought for her sister, who was to be condemned to death in turn five months later.

To Citizen Coutelet, c/o Citizeness Neuvéglise,
the mill of the Jacobins, Rue Saint-Jacques, at Paris.

My dear parents, I am carrying out my last duties. You know what the law has judged me of, they have found crime in innocence and have ordered my death. I hope you can be consoled; this is the last favour I ask of you. I die with the purity of soul that was given me and look on death with joy. Farewell, I embrace you for the last time, I that am the most loving of daughters, the most affectionate of sisters. I find this day the most beautiful given me by the Supreme Being. Live and think of me only to rejoice in the happiness that awaits me. I embrace my friends and am grateful to all those who have been so good as to speak in my defence.

Farewell, for the last time, may our children be happy, that is my last wish.

Coutelet.

KOLLY,[186] Madeleine-Françoise-Joséphine de Rabec, wife of (1758–93)

Mme de Kolly was the daughter of a banker and director of the Compagnie des Indes. She was born at Saint-Malo and married a merchant of Lorient, François-René Foucaud. They had one son. She was widowed while still young and in her twentieth year married again. Her second husband, Pierre-Paul de Kolly, was the son of a court banker of Swiss origin. Their combined wealth was therefore quite considerable. Pierre de Kolly possessed an office as *fermier général*, which gave him 200,000 *livres* a year, and his wife brought him a dowry of 100,000 *livres* and the usufruct of a huge estate in Brittany. Yet, despite this very large fortune, the couple were more or less ruined in under ten years. An extravagant way of life and several unfortunate financial transactions were the main causes of this. When the minister Calonne learnt of their situation, he forced the *fermier général* to give up his appointment. Crippled with debts, Kolly was being pursued by his creditors when the Revolution broke out.

In 1791, specie money was rare, so the municipality of Paris had encouraged the setting up of currency banks with a view to facilitating ordinary transactions by issuing banknotes of small denominations known as '*billets de confiance*'. But they were badly administered and encouraged the flow of forged assignats; they were accordingly abolished by the Assembly a year later, on 30 March 1792.

At this time Kolly was interested in one of them, the Caisse de Commerce, which he imagined he would be able to float by secretly giving it a counter-revolutionary aim.

He took the necessary steps to reopen it and, supported by Santerre, the head of the National Guard, met several deputies, persuaded them of the ill-effects felt by the twenty thousand ordinary holders of the *billets de confiance* and, after a great deal of trouble,

got a decree through the Assembly authorizing the reorganization of
the Caisse de Commerce (28 September 1792).

Immediately, his friend and 'intendant', Regnault de Beauvoir,
armed with a copy of the decree, went to Stenay, in Belgium, where
the émigré princes were residing, made his support known to them,
tied up the interests of the Caisse de Commerce with the restoration
of the monarchy and returned to France (7 October) with the security
of the future Louis XVIII and Charles X, which enabled him to float
the company. Mme de Kolly, who had recently retired with her
children to Boulogne-sur-Mer, was given the precious document for
safe-keeping by Beauvoir himself. All that remained was to find
backers.

With this end in view, Beauvoir joined Kolly in Paris. It was then
that a certain Leblanc was recommended to him by a woman friend
of his, Rose Uzelle, who ran a reading-room in the Palais-Royal.
Beauvoir talked to him about the project. Leblanc asked for time to
think about it.

A few hours later, he alerted the Committee of General Safety. A
scenario was set up by the police: claiming to be a certain 'Marquis
Gérard de Prouville', a rich capitalist, a police officer met Beauvoir
and Kolly on Leblanc's behalf and pretended to be interested in the
project. Things went as planned: when Beauvoir alluded to the letter
from the king's brothers, the pseudo-marquis asked to see it. Kolly
wrote to his wife, asking her to send him the document, which she
did, concealed under the puff of a tin of facepowder. She enclosed a
letter, heavy with foreboding:

> I have found what you wanted . . . Take care in what you are about
> to do, for my sake. I tremble with fear. But I cannot refuse you
> anything. My God! What a shock your letter gave me. But how
> much hope and perhaps trouble I can see ahead . . .

Eight days later, the parcel arrived in Paris. Several search warrants were ready and the police burst into Beauvoir's home just as he
was returning from the post office with one of his colleagues, a
certain Bréard. Pierre-Paul de Kolly was arrested a few hours later,
while two police officers arrived at Boulogne to prevent his wife
from crossing the frontier.

On 2 May 1793, all four appeared before the Revolutionary
Tribunal, which condemned them to death. At the instigation of her
husband and Beauvoir, and for the sake of their three children, Mme
de Kolly declared herself to be pregnant and was given a postpone-
ment, while the three men were taken off to the scaffold. Tisset, in
his *Comte rendu de Dame Guillotine*, describes their end in these words:

Beauvoir was a Turk, born at Constantinople, and the loving admirer of Mme de Kolly. Mme de Kolly was passionately fond of handsome young men and not of old husbands. Kolly loved only his fortune and allowed his wife to be caressed by his worthy friend. Bréard, a great speculator, used the trio for his speculations. A tin of powder upset this union and led the quartet to the Revolutionary Tribunal. The vile émigré princes had no money. The Caisse in the Rue de Bussy remained without any either. The three men had their necks cut, at once. But Mme de Kolly made up her mind only seven months later, having a little Beauvoir to bring into the world.

The *Mémoires des prisons* evokes the horror of Mme de Kolly's detention: apparently, she communicated by means of a sort of gutter with her two eldest sons, who were being held in La Force, in the men's quarters. It was by this means that she conveyed her hair to them before leaving for the scaffold.

She was guillotined on 15 Brumaire. Her death, avoided for so long, was terrible. According to *Le Glaive vengeur,* 'she let out a long, frightful cry before the blade struck her'.

Her three children were taken in by a Jacobin, Ferrières. They never received the extremely moving letter that she wrote to them on the eve of her death:

This 5 October 1793, second year of the Republic.

O my children! You who were my only happiness on earth, I take my leave of you for ever, a barbarous order has snatched me from your weak arms, and ended my peaceful life on earth. You know how much I love all three of you, it is only for you that I thought to prolong my bitter existence. I do not doubt that almighty God, who is giving me the strength and courage to bear my last moments, however frightful they may be, will sustain you, console you and constantly lead you into the paths of honour and virtue.

You, my dear son Armand, who are at this very moment pleading my cause, receive my farewells and my blessings up to my last moment; by this action and all it has cost you you have given the greatest proof of filial love; receive the painful embraces of your unfortunate mother. And you, my dear Foucaud, prisoner as I am and victim of the blackest calumny and of suspicions unworthy of you, of your innocence and of me! And of my piety! Receive my farewells and the testimonies of an unshakeable love that will serve me beyond the grave for all three of you; look after your young brother, teach him at an early age to cherish the memory of the unhappy, innocent authors of his days, tell him that he and both of you are in my heart to my last hour, which will come this evening.

O my dear children, you are happy in that you will no longer see me suffer. For I hope that my resignation to the decrees of Divine Providence will allow me to share in the rewards to come. Pray every day for me and for your father. If God grant me the grace to join him in eternity, we will never cease to pray for all three of you and to bring His blessing upon you. Have courage and never forget the loving, beneficent beings whose memory will, I am sure, survive my life.

I do not need to urge you to gratitude: it is already in your hearts. Although you do not have many relations left to take care of you, I am commending you to benevolent souls whom I shall miss, and embrace most painfully.

Thank God, my adorable children, with the courage that a clement God gives me. I adore you and bear all three of you in my heart to my last moment, farewell.

Never forget your duties, God is our only refuge . . .

She commended her children to her niece, Citizeness Moysoud, Rue Saint-Dominique in Lyon:

5 September old style (5 November 1793).

My dear niece, I have had no news from you for so long. If the misfortunes that have reached your city have spared you, as I hope they have, receive my last farewells. I am about to join the unhappy victim of my sad destiny and leave this earth of pain for ever; you have already adopted my children. I commend them to you yet again, I want them to join you, for they have no one else on the face of the earth, look upon them as your own children. They have the feelings of loving sons for you, receive all my thanks for the help that you have been so kind enough to send me.

What boots gratitude, since, when you read this, I shall be in my gra , I shall be no more and will no longer have to suffer the cruel ills of this painful life.

Give heart to my children, console them for my loss. Alas! they lose a good mother, take my place with them. I am asking our cousin here to send them to you or to your sister. If you are still at Lyon, love them, they are worthy of love, may they never forget me or you and your dear children; remember me to your dear elder daughter; thank her if she is willing or able to adopt one of them. Share all three between you.

Farewell, receive the testimony of a limitless affection that ends only with my sad existence.

De Rabec, widow Kolly.

GORNEAU,[187] Étienne-Pierre (1773–93)

Son of Pierre-Joachim Gorneau, barrister in the *Parlement, rapporteur* in the chancellery of the Palais de Justice in Paris, he was baptized in Paris. He lived first at Bordeaux, where he worked as a notary's clerk, then settled in Paris early in 1793 and, on his uncle's recommendation, entered the Ministry of the Interior. From bravado, he did not hide from his colleagues his contempt for Republican institutions at a time when denunciations, often anonymous, were beginning to pile up on the desks of the Committee of Surveillance for the *département* of Paris. His correspondence with his friends was just as imprudent.

One of his letters, intercepted by the committee, was the cause of his arrest. He was questioned, then sent to the Committee of General Safety of the Convention, where, on 3 July 1793, he was again asked to explain the terms of that letter, addressed to a friend at Bordeaux, a certain Séris. In it he spoke contemptuously of the deputies Treilhard and Mathieu, who had recently been received in Bordeaux, and ridiculed Marat, as well as 'the brave fellows of the sections who could not stop talking and could not even express themselves in French'. Finally, he drew a 'terrible picture' of Paris, where, he says, his stay was 'not very pleasant'.

On 6 July his residence was searched and his papers seized. The same day he was taken to Sainte-Pélagie and his file sent to Fouquier-Tinville. He wrote a memorandum refuting or explaining certain parts of the various examinations to which he had been subjected. On 9 August next, he was examined at the Revolutionary Tribunal, in particular on the subject of new, highly suspect documents found in his house: a letter containing transparent illusions to the country's elected representatives, in which they are compared to the frogs in La Fontaine's fable, and a parody of the *Marseillaise,* signed 'an émigré who mocks the guillotine and does not fear the theft of his property'.

After three weeks spent in prison, young Gorneau was tried at the Revolutionary Tribunal and condemned for counter-revolutionary correspondence. Neither his father's efforts, nor the touching memorandum that he wrote to the public prosecutor, nor even his youth shook the stern conviction of the jurors.

His last letter, addressed to his family, is particularly moving:

To Citizen Gorneau,
Cloître Saint-Merry, no 452.

My dear papa and my dear relations,

I send you my last farewells. My only regret in leaving life is that I cannot embrace you. No other attachment holds me here: he who has never committed a crime, who has done no wrong to anyone, who was a good human being, sensitive and generous, that man dies at peace. I hoped by my work to serve a more securely based Republic. I have always desired the good of my country. I have always abhorred despotism and worshipped liberty. Today, I am the victim of some inconsequential matter, a mere imprudence committed at the age of twenty, and I die without fear.

I hoped, together with my elder brother, to become the support of the latter days of my good parents, who have brought me up with the greatest care, who showed us the most loving kindness during our childhood. All such hopes are now dashed.

And you, true brother, sincere friend, be, in my stead, the intrepid defender of the rights of man. When you have served your country, take care of our young brother, look to his keep and take care of our only sister and shed tears for our friendship only as long as needs be to erase the memory of a brother who worshipped you and who will, in a few hours, be happier than you.

When I entered Sainte-Pélagie, I had reason to say the following lines, which I sent to my cousin:

D'être humain en naissant, l'homme apporte l'envie
Mais il n'est pas je vois de bonheur dans la vie,
Il lui faut, d'âge en âge, en changeant de malheur
Payer le long tribut qu'il doit à la douleur,
Ses premiers jours, peut-être, ont pour lui quelques charmes,
Mais qu'il connaît bientôt l'infortune et les larmes!
Il meurt dès qu'il respire, il se plaint au berceau,
Tout gémit sur la terre, et tous marchent au tombeau,
Époux, père, enfant, il faut qu'on se sépare,
C'est un arrêt au sort, nul ne peut l'éviter.

de Ducis, *Œdipe chez Admète.*

Those lines are very true.

Sooner or later, by some event or other, one must necessarily come to this pass. May *maman* above all try to be consoled for my loss; let her know that I am at peace, as I go towards death and shall no longer be unhappy. I thought the approach of death would be more terrible, but I am experiencing the opposite.

I am leaving a prison that is a true preparation for this eternal act. I was thrown there, on the straw, with some forty other poor devils, all of whom are awaiting the same fate. I don't know whether I should believe in presentiments, but for several days I thought about my affair and the fate that awaited me. When I saw that I was suddenly transferred to Sainte-Pélagie, I said: 'I'm done for.'

Tell my cousin Dupuy to make sure that he collects from Sainte-Pélagie the following objects that he lent me. Here are the instructions that I have given to the citizen keeper:

I beg Citizen Boucherot, keeper of the house of Sainte-Pélagie, to hand over or to have handed over by a chamber comrade, to the bearer, my cousin, the following effects that belong to him: 1. one trestle bed; 2. one mattress; 3. Crébillon, in three volumes; 4. *My mathematics*, by Saurin in five octavo volumes; 5. one telescope.

I have sold to my chamber companion the rest of my books, in exchange for money lent me.

Étienne-Pierre Gorneau.

I take my sincere farewell of all my friends and relations: I embrace them for the last time. I want my father to keep this letter for his descendants, to remind them that I existed and perished on the scaffold, a victim of my opinions, on 14 Frimaire, 4 December 1793 old style, Year II of the French Republic, between noon and one o'clock, or eleven o'clock, on the Place de la Révolution.

Once again, farewell *in vitus eternam*, Father, Mother, Brothers, Sisters, Uncles, Aunts, Relations, Friends, Cousins, who are so dear to me and knowledge of whom has become so sad a matter for me on account of the friendship between us.

In vitam morte datus.

Gorneau, second son.

This 4 October 1793, 14 Frimaire.

DUFRESNE,[188] *Antoine-Pierre-Léon*
(1761–93)

On 2 June 1792, a health officer called Dufresne, a native of Normandy, who had lived for several years in the French West Indies, landed at Bordeaux. He had returned to France, it seems, to marry.

An imprudent correspondence with his friends at Santo Domingo must have led to his arrest and his appearance before the Revolutionary Tribunal. In June 1793, he wrote to Citizen Paraud *aîné*, living at Cap Français: 'Although I am very pleased with my marriage, I have often regretted leaving Santo Domingo: at least one doesn't have one's throat cut by one's brothers there. You can have no idea how hard the guillotine works here: up to twelve, fifteen and twenty men at a time. In the twinkling of an eye, it's all over; there has never been a finer invention in the world for an executioner.'

Another of his letters revealed even more clearly what he thought of the Revolution. In it he paints a very sombre picture of the France of 1793: 'When I left Santo Domingo, I thought I was leaving behind forever the persecutions of anarchy and the horrors of human ferocity. But, to my great astonishment, I have fallen from Charybdis into Scylla (*sic*), France is nothing but a great scaffold in which the strong kill off the weak in the name of the Law. People talk about nothing but battles, fires, massacres, lootings, famine, plague, hail, etc. Our plight is such that I dare to believe that we have fallen to the level of America.'

The same man who spoke so often of the guillotine and often said that he had 'no intention of coming near it' was condemned to it for 'counter-revolutionary propaganda'. His prosecutors had remarked that when he was capable of overcoming his 'sybaritic and effeminate softness' it was 'only for the pleasure of calumniating his country'.

The night before he died, Dufresne wrote to his young wife, who was expecting their first child:

To Citizen Joli, Rue Gallion, no 852,
to be given to his poor daughter, at Paris,

3 December 1793.

Receive, my too adorable wife, the last farewells of your poor
husband. He was not as good as you deserved, but he loved you. I
do not think you ever doubted that. Believe me, dear friend,
always respect your poor, unhappy, respectable father. Be as
steadfast as your husband. His only regret is that he cannot embrace
you.

Your father, dear wife, will always be in your husband's heart,
despite the ferocious cries of his denunciators. If eternity exists, he
will see you there, he had nothing but honest feelings for you,
perhaps not honest enough, for you deserve to be eternally happy. I
have no counsels to give you. You follow those that you have to
follow, but believe me when I say that you should forget your
husband; give your father, who is already too unhappy, a son
worthy of you both. Write to me once more so that I may carry
with me to the grave a line from your chaste hand. I end. My tears
water my letter. Dry your own. Send me about fifteen francs. I
gave sixty francs to Julien who will no doubt pass it on to you.
Thank him and all our friends for me. Believe me, you should retire
to some solitary place and live quietly there. Ask forgiveness of
your father if I have been the cause of his ills. I shall be at the
Conciergerie until tomorrow morning, ten or eleven o'clock.
Farewell, farewell for ever, farewell for eternity.

Your husband, Dufresne.

I shall expect your answer this evening, for I need money.

13 Frimaire, 1793.

Write to my parents, I beg you. You will send my letter to Le
Fourdrai.

Love orders you to do so.

To his denunciator, Le Fourdrai, a paymaster in the navy at
Cherbourg, Dufresne wrote:

I take my eternal farewell of you, villain. I don't know whether you
did it on purpose. Though I knew you for a scoundrel, I cannot
bring myself to believe that you are also a wicked villain. All I can
say is that it is the letters I wrote to you that have brought me to the
scaffold. If it was not wickedness, your turn will come soon
enough.

Farewell, Dufresne.

This 13 Frimaire 1793.

LÉONARD,[189] Guillaume
(17. . –93)

Léonard was one of those petty forgers whose only aim was to get rich without having to invest a large sum in equipment.

A wine merchant, but also a printer working for a works producing assignats, he was arrested with several of his accomplices in September 1793, but freed a month later. Arrested again, he came to trial and was found guilty in December.

Although he was tried in the criminal court of the Paris *département*, this bourgeois forger was probably not entirely without political intentions.

To Citizeness Léonard, wine merchant,
Rue des Lavandières, near the Place Maubert, at Paris.

My dear friend,

I take my leave with tears in my eyes. I am condemned to die tomorrow and I die innocent without ever having committed any crime. I forgive you whatever trouble there has been with your parents and I confidently hope that you will do the same. Write at once to my parents and tell them that I die for finding myself in the company of scoundrels, who were nevertheless not criminals. In all my life, I have never committed any crime; I embrace you with tears in my eyes and I will be your husband to the last hour. You know that I owe five *livres* to Citizen Mauduit, who lent me them on the day I was arrested; do not blush to write of my death to my parents, I knew how to live and I shall know how to die.

Farewell, my more than friend. I am writing to you for the last time and am your husband, Léonard.

Paris, 19 Frimaire, Year II of the French Republic.
And long live the Republic!

PINARD,[190] Charles-Antoine
(1762–94)

❧

RIGAUD,[191] Philippe
(1758–94)

Some thirty individuals at least were tried and condemned by the Revolutionary Tribunal for deliveries of defective material, for 'fraudulent activities in military convoys' or for corruption by functionaries dealing with supplies. These supplies could be anything from firewood to waggons and included artillery horses, food, wine, boots and military clothing.

In December 1793, a certain Pinard, a tailor, was denounced by the army clothing department for delivering tunics of a quality inferior to that agreed to by the department. The deal concerned a thousand uniforms worth about a hundred *livres* each. In collaboration with his suppliers, Pinard hoped to make a good profit out of the inferior merchandise.

He was condemned with several individuals found guilty of the same offence. Among them was a certain Rigaud, a member of the army supplies department, convicted of complicity with the others. On the day of their execution, a police observer saw them leave for the scaffold: 'At the Place de la Révolution, those wretches spat out oaths against the Republic; this did not displease the onlookers, who said that if they were not villains and aristocrats they would not speak in that way . . .'

Pinard addressed his last farewell to his mistress:

To Citizeness Prévost, Rue de l'Oratoire no 141,
Bonnet's house, on the sixth floor, at Paris.

Paris. 19 Frimaire, Year II of the French Republic.

Farewell, my dear friend, when you get this letter your good friend will be no more. I would have preferred to die fighting in the defence of my country; but such a course has not been open to me. I shall accept my fate and carry with me to the grave the peace of a quiet conscience.

Always be faithful, my dear friend, to what you promised me; take care of yourself for the sake of the child you bear in your womb; whether it is a boy or a girl, raise the child in the principles of the Republic. Always be prudent and honest as you have ever been. Farewell, your image is graven in my heart, as mine is in yours, do not forget your friend, but look after yourself and tell your son or daughter that its father died a true Republican.

Embrace my parents, I still love them.

Pinard.

Rigaud's last two letters are also very moving:

To Citizen Rigaud *aîné*, Rue des Singes, no 7,
near the Rue des Blancs-Manteaux, at Paris.

Paris, from the Conciergerie, 19 Frimaire,
Year II of the French Republic.

Farewell, my brother, tomorrow I shall be no more. I must admit that I did not expect this. The peace of my heart is a sure sign of my innocence. You know, my friend, that my estate will not enrich the Republic, but nevertheless the Tribunal has decided that I am guilty and must die. Die! At thirty-six on the scaffold. It is a terrible, unbearable idea . . .

Go back to Montpellier, console our respectable father, shed your tears on my mother's grave, embrace Cyrille and Auguste, those good brothers, and Sophie for me.

Farewell, you must all love the Republic, serve it, it is my mother and can do no wrong. See those of my friends who are in Paris, Saint-Maurice, Chenard and his wife, Marillé, General Sagué, Bastide.

Farewell, I embrace you. See our friend Tayra.

P. Rigaud.

My writing is not shaky, but my heart is still purer than my hand is firm. Do not forget our family, and Jeannette and Suzon (P.T.O.). Embrace François, my friend, for me and weep for my death. Pay him, I beg you, the fifty *livres* I owe to that patriotic woman Rhoze, and do not forget our wig-maker, who is a good Republican. I owe him money since 1 April last, so give him a little New Year's gift. Do the same for Clermont, the porter of the house where I lived; do not go back to my apartment. The few effects that I have there belong to the Republic. Farewell, my brother, farewell, forget me and concern yourself only with the Fatherland.

P.R.

If you do not have the necessary money, I think you will find someone to lend you enough for your journey. In my closet you will find a dozen handkerchiefs marked S.S., they belong to Sophie, the wife of our good Auguste. Mention them to Citizen Dumesnil, whom I greet and who will try to obtain them for you.

A second very beautiful letter is addressed to his wife:

In a few moments, dear and worthy wife, I shall appear before my God, my sovereign master. I still have strength and courage to write to you and to take a loving, eternal farewell.

Although my pen is trembling in my hand, although my heart is oppressed and my tears cover the paper, I still have enough strength to beg you to remember me; I ask your forgiveness a thousand times for whatever ill I may have done you since I have had the happiness of being united with you. I ask forgiveness of my father for all the shortcomings in my conduct towards him.

Forgive me, both of you, I pray you, and remember that when you receive the marks that I have made on this paper, I will already have given an account of myself to the judge of judges for the actions of my life. I hope that he will take pity upon me. I beg you, for the love that you have always shown me, to preserve your health so that you may take care of my venerable father and my children. Tell those children that my last wishes were that they should respect my father, that they should have for you all the care and attention that they owe a loving mother; that they love God above all; tell them that I forgive all my enemies, whoever they may be, from the bottom of my heart, that I forbid them, in whatever position they may find themselves, to seek revenge directly or indirectly against those whom they may think contributed to my downfall, that they may follow the law of God and that, in these sad moments, it is a father who is addressing them. If they love him, they will obey him willingly. May they remember me sometimes as a father who loved them and who regretted the loss of his life more on their account than on his own; I despair at what may follow my sad fate, but God, who never abandons his children, will have pity on mine; may they be good people and he will see that they do not want.

I am sending you, my dear wife, the only thing that still belongs to me; you will receive it in my letter, it is a tuft of my hair. When you look at it, think sometimes of someone who loved you well. As for Auguste, I am sending him the only thing left to me, my collarstud, which I also enclose in my letter. I beg him to wear it always so that he will never forget me. I cannot tell you how much I have suffered so far. God may take it into account.

Farewell a thousand times, farewell for life, pray God that he will receive me in his holy paradise; my heart is full, I cannot say more. Farewell, yes, farewell.

SERPAUD,[192] Jacques
(1738–93)

❧❧

BLOUET,[193] Jacques
(1737–93)

Anne-Léon de Montmorency, a brigadier in the army, one of the biggest landowners in France, owned an estate near Liège, to which he retired in 1791.

His '*intendant*' and general agent in Paris was a former lawyer at the *Parlement*, Jacques Serpaud, with whom he corresponded, at first quite openly, then, after the law on émigrés' property, he tried secretly to transfer large sums of money for him to Belgium. Several people were denounced in the affair. One of them, the porter Blouet, had hidden in the family's Paris house a large part of the Montmorency silver, which ought to have gone to the Mint. With Serpaud, he was condemned to death on 25 Frimaire, Year II (15 December 1793). They both wrote a last letter:

To Citizeness Blouet, Maison de Montmorency,
Rue Saint-Marc, at Paris.

Farewell, my loving friend. I am going to death bravely, a sacrificial victim. I urge you to be steadfast. I am counting on your loving friend, Citizeness Maillard. She will take you in, there you will live happily. It is my hope, it is the only hope that consoles me. You will take counsel for your affairs from Citizen Devilliers, you know what will be left to you. Farewell, Adélaïde, love your mother, respect her and try to console her. Remember me to all my acquaintances, write to my son of his father's innocence, but order him to serve his country. I do not want him to have any other companion; in peace, he may marry whosoever may make him happy.

Farewell, receive my last embraces.

Blouet.

The property of condemned prisoners goes to the nation; it will not amount to much. If the seals have not been placed on the house, that must be done, but I hope they will leave you your furniture, you will keep [illegible word] the rest may bring you some help. I would like to die knowing that you will be happy; you will be, I hope. Farewell, farewell, and for the last time, do not forget me. Remember me to Citizen Herbertot, his wife, and good Citizeness Guérin. Farewell.

Blouet.

Mlle Serpaud, Rue Saint-Marc, no 167, received this note from her father:

Your poor father is about to die with all the courage he is capable of. Mourn not so much his fate, my dear daughter, as your own. Live as happy as you deserve to be. I pray that all the kindness of our friends will be shown you and I embrace everybody for the last time.

6 December 1793.

Serpaud.

My companions in misfortune send you their last farewells. See our friend in the Rue Dauphine if you need advice.

✥

CLÉMENT,[194] Amable-Augustin
(1761–93)

A watchmaker by trade, Clément joined the National Guard as a private and was recognized as one of those who, on La Fayette's orders, had fired on the crowd in July 1791. That tragic event had taken place after the return from Varennes, when a group of republicans had gone to the Champ-de-Mars, to lay on the altar of the fatherland a petition demanding the organization of a new executive power. Martial law had then been proclaimed by the Constituent Assembly and a detachment of the National Guard, commanded by La Fayette and the mayor of Paris, Bailly, had dispersed the gathering. The troops fired on the crowd, causing the deaths of a large number of patriots, including women and children.

It was in December 1793 that the 'section du Contrat social' denounced Clément, who had had 'the barbarous temerity to boast that he had killed four people'. He was also reproached for coming to the assemblies of his section in order 'to ridicule the most useful deliberations' and to insult the patriots. When it was time for him to enlist, he had declared that he would not join the army until fathers of families were also obliged to join. 'Their lives,' he said, 'are no more precious than those of boys,' and he was overheard saying such things before several young men, encouraging them not to join up. His case had been made worse by the fact that a portrait of 'La Corday' had been found in his home. This left little doubt as to his convictions.

He was condemned for 'plotting with a view to disturbing the state in a civil war, arming citizens against one another . . .'

His last letter, addressed to posterity, was accompanied by a quatrain, composed a few minutes before he joined the cart:

Amable-Augustin Clément, born 7 March 1761, died by the sword of the law on 27 December 1793 for having been at the Champ-de-Mars on 17 July 1791 under orders from the municipality of Paris, and condemned out of revenge by Lézerot, who denounced him. That wretched man was under arms and certainly acted no differently from the others, but since traitors are required so that innocence may perish, this man, in order to hide the crime in which he took part, denounced me in order to escape the vengeance of the nation, and committed this base action. But I die without ill feeling towards him, hoping that I am showing him the way and that he will travel along it like the others, for he is as guilty as they, indeed doubly so. But I leave posterity to judge of my innocence. I was born thirty-two years, eight months and twenty days ago, that is a reward for serving my country since 14 July '89.

I hope to bear my sentence with the steadfastness that I have always shown in all matters since the Revolution, unless my strength abandons me. I pray those who will read this sad, last testament to have pity on an unfortunate wretch who is dying for obeying orders, without knowing where he was going. I declare that my commander was as innocent as I, but it will be recognized too late that I did not deserve such a fate.

One of the same batallion, a victim like me, he is called Baron, will accompany me to the scaffold. But it is a theatre of honour when one dies for one's country.

Written on 17 December at half-past seven in the morning.

A. A. Clément, at the Conciergerie.

Immortel dans le coeur de son amie
Ce n'est pas cesser d'être
Quand on meurt pour sa patrie
Et ma dernière parole sera ton nom chéri.

Clément.

DIETRICH,[195] Frédéric, Baron de (1748–93)

Mayor of Strasbourg in 1792, Dietrich achieved celebrity by receiving into his home Rouget de Lisle, a captain in the Engineers at Strasbourg, who composed the *Chant de guerre pour l'armée du Rhin*, which was to become the *Marseillaise*.

Dietrich went into business at an early age, working with his father, Jean, the creator of the Forges du Bas-Rhin, who had been raised to the peerage by Louis XV and on whom the Emperor of Germany had conferred the title of Imperial Count.

He had made a name for himself as a geologist and an economist and, in 1780, he entered the Academy of Sciences, where he became a friend of Turgot and Condorcet.

Elected mayor of Strasbourg in 1790, he was accused of complicity with La Fayette. He was criticized above all for inciting the citizens of Strasbourg not to recognize the Assembly as the supreme authority after 10 August 1792. He proved his innocence first at the Tribunal at Besançon, where he had a large number of friends, but, on 5 Nivôse, he was brought before the Revolutionary Tribunal by decree of the Convention, together with other 'great conspirators' such as Biron and Custine. The investigation preceding his trial was conducted very quickly. He was accused of hiding behind the mask of patriotism, of assisting the plots of Louis Capet and his ministers, of persecuting the people's societies, planning with La Fayette measures that would make it possible to resist the Legislative Assembly, etc. Any one of these charges alone would have been enough to send someone to his death.

His last letter was addressed to his children:

My dear son, you will receive by the first diligence a few pieces of music. They comprise all the music that I have copied out, arranged or composed, in my own hand, during my captivity.

Some of it is very bad, some of it badly arranged, but there are also some charming things; unfortunately, this is all I can leave you.

My dear children, summon up all your strength; your father will no longer exist when you receive these few words.

Look after yourselves for the sake of your mother and your little brother. My heart breaks when I think of the misfortunes that we have drawn on a friend and on his family, I hope my father will take care of him and of you, I beg him to do so again today. Always love your country; do not, at any time in your life, try to seek vengeance on those who have so unjustly persecuted me. If I could do them some good at the moment they are sending me to my death, it would give me great happiness. Be consoled for my loss with the thought that for thirty months your unhappy father endured a torture a thousand times more painful than death.

Try to obtain a reunion with your loving, virtuous mother; I hope that my enemies, satisfied with my death, will no longer oppose it. The future will justify me in the opinion of just men and true Republicans. I await my end with a calm that must serve you as consolation; innocence alone can confront it thus. I embrace you, my dear friends, my dear children; preserve your principles and your virtue and you will be able to bear all events with courage. I clap my friend to my heart. I say farewell to you for the last time.

Farewell.

CUSTINE,[196]
Armand-Louis-Philippe-François
(1769–94)

A cavalry captain in the queen's regiment, he married Delphine de Sabran in 1787 and had two sons by her, one of whom was the celebrated Astolphe, born in 1790. In June 1792, as minister plenipotentiary in Berlin, he handed over the archives of the French legation in Berlin to the minister of the court of Spain.

A supernumerary adjutant-general in the army of the Rhine commanded by his father, a brigadier, young Custine was accused of complicity with his father, then condemned to death for high treason in August 1793. A letter from the son suggested that he was aware of his father's counter-revolutionary plans. This letter was used as evidence at the Revolutionary Tribunal:

> I shall tremble for the public weal at the hands of the party to which perhaps you will soon be obliged, but it will be necessary according to the hypothesis you propose; it will be no bad thing for the nation; it is at least what I wish. When you have to explain the motives for your decision, do so clearly, methodically and frankly, but in prudent language. It is an object worthy of the greatest attention. You know the renewal and present composition of the Committee of Public Safety. It seems that it wishes to say nothing about your despatches and the bad news you gave them, at least the *Journal du Soir* makes no mention of the fact that the Convention was informed.
>
> Farewell, my dear papa. I embrace you lovingly. Do not forget a son who is suffering from all your pains and would enjoy even more than yourself the happiness that you deserve and which perhaps fortune will not always refuse you . . .

Three and a half months after his father's execution, Armand de Custine was condemned to death. During his trial he had attracted the sympathy of the public:

'Poor young man,' one onlooker exclaimed, 'I thought he would
be acquitted!'

Delphine de Sabran, who had attended her father-in-law's trial and
supported him to the end, did likewise for her husband. She even
tried to buy his escape from the prison of La Force. On the eve of his
execution, he wrote his last letter to her. It is said that she joined him
at the Conciergerie to spend a last night by his side. Some time after
her husband's death, she was herself arrested and was in the Carmes
when saved by 9 Thermidor.

At 9 o'clock in the morning.

I cannot begin my last day better than to tell you of the loving,
painful feelings I have for you. Sometimes I reject them and
sometimes they will not be dismissed. What will become of you?
Will they at least leave you your dwelling, at least your room?
What sad thoughts! What sad images!

I have slept for nine hours. How could the night be so calm? For
what I need is your love, not your pain.

You already know the sacrifice I have made. I have a poor
companion in misfortune, who saw you when you were still a little
girl and seems like a good fellow; one is too happy in ending one's
ills, to assuage those of another: tell this to Philoctète.

I forgot to tell you that I defended myself more or less alone and
only for those who love me.

At 4 o'clock in the evening.

I must leave you . . . I send you my hair in this letter. The
Citizeness . . . promised to give them to you. Tell her how grateful
I am.

It is all over, my poor Delphine, I embrace you for the last time. I
cannot see you; and even if I could, the separation would be too
hard, and this is not the moment to break down. What am I saying,
break down? How could I not break down at the sight of you?
There is only one way out . . . To thrust it away with a painful, but
necessary ruthlessness. My reputation will be what it must be; as
for life, it is by nature a fragile thing. Regrets are the only feelings
that, at certain moments, disturb my perfect tranquillity. Take
upon yourself the task of expressing them, you who know my
feelings so well and divert your thoughts from the most painful of
them for they are addressed to you.

I do not believe that I have ever purposely done ill to anyone.
Sometimes I have felt a strong desire to do good. I wish I had done
more; but I do not feel the uncomfortable weight of remorse. Why,
then, should I feel any unease? To die is necessary and as simple as
being born.

Your fate afflicts me. May it be made easier! May it become happy one day! That is my dearest and truest wish. Teach your son to know his father well. May your enlightened care preserve him from vice; an energetic, pure soul has the strength to bear misfortune.

Farewell! I shall not erect into axioms the hopes of my imagination and my heart; but, believe me, I am not leaving you without wishing to see you again one day.

I have pardoned the small number of those who have appeared to rejoice in my arrest. Give some token of gratitude to whoever gives you this letter.

CHARRAS,[197] Anne-Jeanne Roettiers de la Chauvinerie, Marquise de (1753–94)

❧

ROETTIERS de la CHAUVINERIE,[198] Jean-Baptiste-Emmanuel (1747–94)

Like many of those condemned by the Revolution, Mme de Charras was a victim of that very vague notion of 'complicity' in a criminal affair concerning the laws of 'public safety'. A great deal could be said about this notion of 'complicity', the definition of which, in times of crisis, does not trouble overmuch an impatient, overworked tribunal.

Born in 1753, she married in 1772 François de La Laurencie, chevalier, Marquis de Charras, *maître de camp* in the cavalry and inspector of the Maréchaussées de France, the mounted constabulary. In 1793, she divided her time between her apartment in the Rue Buffat in Paris and her château at Asnières, where she lived with her young children and seriously sick husband. She was the sister of Emmanuel Roettiers de la Chauvinerie, director of the Mint during the Revolution.

Through her brother, but also through her best friend, Mme de Billens, the Marquise de Charras was in permanent contact with counter-revolutionary circles. When this friend, charged with extremely serious offences, was investigated, Mme de Charras, was, in turn, investigated.

Indeed, Mme de Billens was highly compromised in the transfer of money and precious metals abroad on behalf of aristocrats living in Paris. Her arrest at Asnières at the château of the Charras in December 1793 led to a whole series of arrests.

A month later, Mme de Charras joined Mme de Billens at the Conciergerie and both were accused of collaboration with foreign powers. A few hours before going to the Tribunal, Mme de Charras complained in writing to Fouquier-Tinville that she had been given an indictment even though she had not yet been subjected to any examination:

Citizen,

I address myself to you, confident that you will grant my request. Yesterday evening I was brought to the Conciergerie. A few hours later, I was handed an indictment in which there is mention of a result after my interrogation; I have not been subjected to one.

Citizen, you are too just to judge me without hearing me. I am depending on your justice to grant me a *défenseur*. If it is necessary, I beg you to examine me promptly and to take into account that I have left a sick husband in his bed and three small children who all have need of me.

I am guilty of none of the things of which I am accused. Grant me justice, I am depending on that of which I know you to be capable. I am asking you this in all confidence and am with fraternity,

Charras.

This octidi of the first decade of Pluviôse.

Of course the unfortunate woman was less guilty than her friend or her own brother Roettiers, with whom she appeared before the Tribunal on 11 Pluviôse Year II. All three were condemned to death. Shortly before dying Mme de Charras had time to write this moving farewell note:

To Citizen Charras and his three children at Asnières.

Oh! My dear husband, my poor children, receive the last embraces of your loving wife and mother. As long as I live, my heart is yours. I am close to the fateful moment. Never forget me. I ask my poor children to keep this last note from me for ever. Farewell, I send you my last breath. I commend you all to the woman who loves you, your aunt and sister, farewell.

Wife Charras.

This 12 Pluviôse.

In another letter, the poor woman wanted to settle her debts to her staff:

I owe Jo and his wife, who served me at Asnières and who have three children, one thousand crowns, partly in wages and partly in money that they had entrusted to me and for which I had promised to give them a receipt. It is all they possess, they have only that to live on with their three children, it is a sacred debt that I beg to be settled.

I also owe a hundred crowns of three hundred *livres* to Citizen Delvaux, who is a servant without position and which I beg to be paid. I also owe a certain Bernard, a grocer living in the Rue du

Faubourg-Montmartre, at the corner of the Rue Provence, for goods supplied, three hundred and I think a few *livres*.

I owe my children's nurse, a certain Paris, at Asnières, a year's wages and interest of fifty *livres* for a one thousand *livres* note that she lent me.

I also owe my cook, Madeleine, at Asnières, a year and a half's wages.

To Joseph at Asnières, I do not remember how much, but the record of what is owing to him will be found among my papers. I beg that this debt be settled.

A. J. Roettiers de la Chauvinerie-Charras.

I beg in general that all my debts be settled.

A. J. R. Charras

Charged with embezzlement, Roettiers, Mme de Charras's brother, was arrested despite the protection of Cambon, president of the Finances Commission of the Convention (see p. 78).

A few moments before getting into the cart with his sister and Mme de Billens, he addressed this last note to his wife:

To Citizeness Roettiers, Rue des Quatre Fils, no 27, in the Marais.

I am close to my end, my dear wife and my dear children. I hold you most lovingly to my heart, which is still beating and will beat until my last breath for you. All three of you must love one another always. Be happy in one another and never forget your husband and father.

Roettiers.

12 Pluviôse at half-past eleven o'clock.

THE COULOMMIERS AFFAIR[199]

In December 1792, while the trial of Louis XVI was taking place in Paris, the municipal elections in the small town of Coulommiers, in Seine-et-Marne, ended in a remarkable victory for the party of order. Le Roy, Marquis de Montsabert, was re-elected mayor, Sieur Prévost de la Plumasserie became first municipal officer, while the rest of the council was made up of notables, all conservatives, if not royalists, with the exception of two patriots. Le Roy de Montsabert, appointed a juror at the Revolutionary Tribunal in March 1793, had to leave Coulommiers and was replaced by Prévost. It was at this time that the Coulommiers affair began; it was to end with the execution of several aristocrats and some artisans.

After the king's death, active counter-revolutionary propaganda tended to stir up the population against the Convention, exploiting in particular a law that imposed on the peasants a maximum price for the sale of their commodities. Thus they were obliged to deliver their grain at a maximum price to commissioners entrusted with the task of providing the capital with food.

The complaints about the price of foodstuffs soon turned against the Jacobin Club at Coulommiers. An incident was to lead to its closure.

Religious feeling, which was very strong among the population, was suddenly exacerbated when laws were passed against the clergy and religious services. Indeed, on 12 May 1793, the notables of the General Council decided to implement to the letter the recommendations made to the municipalities to remove all surviving marks of feudalism in the communes. They entrusted two Jacobin municipal officers with the task of removing the crowns, coats-of-arms and fleurs-de-lis that once covered public buildings and the ancient royal roads. Like many others, the church of Coulommiers was decorated with coats-of-arms and fleurs-de-lis set in stained glass, and pictures and epitaphs marked with royal symbols. In a few hours, the rumour ran through the town that impious plans were afoot to suppress all religious worship. The more religious of the women cried halt to the sacrilege when they heard that some of the stained-glass windows had been removed and that mysterious hands had knocked saints' statues off their pedestals. On Whit Sunday, emotions also reached their height in reparation for the acts of profanity; women organized a collection throughout the parish 'to mend the virgins and to burn a candle before each altar'.

One day, Citizen Leduc, one of the two patriotic municipal officers, who for twelve years had been cantor in the church, unsuspectingly entered the church as usual. As he was taking up his place before the music stand, a small group of excited women tried to eject him. He only saved himself by taking to his heels, to the laughter and applause of the 'holy women'. The parish priest, who saw everything that happened, refused to intervene. The municipality declared that it was incompetent to act in the affair, which assumed a greater importance when Leduc made official complaints about his treatment. 'It has happened,' he wrote anxiously to the deputies of Seine-et-Marne, 'Coulommiers is in a state of insurrection: the priests and aristocrats have removed their masks, the few patriots who remain dare not look up or even go out into the street for fear of being insulted.'

On 1 June 1793, the republican Gillet, a member of the Jacobin Club, wrote to the Convention: 'They have wickedly slipped into the minds of the over-credulous citizens of town and country that it is the Jacobins who have abolished religion, devastating and profaning the church, when, by order of a commissioner, it was simply a matter of removing signs of royalty and feudalism from the windows; Jacobins, it is said, cut off the fingers of the crucifix, whereas they were sawing off fleurs-de-lis over six inches long; Jacobins, it is said, removed the crown of thorns from the head of Christ: there never was one . . .'

While the local Jacobin Club was forced to suspend its meeting, agitation continued to spread. A few fanatics threatened 'to knock the heads off any deputies sent to Coulommiers', decided to tie patriots' wives to the Liberty Tree and applauded 'the infernal war in the Vendée'.

At the market, one woman cried out: 'If any lad or lass was bold enough to shut the door in the Austrians' face, I'd pull a pair of trousers over my backside and go to the head of the Prussians and Austrians and cut the throats of the accursed Jacobins, and I'd lodge the enemies in my house as long as it was left standing!'

The reaction from Paris was not long in coming. The parish priest and several noble families, suspected of stirring up agitation, were arrested and guillotined in Paris. Mayor Prévost was arrested in turn and transferred to Paris, together with fourteen persons held responsible for the disturbances in Seine-et-Marne, one of the main sources of the capital's food supplies. According to the indictment, their aim 'was to establish in that *département* and those surrounding it a new Vendée, assisted by royalism, fanaticism and federalism, in order to destroy the Revolution, by massacring patriots . . . That, indeed, the aristocracy, the nobles, the priests and the rich, protected by the constituted authorities, were laying, in perfect safety, plans to destroy liberty at Coulommiers, persecuting patriots, and had viewed with fury the formation of a people's society composed of the friends of Liberty . . .'

Out of fifteen persons, eight, including two women, were sentenced to death. All left a farewell letter or note before mounting the scaffold on 13 Pluviôse Year II.

BLANCHETON,[200] Charlotte Noirette, wife (1765–94)

DELTOMBE,[201] Marguerite Foi-Franquet, wife (1760–94)

IGONNET,[202] Charles-Jean-Louis (1754–94)

A second-hand dealer and a native of Coulommiers, Igonnet was accused of leading 'all the seditions committed by the women, whom he incited to tumult'. Citizeness Blancheton had been one of the most active of these women. She was accused in particular of encouraging other women to cry 'Long live the King, to the devil with the Republic!' Citizeness Deltombe was also recognized by witnesses as one of the leading agitators. All three belonged to families of small shopkeepers or artisans living in Coulommiers.

Charlotte Blancheton wrote her last letter to her husband, a second-hand dealer:

> I have been sacrificed to the most blatant enmity. I do not acknowledge that I have done anything wrong, but one must know how to die.

I beg you to concern yourself with the fruit of our love, your friendship is sufficient to make you do so. Please convey my last farewell to my brother, my parents and my friends. My strength of character is such that I believe I shall be missed.

Receive my last embraces, share them with our brothers and be certain of my friendship to my last hour.

This 13 Pluviôse.

Noirette Blancheton.

Citizeness Deltombe addressed her letter to her brother-in-law, Citizen Langlois, a maker of edge tools in the Rue Basse at Coulommiers:

Paris, Conciergerie, 1 February 1794.
My dear sister, my dear brother,

I am writing to you for the last time, I ask your forgiveness for not writing for so long; pardon me, as I pardon you. I commend to you my dear husband and my dear child, do not abandon them in these times, you know how sensitive he is, help him to keep his spirits up . . . If I have to leave him, I die innocent.

My compliments to all those who have been so kind as to interest themselves in my fate. Embrace my dear husband, I commend him to you with all my heart.

Your sister Foi-Franquet, wife Deltombe.

Igonnet wrote to his brother, commending his wife to him:

My dear brother and my dear sister,

I thank you for all the kindnesses that you have done me until this day. I beg you to continue them for a woman, a woman I love, and four children that I leave you, and hope that you will show them the same kindness that you have shown me, which is my only consolation at this moment. I hope you will embrace my dear wife for me, and my four children.

I would ask you to tell my wife that I am to die. And that she is left with four children, who require that she live. You will recommend to my father to do everything possible for that dear wife and my mother. I embrace you all and I shall not forget you until my last breath. I am your brother, farewell, farewell, my dear friends, farewell wife and children. Wife, I am your man.

Igonnet.

Citizen Moulin will give you a list of those to whom I owe money.

With them died Mayor Prévost, the municipal officer Merlin and the justice of the peace Maulnoir. The physician Prévost and a nobleman, Ogier de Baulny, were also included in the charge, though the latter was found guilty above all of assisting his son to emigrate.

PRÉVOST de la PLUMASSERIE,[203]
François-Joseph-Toussaint (1749–94)

His last note is addressed to his father, a lawyer at Coulommiers.

I embrace you, my father, I embrace my brother, my sister, her husband, Rosalie, Marianne, farewell. I die innocent.

Prévost.

Farewell to all those who have done me justice, my heart tells me that there are many of them.

MERLIN,[204] Pierre (1765–94)

To Citizeness Merlin, c/o Citizen Auginot,
haberdasher, Rue Saint-Martin, opposite the Rue des Ménestriers, at Paris.

It is all over, my good, most lovable friend. The sacrifice of my life is nothing and of little moment, but I must justify my memory: posterity can and must concern itself with the revision of the sentence passed on my companions in misfortune and myself. My only regrets are for you. I know that I am leaving you a child of four months; I understand that not being sure of your state, you might be in difficulties and this troubles me without any way suggesting that your filial love is not equal to caring for the first born, or for the child that is to be born. I have no wish to cause you concern. I know how sensitive you are. And if you wish to follow the last counsel of your friend, your husband, who will love and cherish you and end his days thinking of you . . . you will try to transfer all the feelings that bound you to me to the unfortunate creatures that I am forced to abandon to your care.

This is evident enough.

Let's talk business: you know that I owe two thousand francs to Citizen Postel of Melun, he has my acknowledgement of it. That sum, as well as that of three hundred *livres* due to Citizen Senard, merchant at Villers-Cotterêts, that which I owe to Citizen Bailli, and any other outstanding debts that I may owe, all that must become the liability of our joint community. You will consult, as best you can, whether you can and must accept that community, but I do not think you do. The imminent confiscation of my property can take place only after you have taken what is legally yours; furthermore, take your marriage licence and, after the inventory has been made, consult with people that you know and you will see what the best course to take is . . .

Embrace my sister for me, and remember me to her husband, my family and hers, our friends and all those who are concerned about us; be not anxious as to my fate, I die a free man, and accept my apologies, thanks, embraces and share them with all those who are dear to me: lastly, accept the last farewells of your best friend, Merlin.

This 13 Pluviôse of the second year of the Republic.

Rereading my letter, I realize that I have omitted to remind you of the two thousand francs I owe Citizen Saron of Meaux. Settle that matter as best you can.

MAULNOIR,[205] *Étienne-François* (1744–94)

To Citizeness Maulnoir, c/o Citizeness Auginot, haberdasher, Rue Saint-Martin, opposite Saint-Julien des Ménétriers, or the Café du Commerce.

My fate is sealed, my dear good friend. For the last eight days I have awaited the misfortune that has now arrived. *I am separated from you for eternity*. I complain not on my own account, I submit to it with resignation, but for you; our dear unfortunate children tear at my heartstrings. I have only a few hours left to live.

As for you, my very dear wife, I find you the more unhappy

since you survive me; I urge you to use all the strength of your character to bear these unfortunate events; if not for yourself, then for the unfortunate creatures who need your care; Auguste, Hypolitte, Lamy, Toinette; and Maulnoirs are able to look after themselves.

Talk often of me, especially to the young ones who will scarcely remember seeing me. Keep this letter and read it to them that they may see that all my wishes were for their happiness and to give them an upbringing that may enable them to earn a living, since I leave them no fortune. Thanks to Toinette's virtuous godfather, the little he has left her will provide her with the poor necessities, that cannot be taken from her and with her work she will at least be able to buy her bread. The boys will work, they are made for that, but they will still need a proper status: your prudence and steadfastness will procure that for them.

My property has been confiscated by the Republic, but alas you will have to prove how very little I owned: I have a large family and my dead parents left me no more than an upbringing.

All we possessed – and that is accounted for by many commitments – comes from your side: our marriage licence is in our family papers, in the cupboard that does not contain any others. You will also find the various deeds signed with your aunts and brothers. They will serve, as will also the last deed signed before P . . . [illegible] to settle your claims, which will certainly exceed anything we owe . . .

I urge you, after settling your rights, to sell the house in which we lived together; it is too large for your position. If, which I doubt, you wish to go back to Coulommiers, I think you would do well to retire to another, more distant quarter.

But if, which I would prefer if I were in your place, you are thinking of leaving Coulommiers, then you should go either to Courgivaux or to Réveillon, where you could find suitable, but cheap lodgings, or better still to Sézanne, which would offer better facilities for the education of your boys and where you would find friends if not relations . . .

Farewell, my dear wife, I do not urge you to remember me, I know your feelings too well to have any doubt in that regard. The pen is falling from my hand, our friends will wish to console you, I sincerely hope. I must mention the Clément family as being most attached to you, Chicard and others, tell them all a thousand things on my behalf.

You will be able to send this letter to my son, whose sensibilities you wish to spare. He will learn of my death at the same time as my imprisonment.

Maulnoir.

MARTIN,[206] Guillaume (1729–94)

He was the only one of the condemned group who was not a native of Coulommiers – he came from Lavaur, in the Tarn – and wrote his letter to Citizeness Dufrene, at whose home he lived:

> 1 February.
>
> Farewell, my good friend, I am truly sorry for the trouble I have caused you: it is to be hoped that it will not be for long. I wish every kind of happiness to you and to my friend Dufrene, who will prove to you that he loved me; and loving and respecting you and conforming to your wishes, I am about to embark on a long voyage. My last but one breath will be for Dufrene and for you, and the last will be for my God who, I hope, will receive me in his mercy and in whom I have every trust.
>
> Farewell to our friends and neighbours.
>
> Martin.

OGIER de BAULAY,[207] Étienne-Thomas (1748–94)

A member of the minor nobility of the region of Brie, a landowner, it was impossible for Ogier de Baulay to prove that he had not taken part in the plot to bring about an uprising in the region. He was accordingly sentenced to death. His last letter was addressed to his wife:

> From the Conciergerie, Saturday 1 February (old style)
> 9 o'clock in the morning.
>
> Ah! My good friend, my loving friend, I am writing these few words to inform you that today at midday, you will no longer have a husband. If I have done anything to harm you or treated you badly, I beg you to pardon me as I pardon you any ills that you may have caused me. Embrace Amédée for me and tell him never to forget his dear, loving papa.
>
> I beg you always to take care of him, but I have no need to commend him to you, knowing your love for him and the good care that you have always lavished upon him. Farewell, my dear friend, never forget me as long as you live, farewell once again, I embrace you for the last time.

TROUSSEBOIS,[208] Jean-Jacques, Comte Baillard de (1743–94)

Son of Marcellin Baillard des Combeaux and Louise-Madeleine de Troussebois, Jean-Jacques Baillard, Comte de Troussebois, was born at the Château de Chervil, in the Vivarais. A lieutenant in Monsieur's regiment, he joined the infantry at the age of fifteen, was taken prisoner at the Battle of Rosbach and was then raised to the rank of colonel. In 1788, after the Corsican campaign, he was made a brigadier.

He then lived separated from his wife in his Château de la Mothe-Mourgon, near Cusset, with his sister, Mlle des Combeaux, a spinster 'of rather determined appearance', and his brother the Chevalier de Chervil.

In 1789, when the new ideas were being expressed, Troussebois, the eldest son, armed with his seigneurial prerogative, exercised almost feudal authority over the local population and his employees.

In June 1791, he took with him his only daughter, Armande, to the court of Turin to claim a pension that she had inherited from one of her mother's aunts. Full of his own importance and dignity, he then set about marrying her to a member of the Harcourt family. But the girl secretly loved a young penniless nobleman, Bellescize, with whom she returned to France early in September 1792. The principal laws on emigration had already been passed and the young couple risked death.

Troussebois also returned to France in order to avoid the sequestration of his considerable property. He was arrested while, with the help of a forged certificate of residence, he was trying to obtain a certificate of civic spirit. By means of a document in proof in which he denounced the emigration of Bellescize, who was now his son-in-law, he succeeded in proving his residence in France for over six months and was released.

He was arrested again and held in the Abbaye just prior to the passing of the law on suspects (17 September 1793). He tried without success to get the support of Danton.

Together with his brother Chervil and his sister des Combeaux, he was brought before the Revolutionary Tribunal, convicted of consorting with the enemies of the Republic and condemned to death on 29 Pluviôse Year II (8 February 1794).

Before sentence had been passed, those familiar with the workings of the Tribunal were already convinced of the Troussebois family's complicity with the émigrés who had taken refuge at the court of Turin: 'There mustn't be any jealousy between them,' they said, 'they must all go through the little window' (the lunette of the guillotine).

Denounced once again by his father-in-law, young Bellescize was tracked down and arrested a few days later, condemned to death and executed. Armande, aged eighteen, who had no wish to survive him, accused herself of the offence that had condemned her husband and mounted the scaffold in turn.

Shortly before the preparations for his execution, Troussebois addressed a farewell letter to his wife, who had herself been arrested, that revealed something of his strange personality.

To Citizeness Troussebois.

You will no doubt be very surprised, my dear friend, when I tell you that des Combeaux has borne her arrest with heroic courage and still maintains, to the extent that she has not shed a single tear, that she is more at peace than she has been at any time in her life. We have talked with quite astonishing tranquillity, calm and coolness and she almost won us over. Half-an-hour later, we all three had eaten and drunk with appetite. Without what happened yesterday, you would never believe what I am telling you in all truth.

What useful things, my dear friend, will those events bring you at all times for your greater happiness: they have taught you in a moment to know the world and men, they may teach you the true source of our misunderstandings and those of your mother, and all the other misfortunes that have come in their wake and which beset the world. You should therefore regard that day as the finest in your life, despite the pain and affliction into which it has plunged you. Ascribe it, therefore, my dear friend, to your own happiness for the time that remains to you to live in this wretched world, in which it is nevertheless possible to be in some manner happy and content as you see, despite the misfortunes with which it is filled.

Anything may be turned to one's advantage and profit; it is like the true alchemy by which all the bodies of nature may be turned to one's profit, by which even from poisons their most subtle elements may be drawn to produce the most salutary remedy for man. I was close to the point of being able to use it to cure the poor incurables of the Republic in an establishment that I was planning (which would have been free of charge, of course). I had abandoned minor ailments to the vulgar medicine. But that same Providence that directs all has not wished to enjoy this advantage and the effects of this science that it thought fit to provide me with [illegible word].

You have been able to judge, by the small sample of patients that I have treated, something of what it might have been possible for me to do one day, which you would not have believed at one time.

Lastly, my dear friend, I exhort you to be mistress of yourself and to moderate your feelings on every occasion in order to be happy to keep the promise that you made: always keep before you the example of my sister and live as a Sans-Culotte, as you know that has always been to my taste. All I am telling you applies also to your mother, to whom I can wish only the same happiness. I would be most happy if you could spend your lives together, turning to profit all that you now know of the manner in which happiness may be achieved. Chervil told us something rather odd and that is how we were all three born in the same place and how we shall all three die in the same place and how it required an extraordinary event to bring us together in the same place and how, lastly, I am his godfather and des Combeaux his godmother.

Des Combeaux is very angry about one thing and that is that she thinks, at a time when she can do nothing about it, that she has left at Moulins, without any means of support, the maid called Marion, who used to serve her. That poor old maid, who is infirm and not of that country, even went so far as to bring her the few assignats she had, thinking that she might have greater need of them in Paris, where she was being taken. If you can find some way of helping her some time or other, please perform this act of charity. Marion was in the town's *maison de réclusion*, and there are two or three hundred *livres* owing her; she still owes something for food at an inn. It was a certain Mademoiselle de Palladu, who was also in the same *maison de réclusion*, who paid for her. That debt does not, as far as she knows, exceed forty *livres*. You must write to Marion and to this lady.

This Saturday 8 February, old style.

Troussebois.

I shall finish now, being constantly interrupted by the noise and comings and goings.

My sister also wants me to tell you that she has received from Mme de la Gouttenesle du Donjon, who was in confinement with her, the sum of two hundred and fifty *livres*, for which she gave her an acknowledgement, which is only for two hundred *livres* because she gave it to her twice. She also owes one hundred and twenty *livres* to Citizeness Dupuis de la Jarousse, who has been arrested at Cusset and who has no acknowledgement of it. She also owes money to several other persons: so it must not be assumed that she owes nobody anything because it is not listed here.

MILLIN de LABROSSE,[209]
Claude-Valentin (1752–94)

A former captain in the regiment of the Île Bourbon, Millin de Labrosse was a pensioner of the Order of Saint Louis, and at the time of the Revolution was living in lodgings at the Hôtel Notre-Dame, 186, Rue la Harpe. It is possible that he would not have got into trouble if he had not been such an aggressive individual.

One day, reading the newspapers on the Quai de Conti, at the corner of the Rue de Thionville and the quay, he did not refrain from criticizing aloud the attitude of Turkey, which had just come in on the side of France against the coalition of despots. It would have been better, he declared, if she had supported the Austrians.

Thereupon, an argument broke out with a certain Joly Braquehaye, a sort of *agent provocateur*. They came to blows. A rendezvous was arranged for a duel the following day. But when Millin de Labrosse arrived at the appointed hour, clutching his swords under his coat, Joly Braquehay, accompanied by three armed men, promptly arrested him. He was confined as a suspect in the *maison d'arrêt* of the Mairie of the Paris Commune. An affair of honour had turned into a sordid legal wrangle. Millin remained in prison for fifty-one days before being examined. One can imagine the state of exasperation into which our knight was thrown: he must have been fairly violent, judging by the tone of the letters that he wrote to a former friend of his mother's, letters that were filed in his indictment in the national archives. Here is a sample:

24 Nivôse Year II

My last linen is dirty, my stockings are rotting, my breeches are threadbare, I'm dying of hunger and boredom . . . I shall not write to you anymore, the world is execrable. Farewell!

Meanwhile, he had the misfortune to be appointed by the other prisoners secretary of their association and, as such, had the task of keeping silence in the prison after 11 o'clock in the evening. This brought him into conflict with certain recalcitrant prisoners who ignored the regulations. On one occasion a brawl ensued, the gaolers intervened and threatened to put Millin in chains. Millin was furious and rash enough to declare that, as far as he was concerned, the Republic could go to the devil. He insulted the 'divine Marat' and threw his shoe at the head of one of the prisoners. He even went so far as to threaten him, for want of a sword, with his knife. As a result, he appeared before the Revolutionary Tribunal. As if he were afraid of having to wait too long for death, he thought nothing better than to write to Fouquier-Tinville asking him to bring him to trial without delay. Sentenced to death, he wrote a second and last farewell letter:

To Citizen Fouquier, public prosecutor
at the Revolutionary Tribunal, in his office.

Conciergerie, death cell, 24 Pluviôse Year II
of the one and indivisible Republic.

Citizen Prosecutor, though I have been imprudent, though I have said things and written two letters that I would have done better to keep to myself, I nevertheless did not expect to be treated as harshly as I have been by your Tribunal, equality section. I will say nothing more about that, but I would point out to you that I leave behind me the cardboard model of an entirely new aerostat that would have the advantage of direction. I would like to give to the Revolutionary Committee of my section, or, at least, to two of its members, the explanation of the theory behind its construction. I would then offer it to my section, if it seemed worthy of it. This would take less than two hours and I would die as a result within the twenty-four hours ordered by the court. This, citizen prosecutor, is what I take the liberty to propose to you. Pass this note on to the Committee of Public Safety, if you think it necessary, and obtain its permission. I am resigned. I shall die resigned. I am not trying uselessly to prolong my life, but I admit that I am still thinking of what might be done so that my name may be remembered, when the time of anger is past.

I greet you respectfully, there is, alas, no longer any fraternity.

Millin Labrosse.

P.S. Citizen Harny knows my aerostat, and I appeal to his conscience, though he has grievances against me. I have no more paper.

FOURCAULT de PAVANT,[210]
René-François (1750–94)

Son of Jean Fourcault, an honorary notary at the Châtelet since 1762, a freemason (Saint Alexandre d'Écosse, 1786), and himself a notary at the Châtelet since 1783, his Paris office was situated in the Rue Sainte-Croix-de-la-Bretonnerie, no 27. Among his clients were Pierre-Charles Chevenon, Marquis de Bignay, a big landowner in the district of Saint-Amand, who lived at Bourges. In August 1792, Fourcault acted as an intermediary on his behalf to obtain a mortgage on his Berry estates, but, when sending him the money, he was imprudent enough to admit that he had been 'very busy, particularly with correspondence concerning his émigré clients'.

Fourcault was a friend and business adviser of the Duchesse de Caylus, the Rohan-Chabots, the Nicolaïs and other émigrés, whose interests he continued to serve. He received from abroad large sums of money in assignats, which he then set about exchanging on behalf of his clients, for specie or national property. He was even prudent enough, in July 1793, to declare thirty-nine parcels containing assignats, 'which seemed to him to be suspicious' and which came from Philippeville, near Liège.

When the Marquis de Bigny was arrested at Bourges, letters from Fourcault de Pavant were found among his papers. He in turn was arrested, seals placed on his office and, a few days later, a search of his home ordered. On 28 Pluviôse Year II, he was given notification of the indictment drawn up by Fouquier-Tinville and learnt that it had emerged . . .

. . . from his examination . . . and from the documents addressed to the public prosecutor by the Committee of General Safety of the Convention that the said Fourcault, like many other notaries in the Commune of Paris and all the bankers, stockbrokers, dealers and other bloodsuckers of the people, has been the agent of the accomplices of the infamous Capet and Messaline Antoinette, that he has provided them with funds, received, paid, administered, speculated, exchanged for them assignats against specie, which he passed on to them, either in France, to facilitate their leaving the country, or at Koblenz and elsewhere, to provide them with the means to implement their plans against their country, and an invasion of French territory; that this complicity with the conspiratorial villains has been established in a quite unequivocal manner and admitted by him; that one has only to name the counter-revolutionaries who were in his confidence to demonstrate the extent to which he has assisted in the execution of their liberty-destroying plots, by assisting them with money, given or lent, and in other ways that his profession enabled him to procure for them, contravening the laws directed against them and their agents: Marbeuf, former archbishop of Lyon, the widow Marbeuf [his aunt, recently guillotined], Choiseul, Montbard, Rohan-Chabot, Caylus, former duchess, and others of the same kind, all émigrés and counter-revolutionaries . . .

In a letter to Fouquier-Tinville, Fourcault protested against the charge of conspiracy and coalition with those arming themselves against the fatherland: 'one may consult my registers, question all my juniors, examine my accounts. I swear that I have made no payment to the émigrés since January 1792 . . .'

At the Tribunal, the jury replied in the affirmative to questions concerning his correspondence and collaboration with the internal and external enemies of the state.

He was sentenced to death. Shortly before getting into the cart. Fourcault wrote a last letter to his head clerk and close friend, Citizen Dessouches:

To Citizen Dessouches,
Rue Sainte-Croix-de-la-Bretonnerie, no 27.

I have been sentenced to death, my friend. Furies have passed judgement on a hastily written letter that did not faithfully represent my thoughts. They did not wish or, given the law, perhaps were not able to take into account my conduct and principles since the Revolution, and the purity with which I have carried out my professional duties. I am counting on you, my friend, to defend my memory. I know that under a revolutionary government one cannot avoid the full rigour of the law and I forgive those who have sentenced me to death. I hope that the *département* will call upon you to give information concerning my accounts. Look after my unfortunate creditors, for, given the order at present in force concerning the liquidation of our notarial appointment, considerable liabilities will be found. I am depending on the nobility of your feelings and on those of my family to come to the help of those who will have greatest grievance. Above all warn the creditors of the émigrés to comply with the regulations before 1 Germinal, the fatal date. I perish a victim of the manoeuvres of their cruel debtors. You know, my friend, that I never approved of their atrocious conduct and how loyal I have been to my country. I am ready to appear before God and am not trying to deceive men. This is the last time I shall concern myself with their interests. All human affections will cease, but up to my last breath I shall carry you in my heart. Console my mother, my friend, I am more sorry for her than for myself. Swear to me that you will live on. Reward, if you can, my faithful servant, assure my friends and all my fellow-citizens that, although guilty in the eyes of the law, I die innocent.

Farewell, my loving friend, I embrace you for the last time.

2 Ventôse, noon.

Fourcault.

MAUSSION de CANDE,[211]
Étienne-Thomas de (1750–94)

Rapporteur of the Council of State in 1775, he married the daughter of the intendant of Orléans, Cypierre de Chevilly, through whose influence he had himself been appointed intendant of Rouen in 1787. He was very unpopular and his Paris house was sacked on the night of 3 August 1789.

Fiercely hostile to the Revolution, he emigrated to Rome in 1791 in the company of '*mesdames tantes*', the daughters of Louis XV, Adélaïde and Sophie, whose financial agent he was. The laws on the confiscation of émigrés' property then led him to return to France in order to protect his immense patrimony and he justified his residence with forged certificates. In fact, from 1792 on he spent enormous sums in the counter-revolutionary cause and made several journeys abroad. When in Paris, he occupied a discreet lodging in the Rue du Faubourg-Saint-Honoré, which was kept for him by Marion Latour, the wife of Condé's agent, Josset de Saint-Laurent. (Later, the authorities discovered that 'the house was the den of a crowd of conspirators'.)

Arrested in January 1794, he obtained a transfer to Citizen La Chapelle's *maison de santé*, where the richest detainees benefited from more favourable treatment, but he stayed there for only three weeks. In February, he appeared before the Revolutionary Tribunal and was accused of emigration. He was also charged with 'trying to starve the people by hoarding cereals', when he was intendant of Rouen, and, in 1789, of condemning to the gibbet two Rouennais held responsible for a riotous attack on the grain barns. He was sentenced to death and a few hours later wrote this farewell letter to his niece:

To Citizeness d'Escayrac, house of C. du Ruey,
3rd *porte cochère* on the left on entering from the boulevard, Rue de Richelieu.

I know, my dear niece, that you were at the Café Valois yesterday. God knows that my only anxiety was that you should be present at my trial. I know how much it must have hurt your loving, sensitive heart.

Two points, in particular, were brought up in the cross-examination: first, the Bordier affair – you know that I had nothing to do with that; secondly, a supposed emigration – nobody knows better than you when I came back to France and that it occurred two years before the date fixed by the decrees. However, I am not complaining about my sentence.

I worship the decrees of Providence and I bless the hand that strikes me. I believe I defended myself with simplicity, presence of mind, sang-froid and courage: however I would have said more in my defence had I not had behind me my *défenseur*, on whom I was counting: I do not know why he said so little. However, it is no great matter, I have no resentment against him and I know very well that it was not in his power to save me. But I am angry that the witnesses who signed my certificate and who attested only to the truth should have been led in as if they themselves were guilty. I am ready to appear before the fearsome tribunal of the Supreme Being; I protest my innocence once again and have no fear that it will be disproved. Having no money in prison, I have been unable to pay what I owe to my *défenseurs*.

It seems to me that the Nation, which has seized all my property, ought to discharge this debt. In the event that this should give rise to any difficulty, my family is too honest not to discharge it and my children will not refuse to pay this debt out of the estate that must come to them. I commend you, therefore, to discharge my debts to Citizens Chauveau and La Fleutrie.

I leave you my unhappy children and cannot but appeal to your love for the care that you will lavish upon them. Take great care with their upbringing: it is the best legacy that one can leave them. May they be inculcated at an early age with the principles that may serve them as rules of conduct throughout their lives, and may the unhappy example that they have before them teach them while still young the truth about evil things and to concern themselves with more certain, more lasting matters.

If, in my testament, I have seemed to depend more on your father than on you for such cares, it is because his position, my dear niece, made him more able than yourself to take care of my children. I beg him to adopt them and yourself and I beg you to be the interpreter of my feelings to all my family.

Farewell, my dear niece, farewell for the last time.

Maussion.

PRUNELLE,[212] Louis
(1758–94)

The Prunelle affair was connected with that of the inhabitants of Coulommiers (see p. 160), with what was called the '*petite Vendée briarde*'.

In the middle of December 1793, an insurrection broke out in the name of religious liberty, led by royalists in the communes of La Ferté-Gaucher, Maupertuis and Meilleray. The representatives of the Committee of Public Safety saw it as an attempt to manipulate people's minds: 'In attempting to achieve this criminal end, men unworthy of the name have not feared to hide behind the mask of a religion that, as they are well aware, holds enthralled uneducated, feeble intellects.'

As an article that appeared in the *Révolutions de Paris* on the subject of the war in the Vendée shows, the rural populations of that period were particularly superstitious; the Vendéens 'would have given up already if they had not been sustained by fanaticism. It is all too true that they believe that they will rise again in three days. In a village near the Châtaigneraie a woman, when asked for her husband, went to fetch him in a ditch. She gave him a kick and said, "Get up, then, Toussot, the three days are up." The body was infected. The visitors tried to enlighten her as to her mistake. She replied that obviously he had not expiated all his sins. Never has fanaticism been pushed so far. The parish priest of Sainte-Cécile often takes them into a church and there incites them, in the name of Christ, to murder and counter-revolution.'

Indoctrinated and armed by agents of counter-revolution, it was peasants, artisans and minor functionaries like Louis Prunelle who led such seditious activities: 'Men affianced to the intrigues of rebellion have visited the various communes, rung the tocsin bell, terrified certain of the inhabitants, telling them that the Jacobins of Coulommiers wanted to murder them, and forced those who refused to believe in such an absurdity to go along with them . . .'

Despite the efforts of the local authorities to calm the population and the instructions given to the National Guard not to provoke a general riot, they were forced to intervene after the municipal buildings had been sacked by rioters, crying: 'Long live religion, the Catholic Army! Down with the clubs and the heads of the Jacobins!'

A carter, a miller, a weaver, a blacksmith, a hemp-grower, a former priest, a sawyer, a thresher and the schoolmaster Prunelle were arrested. They were convicted at the Paris Revolutionary Tribunal, 'of taking part in all the crimes committed at La Ferté-Gaucher on 24 Frimaire and of inciting the inhabitants of Villemain to take up arms and to defy death'. They were sentenced to death.

Before dying, Louis Prunelle wrote this letter to his wife:

To Citizeness Prunelle, former schoolmistress,
near La Ferté-Gaucher in Brie, at Meilleray,
From Paris, this 12 Ventôse of the second year of the one and indivisible French Republic.

My dear friend, I must now inform you of sad news for yourself and your poor children. Above all, I beg you, do not be afflicted. Always put your trust and the children in the hands of the Supreme Being, who must be all your strength and your support. It is two hours now since I was sentenced to death through the negligence of the municipal officer of the commune of Meilleray, who did not send what I asked of them.

Learn, dear heart, to be consoled for I shall never see you again. Take good care of your children and raise them well. I suffer death in innocence, accused of being the conspirator of the Meilleray riot when we were at La Ferté-Gaucher, which is false, but I suppose someone has to pay the penalty. Cast yourself into the arms of God's mercy. Show this letter to all my relations and tell those at Champguion so that they look upon you and your children as if I were there, and that they do not cause you pain in anything, that they always take care of you and take pity on my poor little children.

Farewell, my friend, my dear heart, I leave you embracing you, bursting into tears. I beg you to embrace my poor children for me and my father and mother and all my relations and friends. All of you pray to the Supreme Being for me; I am leaving you for ever.

Prunelle, your dear friend.

VILLEMAIN,²¹³ Claire-Madeleine de Lambertye, Comtesse de (1750–94)

In 1770 she married Nicolas-Pierre-Geoffroy, Comte de Villemain, Seigneur de Mesnil, attaché to the King's *cabinet*, but, on the eve of the Revolution, she found herself the mistress of the Duc de Polignac, who benefited from the favours that Marie-Antoinette lavished on his wife.

The Polignacs had been among the first to emigrate in 1789, followed in 1791 by Mme de Villemain's brothers. She herself went 'to take the waters' at Spa, where she received instructions concerning the Polignac family property, which had so far escaped sequestration.

Mme de Villemain returned to France, under the pretext of 'collecting a collateral inheritance', and set about gathering together and storing in her house all sorts of valuable objects belonging to the Polignacs and, it seems, to the Comte d'Artois. In October 1792, as a result of a denunciation, her house in the Rue de Provence was searched. The charge drawn up on this occasion shows that there was found on the premises 'hidden in a walled-up closet', a hundred and thirty marks of silver bearing the arms of the Polignacs and various objects whose provenance Mme de Villemain had some difficulty explaining. She indicated to the authorities that she had wanted to protect these objects from looting and that, moreover, they had been given to her by an 'unknown person' for a sum of thirty thousand *livres*.

She appeared before the Revolutionary Tribunal on 27 March 1794, and was convicted, without much difficulty, of communicating with the enemies of the Republic and sentenced to death. Being sick after a long period of detention, she had been admitted to the diocesan prison, then being used as a hospital by the Revolutionary Tribunal, from which, without any illusions as to her fate, she made her last legacies to her staff, in particular to Citizen Lhomme, her servant, who was executed three months after her for complicity. Before facing the Tribunal, she wrote her last letters to her husband, her mother and to the devoted Lhomme.

To Citizen Villemain, Rue de Cerutti.

I have just been given orders to go to the Tribunal, it is ten o'clock in the evening, and I can hardly sustain myself. Since one cannot depend upon human justice, I want you to know that I thought about you in my last moments and that I shall end my career protesting that I have nothing to reproach myself with and that the wishes of my heart were and are to know that you are happy; as a favour I would ask you to carry out the small commitments that I have made towards those who have served me, and to my servants, you are too honest to refuse me that; this is not a testament, but a favour I am asking you; I send each and every one of them God's blessing. My friend, I cannot regret life since you have ceased to be just towards me, be happy, that is my heart's wish.

Lambertye de Villemain.

I declare that for some time I have owed six [*livres*] to Citizen Jumilhac, which he lent me and for which I gave him an acknowledgement. Citizeness Ferrière will give you the acknowledgement for what I owe her; she is a most honest woman, you know her, I owe her three or four hundred *livres*.

To Citizeness Lambertye, near Moulin, at Montluçon.

Do not weep over your daughter, my dear *maman*, she has died worthy of you, she loved you until her last breath, live and look after yourself and pray for her.

Farewell, my last breath will be for you.

L.D.V.

I have felt, as I should, the value of your good care, my dear citizen, and I shall take with me to the grave my undying gratitude. Do not pity me; do me the pleasure of accepting the enclosed bond and pass on exactly all the letters and bonds enclosed.

I write with difficulty, my faculties have been destroyed, but my heart will go on beating to the last moment, concerned solely with all those who are dear to me and you are among them.

Look after Monsieur de Saint-Sernon. I dare not write to him, but tell him that I love him. If I cease to be, give him my jams, my sugar, my provisions, farewell.

Wife Villemain.

Her husband, from whom she was separated, had more luck than her and miraculously escaped the guillotine. He was regarded as an ardent patriot by the members of the Revolutionary section of his quarter, which happened to be a very moderate section. However, he was suspected by Mosnier, the commissioner concerned with hoarding, of not declaring commodities.

Villemain denounced him in turn for 'abuse of power' and a rapid exchange of memoranda ensued. However, the General Council of the Commune arbitrated in Mosnier's favour and the 'patriot Villemain' was arrested in December 1793. He was freed some time later.

POIRÉ,[214] Louis-François
(1758–94)

Son of a wood merchant, Poiré had been employed as secretary first in the house of Talleyrand-Périgord, then by Diane de Polignac, the sister-in-law of Marie-Antoinette's favourite. He was arrested on 9 December 1793, on the orders of the Revolutionary Committee of Finistère, for having opposed the 'days' of 31 May and the fall of the Gironde. He was also criticized for having plotted against the election of Hanriot as commander of the National Guard in Paris:

> For too long the rich have laid down the law, the general maintained, it is now time that the poor did so and that equality should reign between rich and poor.

For his part, Poiré drew a distinction between:

> . . . the honest rich, who owe their fortune to their labours and to useful, legal speculation, and the guilty rich, who owe their gold only to intrigue and criminal calculation.

In fact, Poiré had remained profoundly royalist, as his correspondence, which he had not taken the trouble to destroy, clearly shows. In September 1792, through his friend, Rose du Rempart, a friend of the banker Ker, who was the secret agent in Paris of the English minister Pitt and in close contact with several deputies, he obtained a post as clerk to the Convention. He was then put in touch with a certain Mr Knight, living in London, who offered to pay him a substantial sum in exchange for detailed reports on the debates in the Convention and on the conversation that he might overhear between deputies in the corridors of the Assembly.

In October, Poiré began work, his reports being 'officially' intended for an English newspaper, *The Courier,* whereas those written by his friend Rose du Rempart, also a clerk at the Convention, were intended for the *Morning Chronicle.* In their letters, his

English correspondents asked him not to send them 'either conjecture or rumour, but facts. Above all,' they added, 'we want nothing that might have appeared in any other public sheet.' Some time later, in December 1792, they insisted that he give them details 'on food supplies, the affairs of Holland, the opening of the Scheldt, the probabilities of war with Holland and England . . . suspensions of hostilities for this winter . . . and the mentality of Assembly members at the present time'. After the execution of Louis XVI, he was asked for 'all the little details especially concerning the dead man and his family that might be of interest to England'.

In order not to attract attention, Poiré addressed his mail to François d'Affrengues, a former officer who had become a postal clerk at Calais, and on one corner of the envelope wrote, 'For Citizen Boosey'. After the arrest of Affrengues, followed by the prohibition of any communication between France and England, the postal services of Calais and Boulogne were closely watched. The counter-revolutionary mail then found its way to Belgium, reaching England via Ostend. But after the decree calling for the arrest of foreigners living in France, the papers of the bankers Boyd and Ker were seized in Paris and examined: a large number of their collaborators and French friends were mentioned in those papers, including Rose du Rempart. All the clerks at the Convention were arrested, Poiré among them.

A letter seized at his house gives some idea of the prudence with which the counter-revolutionaries communicated with one another and the difficulty for the revolutionary authorities (and for the historian) to grasp the meaning of an apparently ordinary correspondence:

> When we are forced to write to you by post, you must grasp the spirit and not the letter of what we write to you, sometimes even, you must understand the exact reverse of the letter, given that your address [the Convention, where Poiré worked] is of a kind to arouse suspicion and surveillance and we have no reason to depend over much on the loyalty of the postal service.

Accused of conspiracy against the French people, of corresponding with the enemies of the Republic and becoming an accomplice of the agents of the faction abroad, he was sentenced to death.

To his wife he wrote:

To Citizeness Poiré, Rue Saint-Dominique,
near the Rue des Saints-Pères, no 1023.

9 Germinal.

Loving friend, I die content since the sacrifice of my life is considered necessary for the good of my country; but you, my friend, must go on living in order to take care of my child and my poor father, now reduced to poverty, and to console my brothers in the army with whom I corresponded.

I know that it is cruel to lose one's friends, but one has to expect anything in a time of revolution. For the sake of our son I beg you to rise above this unhappy event. You are now reduced to the most terrible poverty, I call on the humanity of the good citizens among our friends who know the purity of our intentions. Retire to my poor father's house, he will give you words of peace and will prove the most loving friend.

I enclose the bill of what I owe the keeper at the Luxembourg.

Farewell, farewell.

Poiré.

26 Ventôse, received from Citizen Benoît, keeper, six pounds of meat at fifteen *sols*, making the sum of four *livres*, four *sols*.

3 Germinal, received seven pounds of meat at fourteen *sols*: four *livres*, eighteen *sols*.

GATTEY,[215] François-Charles
(1756–94)

He was living at Rouen in 1787, when he was appointed first secretary to the Contrôle Général in Paris. When his post was abolished at the Revolution, he turned to publishing and distributing books and pamphlets favourable to the *ancien régime*. A decision of the police tribunal of 5 May 1790 ordered the seizure and prohibited the sale of a work published by him entitled 'Extract from the records of the conclusions of the chapter of the Church of Paris', itself forming part of another work entitled *Declaration of part of the National Assembly on the decree of 13 April 1790, concerning religion.* According to the statement issued at the trial, this work tended 'to inspire in the people false alarms concerning the maintenance and preservation of the Roman, Catholic, apostolic religion', displayed 'a truly criminal spirit of opposition to the decrees of the National Assembly' and tended to 'proclaim seditious maxims, intended to bring the constitution and the rights of the nation into contempt and to arm fanaticism against the law'.

Up to 10 August 1792, Gattey published or distributed the most counter-revolutionary pamphlets and newspapers in his bookshop under the arcades of the Palais-Égalité (Palais-Royal) – so much so that one day the shop was looted and several copies of the Royalist newspaper *Les Actes des Apôtres* were burnt in front of the door.

In 1793, fearing censorship, he secretly sent virulent royalist works to England. A bookseller called Bernard, who had settled in Haiti and shared Gattey's opinions, suggested that he send him his publications through a certain Grandmaison, his clerk.

The inventory of a trunk seized at Le Havre revealed that Gattey, despite the law suppressing counter-revolutionary writings, was continuing to deal in such works. These included an *Histoire de la Révolution de France* by the reactionary Abbé de Montjoye, the works of the 'traitor' Pétion, a former mayor of Paris proscribed with the

Girondins, the *Petit Traité de l'amour des femmes, pour les sots* by Rivarol's friend, the Chevalier de Champcenetz, who was arrested four days after Gattey, and *Mon agonie de trente-huit heures*, by Jourgniac de Saint-Méard, concerning the massacres of September 1792.

At the Revolutionary Tribunal, at which Gattey appeared with other booksellers and publishers, it was established that there had existed 'a conspiracy tending to disturb the state of the colonies by means of civil war, arming citizens against one another'. Gattey was found guilty and sentenced to death. As she left the hearing, his sister Marie-Claudine shouted out several times: 'Long live the King!' and was immediately arrested. Regarded as mad, she was taken to the hospital of the Revolutionary Tribunal, but the physicians soon realized that she was perfectly sane and sent her back to Fouquier. She persisted in proclaiming her opinions and was duly sentenced to death.

A few moments before getting into the cart, Gattey took his last farewell of his wife:

To Citizeness Gattey, Maison Égalité, no 14.

I die, my dear friend, with a pure, innocent heart, no one could have understood my feelings better than you. I commend my children to you: bring them up according to the new laws. I know the purity of your soul. If sometimes I have allowed myself to scold you, attribute it to my overhasty temper, but never forget that you have been loved and cherished by me. Needless to say, I commend myself to your parents, they are as dear to me as my own: grieve over my fate with them. Yet why grieve over me, I am innocent, the hour of death approaches, I am about to begin a journey the thought of which should make the despotic tyrants tremble. Allow me, before leaving, to throw myself at your feet, to ask forgiveness for any offence I may have done you; and do not mourn for long; your friend, brave and emboldened by the purity of his intentions, is about to pay the tribute he owes to nature. If he has any regrets, it is not to die in your arms, not to be able at last to express to you all the feelings for you that nature has always inspired in him. Farewell, forget your friend and be happy, his children will one day be your happiness. Embrace them tenderly and always inspire in them the sentiments worthy of a true patriot. Death is nothing. I have never been a conspirator, but my denunciator should live in shame. Farewell, and embrace for the last time my children, your parents and mine, and do not forget my friends.

This 25 Germinal '94, on my knees.

Gattey.

If this note reaches you, I shall die happy, do not forget my adopted nephews.

It is three o'clock. We are about to go.

Gattey.

LAVOISIER,[216] Antoine-Laurent de (1745–94)

Since 1779, Lavoisier, the famous French chemist, a member of the Academy of Sciences, had held the post of *fermier-général*. A substitute deputy in the States General, he had become a member of the commission appointed to set up a new system of weights and measures and, in 1791, secretary at the Treasury. It was as the holder of these posts that he had proposed in a treatise entitled *On the Territorial Wealth of the Kingdom of France*, a whole plan for the levying of taxes.

Though the owner of considerable estates in the commune of Blois, which brought him in an income of 30,000 *livres* a year, Lavoisier owed most of his fortune to his wife, a shareholder in the Compagnie des Indes and daughter of Jacques Paulze, also a former *fermier-général*.

On 24 November 1793 the Convention decreed the arrest of the former *fermiers-généraux*. All were brought before the Revolutionary Tribunal and found guilty of a charge of 'exactions and extortions', of defrauding the nation of 'the huge sums necessary to wage the war against the despots in coalition against the Republic'.

A report concerning Lavoisier and his work was demanded by the Bureau de Consultation des Arts et Métiers. Submitted on 4 Floréal Year II, a few days before the chemist was sentenced to death, it concluded: 'The picture that we have sketched presents a series of facts, the number and scope of which are such that one can scarcely believe that they belong to the history of a single man . . . Citizen Lavoisier deserves to be placed among the men whose work, in pushing back the boundaries of human knowledge have done most to advance the arts and glory of the Nation . . .'

This official document, hitherto unpublished I believe, is to be found in Fouquier's papers. It would seem that it was never used during the trial.

One of Lavoisier's last letters was published in the *Mémoires* of Berryer, whom he had known in the Treasury:

'I have had quite a long career,' he wrote to his wife, 'and, above all, a happy one and I believe my memory will be accompanied with some glory. What more could I wish for? The events in which I find myself caught up will probably spare me the inconveniences of old age. I shall die in perfect health, that is one advantage that I must count among the many that I have enjoyed . . . I am writing to you today because I shall probably not be allowed to do so again and it is a sweet consolation for me to concern myself with you and those dear to me in these last moments.'

LUBOMIRSKA,[217] Rosalie Chodkiewicz, Princess (1768–94)

❦

SALM-KYRBURG,[218] Frederick, Prince of (1747–94)

Born at Czarnobyl in the Ukraine, Rosalie Chodkiewizc, who came from a powerful Polish-Lithuanian family, had married at a very early age Prince Alexander Lubomirski, whose father had been a candidate for the throne of Poland in 1764.

A passionate lover of literature, music and travel, the princess wandered across Europe during the years prior to the Revolution. She was twenty years of age, 'beautiful as a painting of Venus', and she was to be seen at Vienna, London, Nice and Paris, where, like many young liberal aristocrats, she applauded the events of 1789.

In 1791, she returned hastily to Warsaw to support the efforts of the 'Polish patriots', in particular those of her friend, Senator Mostowski, one of the authors of the Polish Constitution of 3 May. But in 1792 Russia and Prussia suddenly came to the conclusion that the Poles had gone beyond the 'madness' of Paris and that it was high time to extinguish that 'hotbed of Jacobinism'. For a few weeks the Polish army resisted the Russians and Prussians, then the country capitulated: the Confederation of Targowica was no more than a caricature of the democratic hopes of the Poles.

In order to avoid deportation to Siberia, the patriots had to flee. Disguised as 'William', one of Princess Lubomirska's servants, Senator Mostowski travelled with her to Vienna, then on to Lausanne, arriving in Paris in November 1792.

While Mostowski was trying to interest the French government in the Polish cause, the trial of Louis XVI was taking place. Rosalie was staying with her friend Frederick of Salm-Kyrburg, who was living with his sister Amelia of Hohenzollern in the magnificent Hôtel de Salm, on the banks of the Seine (it is the present Musée de la Légion d'honneur). It was there, on January 1793, that she heard a gun salute announcing the execution, a few doors away, of poor Louis XVI.

At the time, her host and no doubt lover, Frederick of Salm-

Kyrburg, was in his principality of Salm. Favourable to the Revolution of 1789, he had welcomed it, when, after Valmy, his territory was invaded by French troops (it was to be annexed in 1793). 'Imbued with the truth' of Republican principles, he wrote on 19 December 1792, to the Convention: 'I went among the men whom I once called my subjects and whom I now call my fellow-citizens, my friends, my children, in order to abolish personal serfdom among them, the rights of mortmain, guild-mastership, in a word, all the barbarian remnants of feudalism'.

But, in late winter 1793, the Republican army was beginning to retreat. The foreigners had recaptured Mainz and were advancing on the Moselle and the Nahe. The Prince of Salm was no longer safe in Kyrn, his 'republicanized' capital. Fearing the reaction of the German princes to his defection, he returned to Paris.

The death of Louis XVI had caused a break between those who had rallied to the Comte de Provence, the future Louis XVIII, who had proclaimed himself regent, and the advocates of constitutional monarchy, who recognized Marie-Antoinette as regent. Salm-Kyrburg was close to the second party. Most of his friends were army commanders, supporters of Dumouriez, who believed that they were called upon to play a political role. They included Castellane, Broglie, Hénin and above all Dillon, who was suspected of wanting to free the queen from the Temple prison. After Dumouriez's attempted military coup d'état, all were prosecuted as his accomplices. No doubt through the intervention of their secret protectors in the Convention (Danton, Desmoulins, Merlin de Douai, Cambacérès, etc.), they were able to get their sentences limited to house arrest.

Castellane managed to reach Switzerland, but Dillon and Salm were caught. A denunciation dated 20 August indicates that, under false names, they remained in hiding 'with several individuals' at the house of a certain Citizen Berquet, a grocer, at Vitry-le-François. Their hiding-place was discovered and they were arrested again and placed under house arrest. When the Dantonists were brought to trial, Salm's situation worsened. On 11 Germinal, the *département* Committee of Surveillance decided that 'certain of its members would be posted at the exits of certain Paris theatres and would arrest and bring before the Committee all those who seemed suspect and were unable to justify their "political existence".'

So, two days later, on 13 Germinal, the same *département* of Paris had to decide on a report according to which Salm, while under house arrest, had gone to the theatre with his guard and 'had there made certain statements tending to blame and to stir up the citizens against measures that the Committee had considered necessary, namely, surrounding the Vaudeville theatre, with a view to discovering and arresting a large number of individuals lacking conviction and consequently suspect. Considering that such conduct is not that of a friend of the measures of general safety that usually produced great benefits . . . [the Committee has decided] to withdraw the permission granted to the said Salm.'

The Committee of General Safety immediately ordered his imprisonment. He was to survive Dillon by two months: Dillon was to be guillotined with his friend Lucile Desmoulins a week after the Dantonists.

Rosalie Lubomirska had resolutely sided with those royalists who had rallied to Louis XVIII and had made several journeys abroad on their behalf.

In April 1793, her differences of opinion with Salm-Kyrburg led her to rent a private house at Chaillot. No sooner had she moved than a report was submitted to the Committee of General Safety concerning her relationship with the Polish Count Potocki, who had been denounced as a spy by Russian agents. When questioned, she declared that, since she was of foreign nationality, it was a matter of indifference to her whether she had a police record, that being Polish it was quite natural that she should receive Polish friends.

Though 'Polish', many of her guests were English spies or agents of the exiled princes. Among them were Salm-Kyrburg's nephews, the Prince of Talmon, head of the Vendéen Insurrection, and his younger brother, the handsome Abbé de La Trémoille, the very embodiment of the chivalric hero. In Bailleul's *Almanach des bizarreries humaines*, reference is made to Rosalie, but also to La Trémoille, who was her lover:

> All kinds of valuables were secretly given away in order to avoid sequestration and confiscation. His particular role was to look after their common interests. He travelled to England six times. He speculated on the sale of national property. He was privy to all the intrigues surrounding the government committees of the time. He often spoke of the corruption of several of their members and of deals that had been made as a result: however, he did not reveal the secret of these intrigues, except to suggest without too much mystery that Chabot was one of the men who did best out of them.

Rosalie's name cropped up during the Comtesse du Barry's examination and she was arrested on 9 November 1793. She spent two months at the Petite-Force and tried in vain to get the support of the deputy Hérault de Séchelles, who was already compromised in important politico-financial scandals. In late January, she managed to buy her transfer to the La Chapelle *maison de santé*, where she was allowed to keep her five-year-old daughter, Alexandrine, with her. Despite several interventions by members of the Polish government, she was sentenced to death on 30 Germinal as an accomplice of Mme du Barry.

Terrified, she delayed the time of her execution by declaring that she was pregnant. That same day she was transferred to the Tribunal hospital, which had been set up in the Maison de l'Évêché, the former diocesan premises, near Notre-Dame. Of the score of women there, several had had death sentences deferred. It was of these women, who were taken to the scaffold after giving birth, that Alfred de Vigny was thinking when, in *Stello*, he put these moving words into the mouth of his heroine:

> It is my duty to bring my child to the day of his birth, which will be the eve of my death. I am left on earth only for that, I am good only for that. I am nothing but the faithful shell that protects him and which will be broken once he has seen the light of day. I am nothing else.
>
> Do you think they will leave me at least a few good hours to look at him when he is born? Were they to kill me immediately, it would be very cruel, would it not? Well, were they to give me just time enough to hear him cry and to hold him in my arms for a day, I would pardon them, I think, so much am I looking forward to that moment.

Six months after his arrest, the Abbé de La Trémoille had managed to buy his transfer from the prison of La Force to the Maison de l'Évêché. He knew that Rosalie was not really pregnant and that her days were numbered. For her, he was ready to do anything. What happened at the Évêché? One witness has recounted how La Trémoille managed to outwit the guard's vigilance, how he had joined the beautiful princess in the prison bathroom and how they had been caught *in flagrante delicto* . . .

La Trémoille was sent to the Conciergerie and was guillotined a few days later. Rosalie, who would have given anything to escape death, had already had her agony postponed by two months. The '*mouton*' of La Force, Ferrières-Sauvebeuf, who had already alerted the Committee of General Safety about La Trémoille's activities, drew its attention once again to Rosalie's case. Her pregnancy was less than apparent and every night she was haunted by the squeaking of the wheels of the cart that would take her to her death.

On 1 Messidor, she learned of the execution of Beaussancourt, another of her lovers, on whom a bracelet enclosing a lock of her hair and her portrait in miniature had been found. That day, one of the prisoners in the Évêché, General Carteaux, who had difficulty breathing, found a subject for romance in the love of the Abbé de la Trémoille and Princess Lubomirska: he sang his couplets loud enough to be heard in the women's quarters. The effect was reported that day to Fouquier-Tinville by the prison bursar:

> As a result she [Rosalie] entered into an astonishing state of convulsion that lasted for a long time. What was even more surprising was that her state spread to three or four other women, as if by a physical effect. Today everything is calm and quiet once more . . .

The young woman's purgatory ended ten days later. One of her companions, Victoire Lescale, had just given birth to a girl, Virginie. Rosalie still did not show any sign of pregnancy. One evening, a cart took both of them away. The next day, 12 Messidor, a warm morning, the beautiful Polish princess took her farewell of Amelia of Hohenzollern:

> Farewell, Amelia, soon I shall cease to be alive. Remember your friend and love me in the person of my child.
>
> Rosalie.

Three weeks after her death, the Prince of Salm was implicated in the 'conspiracy' at the Carmes. Before dying, he, too, wrote to Amelia of Hohenzollern:

> When you receive this letter, my dear Amelia, your unhappy brother will be no more. I am accustomed to the idea of my imminent destruction, but I cannot bear the thought of your despair. May the memory of our holy friendship imbue your whole life with its consoling, painful spell. Look after yourself so that you may cherish my memory and bring up my little Ernest. He will not be an orphan, Amelia, because you will become his mother. Farewell, my loving sister. The religion that took me to its bosom on my entrance into life assists me in prison and will accompany me to the grave. Its fatherly but severe voice summons up over my past sins the tears that nature demands for my sister and son. May you one day learn all that your brother and his companions in misfortune owe as consolation to the courageous and charitable ministers of that divine religion! Farewell, promise to live for my son Ernest. Remember your unhappy brother.
>
> Frederick.

After 9 Thermidor, the Princess of Hohenzollern took in Alexandrine Lubomirska and Ernest de Salm for a time, then had the common grave at Picpus, into which their parents' bodies had been thrown, enclosed.

COSTARD,[219] *Avoye Paville*
(1768–94)

In May 1794, Citizen Brunet's *maison de santé*, at 4 Rue Buffon, now transformed into a *maison d'arrêt*, housed a detainee who would probably not have attracted the attention of the Committee of General Safety if love had not bound her to a man whose counter-revolutionary opinions and involvement in certain events had not brought him to prominence.

Early in 1790, Avoye Paville, separated from her husband, met a young journalist, Jacques-Marie Boyer-Brun, a Catholic and a convinced royalist. She followed him to his native city, Nîmes, where certain disturbances were beginning to take place.

At the head of the municipal adminstration in Nîmes was a certain Antoine Teissier, Baron de Margueritte, who was assisted by a former lieutenant in the Royal-Vaisseaux regiment, François Descombières.

Through them, Boyer-Brun soon obtained for himself the post of deputy prosecutor for the commune. About the same time, he founded the *Journal de Nîmes*, whose opinions were overtly Jacobin. In May and June 1790, riots broke out in the city; these were brutally repressed and the municipality fell into the hands of the patriots. Descombières was arrested, Margueritte took refuge at Lagny (Seine-et-Marne) and Boyer-Brun returned to Paris with his mistress. In the *Journal du Peuple,* he continued his campaign of denigration of the Nîmes revolutionaries and published a *Précis historique sur les troubles de Nîmes* and a *Histoire des caricatures de la révolte des Français.* The distribution of these works was in the hands of a royalist bookseller at the Palais-Royal, Gattey (see under his name), who was denounced for selling odiously reactionary books. Boyer-Brun was arrested with him in Pluviôse Year II. The procurator-syndic of the commune of Paris, Chaumette, congratulated himself on this arrest in a letter to Fouquier-Tinville, written while travelling in the Gard:

'So the infamous Boyer-Brun has been arrested at last! I must admit that I am astonished that such a monster could go unpunished for so long. How did he manage to elude the searches of the Sans-Culottes? The wretch! He deserves a thousand deaths!'

Indeed he was sentenced to death with the Baron de Margueritte and Descombières 'for inciting civil war in the *département* of the Gard'. Among the witnesses for the prosecution was the cousin of Voulland, deputy of the Gard and member of the Committee of General Safety, a certain Citizen Ribeau, whom Boyer-Brun had denounced to the Assembly a few months earlier, as one of the 'murderers' of the Nîmes population.

Meanwhile, Avoye Paville had also been arrested. One of her companions in captivity later reported how she took the news of the execution of the man she loved: 'This event made Citizeness Costard lose her head. She was out of her mind for three days; she knew that the wife of Lavergne, commander of Longwy, had cried out "Long live the King!" as her husband was being tried and she was thus condemned to death and taken away in the same cart as he.'

That night she wrote the same letter to the National Convention and to Fouquier-Tinville. This letter, written in a paroxysm of grief, is often incoherent, with parts of whole sentences missing, which proves that thought is more rapid than the pen.

You have sentenced to death Boyer-Brun. Why have you condemned him thus? Because he loved his God, his Roman, Catholic, apostolic religion and his king. If he had been of the party of certain members that you have among you, who are constantly complaining about massacre and looting, as he had done at the massacre of the Catholics of Nîmes [the sentence is incomprehensible if one does not add 'you would not have condemned him'; the 'he' refers no doubt to Voulland, of whom she speaks later and whose memory haunted her thoughts]. On the occasion of Boyer's first address to the Assembly, justifying the conduct of the Catholics massacred at Nîmes by Protestants, in which he said that Ribeau had been among the murderers, Voulland wrote a long letter in reply to the first address. Then Boyer made a second address in response to Voulland's letter in which Boyer told Voulland that he was wrong to say that his cousin Ribeau had not been among the murderers, thinking that it was he who had delivered the first blows. Then Voulland swore to be revenged: he had to find something to bring about his downfall [i.e., Boyer-Brun's downfall], because a villain like Voulland trembles and blushes before an honest man. And he knew that Boyer knew all about his villainy and that if things changed his crimes would soon be punished, but he would be able to bring about the deaths of all those who knew what he had done and we would be avenged.

You should have referred to his works [Boyer-Brun's writings] though he had them published after the freedom of the press had been decreed: he wrote *Défense des Catholiques de Nîmes*, the *Histoire des caricatures* and the *Journal du Peuple*, in which many harsh truths were said about Voulland.

Well, you have not punished all the guilty. You know that, during the four years that Boyer wrote his works, I was associated in everything he did, he was my friend, I think as he does and I cannot live without him.

It is impossible to live under a regime like yours, in which one sees nothing but murder and looting. Before my friend's death, I patiently suffered the ills that were sent me, because he consoled me and because I hoped that we would soon see a king and avenge all the ills that you have made us suffer. But now I have nothing left in the world since I have lost my friend.

Strike, end a life that is odious to me and which I cannot bear without horror.

And in the exaltation of her grief, she wrote her signature and the flourish at the bottom of the letter, not in ink, but in her own blood, adding these words:

Long live the King? Long live the King! Long live the King! Don't pretend to believe that I am mad, no, I am not. I believe everything I have just written and I sign it in my blood.

You will find me at the *maison de santé*, Rue de Buffon, no 4.

She was sentenced to death and executed two days later for calumniating the National Assembly and insulting the public authorities.

DUFOULEUR de COURNEUVE,[220] Jean-François (1755–94)

The affair by which the notary Dufouleur was condemned to death concerned the falsification of legal documents. Leduc de Biéville *fils* had emigrated and his property had been sequestrated. In order to elude the law, he appointed Maynard, his agent in Paris, to sign at Dufouleur's an acknowledgement of one hundred and fifty thousand *livres* in favour of Biéville *père*, who, because he had remained in France, was not affected by the law concerning émigrés' property. Now any legal document, authenticated by a notary, especially one concerned with the transfer of property, drawn up by an émigré, was invalid unless antedated. At this time, legal documents were not numbered, initialled, or signed: one could easily destroy one page and replace it by another on which an earlier date appeared.

Thus the transaction between Biéville *père* and Biéville *fils* was dated 1789 (January) and not 1792, the real date of the deed. It was an unfortunate letter found in Maynard's correspondence that revealed the subterfuge and led to Dufouleur's arrest. It must be said that this was a means frequently used by many émigrés to protect part or all of their fortune from confiscation. It was not until 14 March 1793 that Fouché, in the name of the Fraud Committee, presented to the Convention a bill intended to outwit 'the criminal manoeuvres of the émigrés':

> Citizens . . . Émigrés who have returned to France issue obligations of various kinds, given either verbally or in writing, whose sole purpose is to allow émigrés living abroad to regain possession of their former property. To do this they depend on accommodating notaries and, to achieve their ends, they give their collaborators a percentage of twenty-five per cent and a bribe to those who are willing to give the names of those notaries willing to make out such deeds. It goes without saying that the notaries are employed, at the

expense of the owners of the property, to issue new deeds registered at earlier dates . . .

With a view to countering these new manoeuvres your Fraud Committee proposes that, within twenty-four hours for Paris and four days for the *départements*, notaries be obliged, on pain of a twenty thousand *livres* fine, to present to the Directory of the *département* lists of deeds made by them or their predecessors after 1 January 1753.

Dufouleur was executed with Maynard and Biéville in June 1794. Before dying he wrote a last letter to his wife, who, a month later, gave birth to a child:

To Citizeness Dufouleur, Rue Montmartre, no 205, opposite the Rue du Jour.

I can only write you a few words and take my eternal farewell of you. As heaven is my witness, the only things I regret in life are my poor Angélique and my dear little Alphonse. Your condition makes me tremble, but think that you owe it to the fruit you bear and to our poor child, embrace him for me. But have courage, you must. You will no doubt be informed of the reason for my death. Maynard is its involuntary cause and I had nothing to do with it, but regrets are useless. Farewell, I embrace you a thousand times. Remember sometimes your unhappy husband, what am I saying, on the contrary, do everything you can to efface him from your memory, if that is possible. It is frightful to die when one leaves behind so many treasured objects.

Your good, loving friend, your unhappy husband Dufouleur.

RAUCOURT,[221] Jean-Baptiste-François
(17. . −94)

Accused at the Revolutionary Tribunal of publishing a work entitled *Opinion dans le procès de Louis XVI*, Citizen Jean-François-Stanislas Vuibert was sentenced to death. His printer, Citizen Raucourt, who appeared the same day, was acquitted, contrary to all expectations. On the eve of appearing before the Revolutionary Tribunal, Raucourt wrote this fine farewell letter to his wife, whom he was able to embrace . . . two days later:

To Citizeness Raucourt, at the house of Citizen Le Cleso, bookseller, Quai des Augustins, no 34, at Paris.

My dear wife, I have reached at last the very confine of what will be our reunion or our total separation: what terrible uncertainty! In a few hours I shall know my fate. I commend myself to the equity of my judges, but whatever the outcome, arm yourself with courage, preserve yourself for our dear children's sake; bring them up in love of country. How sweet it would have been to share those labours with you! Speak to them sometimes of their father; tell them how dearly I would have wished at this moment to press them with you to my bosom! Tell my parents and friends that my thoughts were with them to the end; tell my enemies that I pardon them the terrible plight to which they have brought me and which I have not deserved. If a few light clouds have sometimes darkened the clear days that we have spent together, think not of them, but remember only my love. I do not have the strength to speak to you of business matters and, indeed, how could I? What a barrier of obstacles has always come between us since that fatal blow struck me! Why am I reduced to desiring nothing more than to hold you in my arms and to wet your face with my tears: vain regrets, I do not even know whether you will receive this last expression of my suffering. All is not yet lost, but, in uncertainty and no longer expecting to speak with you again, I am making a most sweet and yet most bitter use of this present moment. My heart cannot bear it: I embrace you, my dear good friend, with all my soul. Receive the farewells of your loving friend and husband Raucourt.

From the Conciergerie, 12 Messidor, in the morning.

You will now have been persuaded how certain persons, under the appearance of interest and service, have proved most false and cruel.

GOUY D'ARSY,[222] Louis-Henri-Marthe, Marquis de (1753–94)

Son of a blacksmith in the king's army, Chevalier de Saint-Louis, lieutenant-colonel in the queen's dragoons, he married a rich Creole woman from Santo Domingo.

On 13 June 1789, he was elected to the Assembly as deputy for that colony. He proved fiercely hostile to the abolition of slavery and, with the members of the Club de Massiac, violently opposed the efforts of Brissot and the Abbé Grégoire, the 'Friends of the Blacks'.

He was a member in turn of the Finance Committee and the Land Committee, then a commissioner of the Assembly. At the end of the session, he rejoined the army and served as a brigadier. Suspected of calculated inactivity in the missions entrusted to him and accused of being a supporter of La Fayette, he was arrested in his Château de Moret, a locality of which he was mayor. He was released, then again imprisoned as a suspect on 31 March 1794. Confined in the Carmes, and knowing that he was condemned in advance, he wrote several versions of a farewell letter to his wife. This very beautiful letter was published after the Revolution. Unfortunately, its length does not allow me to reproduce it in its entirety:

> . . . So what remains for me to do . . . Ah! My friend, the most painful of acts . . . It remains to me to leave you! Here I admit, to the shame of human weakness, but to the glory of my heart, that all my physical strength deserts me. My moral faculties are destroyed, tears flood my face; and because I feel so much, it seems to me that I have ceased to be, before suffering death. This state of nothingness and pain is horrible; the yearnings I feel are frightful . . . To leave my family, to be separated for ever from my dear companion, to be far away from my dear children, to abandon all that in the flower of my age, without accident, without glory, without disease, to be in full possession of my faculties to appreciate what I am losing, all my affections to know what I am leaving, all my senses to struggle

against the mortal stroke that is to separate me from the living, all that, my dear, is more than I can bear and is killing me in advance; so conjugal love, which has brought me so much delight, now causes all my pain! Thus fatherhood, which has brought me so many sweet moments, now gives me so many regrets! And one cannot leave it! And yet, in a few moments, I shall be in another world!

Ah! My God, where shall I find the strength to undertake such a journey. Without friends, with no one to console me, isolated from all that I love, I feel around me nothing but prison, judges and executioners! But my conscience sustains me, my innocence consoles me, pity comforts me and God calls me: it is on his paternal bosom that I shall throw myself . . .

Do not pity me, my friend, in a few hours I shall be happier than you; your ills alone torment me, they will be excessive, I see from here your pain, I sense your tears flowing . . .

Ah! How sweet it would be to wipe them away, to embrace you again, to hold my children in my arms once more . . . But no . . .

Farewell, all my beloved children! Farewell, my dear Baptiste, my beloved; I die your friend, your husband, your lover; I excuse my judges, I forgive my executioners, I wish every happiness to our country: I shall not cease to say so, for your consolation, for your happiness and that of our children.

Farewell! Farewell! You who were everything for me in this world, and whom I shall never forget in the next, farewell, for a time; that hope sweetens this cruel moment for me . . . Farewell, dearest half of myself; we must make an end; farewell! I tear myself from your arms, I throw myself into God's bosom; come and join me there one day, with all our children. The others await me, farewell! Receive my last kiss, it is loving, pure, it is the price of the great courage of which you have given me such honourable proof, so worthy of the esteem of my loved ones!

My body perishes, my soul flies up, my heart will not leave you . . .

I enclose a few letters; those from my children, for example, from my mother, my sister, which I managed to hide from the searches of the investigators sent into the prison by our tyrants, our executioners . . . Plus my hair, which I cut off myself; I didn't want it to reach you sullied by the hands of Robespierre's executioner. Farewell again, a hundred kisses for each of our children! A hundred kisses for my father and mother! A thousand for you, my friend! To my eldest son I send the key to my little case; I have wrapped it in paper, which contains a few important words for him and his brothers; you will give to all the others some other object that belonged to me and which may prove to them that I love them all equally. Let them copy out this letter and you, my dear, keep the original, for it concerns you. Can I write anything without your beloved name finding itself naturally on the paper! It is in my heart, on my lips and everywhere. Farewell, yet again: how heartrending that word would be were I not sure that you would do everything in your power to join me one day: our little ones await us; already, I hear them calling me; the others will join us later; take care to bring them up well. Ah! My friend! My beloved friend! How I owe you everything that I have demanded of you in the name of the bitter sacrifice of all my joys, all the happiness and all the compensation that perhaps I was worthy of tasting after so many ills!

What a sin it is to murder a citizen thus! But . . . what am I saying? I promised to endure my sacrifice without complaint and I am already forgetting my oath.

Ah, my God! Forgive mankind, surrounded by weakness and woe. And you, my dear wife, be comforted; I summon up all my courage to offer you the homage of all that remains of my virtue: farewell, receive my last kiss . . . My body perishes, my soul flies up, my heart does not leave you . . . It could never leave you . . . O my country! . . . My country! May you soon be delivered at last from the bloody executioners who wish to dishonour you before all nations!

FOUQUIER-TINVILLE,[223]
Antoine-Quentin (1746–95)

After the death of Robespierre and his friends, the executions and therefore the farewell letters became rarer. In any case, most of them reached their addresses. On the other hand, the last two notes from Fouquier-Tinville to his wife were intercepted.

Born at Hérouël in the Aisne, Fouquier called himself de Tinville as his brothers called themselves d'Hérouël, de Vauvilliers and de Foreste. In 1774, he was appointed 'procurator postulate at the Châtelet and presidial seat of Paris'. He fell into debt and had to sell his post in 1783 and borrowed twelve thousand *livres* from the Abbé de Lamarlière, a councillor in the Grand Conseil. We do not know whether this debt was repaid to the Abbé or to his heir and nephew, General de Lamarlière, who was sentenced to death in 1793 by the Revolutionary Tribunal.

The Duchesse de Fleury cites Fouquier as an agent of Louis XVI's secret police. In any case, he became a member of the prosecution jury at the Tribunal of 17 August set up to judge the 'murderers' who had fired on the people a week before in the Tuileries. When the Revolutionary Tribunal was set up in March 1793, he was appointed public prosecutor. His salary amounted to six hundred and seventy *livres* a year.

On the evening of 28 Prairial Year II, a day when fifty-four individuals were sentenced to death in a single session – the biggest 'batch' of the Terror – he was crossing the Pont Neuf incognito: a young man named Falempin, a guard on the bridge, demanded his security card, then insulted him and began to strike him. The young man was arrested and imprisoned in the Luxembourg, where, miraculously, his name did not appear on the list of 'prison conspirators'.

After 9 Thermidor, Fouquier-Tinville was held responsible for serious irregularities in the exercise of his functions. In fact he was made the scapegoat for many individuals, in particular for the members of the Committee of General Safety, whose directives he had conscientiously implemented. Having no illusions as to the outcome of his trial, he had advised his second wife to renounce their marriage and to take whatever movables of theirs she could to some safe place.

After Fouquier was condemned to death, his property was confiscated, listed and valued: it amounted to very little. Anyway, if Fouquier had got rich under the Terror – which is not certain – he probably had the elementary prudence to place his deeds of ownership in the name of a third party. He had a son and two daughters from his first marriage with his cousin and a daughter from his second marriage to Henriette-Jeanne Gérard, to whom this letter was addressed:

> From the *maison d'arrêt* of Le Plessis, known as Égalité.
> 22 Brumaire of Year III
> of the one and indivisible Republic.

Though I have not yet been interrogated, I must expect, my good friend, to be sent to trial before long; in another time, trusting in my innocence, I would have had nothing to fear from the approach of the trial; but in the sorry circumstances in which we find ourselves, and after all the calumnies, the horrible abuse, the vociferous attacks of all kinds that have been directed against my person since my confinement here, it would be idle to harbour any illusions as to my fate. Being subjected to all that frightful abuse, hearing myself called such things as abominable conspirator and bloodthirsty tiger, though supported by no facts, all this is merely the prelude to my trial. It is a tactic employed by those enemies of liberty to destroy me all the more surely.

I therefore expect to be sacrificed to public opinion, which has been stirred up against me by all manner of means, and not to be sent to trial. I arrived at this conclusion long ago, though I said nothing of it until now so as to spare you, for as long as possible, the blow that this outcome may bring you. So I shall die for serving my country with too much zeal, too much application, and for carrying out the government's wishes, my hands and heart free of all blame. But, my good friend, what will become of you and my poor children? You are about to be cast down into the most terrible poverty; that, at least, will be the most telling proof that I have served my country with the selflessness of a true Republican; but what *will* become of you all? These are the sinister thoughts that assail and torment me night and day! Was I born, then, to suffer thus? What a terrible notion! To die as a conspirator, I, who have not ceased to wage war upon such men. Is this to be the reward for my patriotic zeal? Through all these disastrous events, there has remained to me one ray of satisfaction, or rather of consolation, and that is the knowledge that you are convinced of my innocence, that knowledge at least gives me hope that you will not fail to repeat to our children that their father died wretched, but innocent, that he always enjoyed your trust and esteem; I beg you not to abandon yourself to grief and to preserve your health for your own sake and for that of our poor children. Forget any slight differences we may have had; they were but the product of a hasty temper, my heart was never in them and has never ceased to be attached to you. Alas! my good friend, who would have thought that I would have such an end, I who have never known intrigue, never been tormented by the lust for wealth.

It is hard, my good friend, to share such gloomy thoughts with you. I have pondered much upon it, but considering that once my trial begins it will not be possible for me to do so I have resolved to convey to you my last feelings for you and my thanks for all the pains that you have taken since my confinement: I say again, do not abandon yourself to grief and, I beg you, do not spurn opportunities that might bring you a happier lot; for the last time, with an aching heart and tears in my eyes, I take my leave of you, your aunt and my poor children. I embrace you a thousand times. Alas! what sweet satisfaction it would give me to see you again and hold you in my arms! But, my good friend, it is all over with me, we must not think on it further!

Farewell, a thousand times farewell, and to the few friends that still remain to us and above all to her who has proved the best of all friends: embrace our children and your aunt for me; be a good mother to my children, whom I exhort to be good and to do as you bid them; farewell, farewell.

Your faithful friend.

The only token of my friendship that it is in my power to give you is a lock of my hair, which I beg you to keep safe.

After sentence of death had been passed, Fouquier-Tinville also wrote this last note before mounting the scaffold:

I have nothing to reproach myself with; I have always conformed to the law; I have never been the creature of Robespierre or of Saint-Just; on the contrary, I was on the point of being arrested four times.

I die for my country, without reproach, I am satisfied; later, my innocence will be recognized.

A.Q. Fouquier.

BABEUF,[224] François-Noël, known as Camille, then as Gracchus (1760–97)

Gracchus Babeuf occupies an important place in the history of socialism. He had been held in Sainte-Pélagie and survived only three years after the events of Thermidor. His last letter, written in 1797, found its place in this collection.

Born at Saint-Quentin, he had begun to earn a living as clerk to a land commissioner, then as a household servant and, finally, in 1784, as assistant to a surveyor at Noyon.

In 1790 he became editor of the *Correspondant Picard* and, in 1792, after being elected to the General Council of the *département* of the Somme, he became administrator of the district of Montdidier, concerned with the sale of national property. The departmental administration was then in the hands of reactionaries, whom the revolutionaries were trying to oust: accused of not valuing national property at its true value, he was sentenced in his absence by the departmental tribunal of the Somme.

He came to Paris in 1793. He supported Fournier the American in his polemic against Marat and found work as secretary to the Administration des Subsistances of Paris. He was arrested, then, set free on the intervention of Thibaudeau, he worked temporarily on *Les Révolutions de Paris*. Arrested again, he was sent to La Force, then, on 1 Germinal, to Sainte-Pélagie.

His trial before the Criminal Tribunal of the Somme had been quashed by the Tribunal de Cassation, so he was sent to appear before the Tribunal of the Aisne, and transferred to the prison of Laon on 9 Messidor.

Charges against him were dropped on 30 Thermidor Year II (17 August 1794). He was freed and, two weeks later, launched the *Journal de la Liberté*, in which he praised the Thermidorians and identified himself with the counter-revolutionaries.

On 4 October, the tone and spirit of the newspaper changed. It was now called *Le Tribun du Peuple, ou le Défenseur des droits de l'homme*, edited by Gracchus Babeuf.

He demanded that the 'common weal' become the reality of the Republic. In the issue for 31 Pluviôse (28 January 1795), when a warrant had again been issued for his arrest and he was in hiding, he expatiated on the concept of the right of insurrection.

Arrested in 17 Pluviôse (5 February), imprisoned first in Paris, then at the prison of the Baudets in Arras, then again in Paris, he continued to write for the *Tribun du Peuple* and, in one of its numbers, called on 'plebeian republicans' to join together and to struggle against the growing influence of royalism over the increasingly poor people. He associated with former Robespierrists and brought together democratic revolutionaries of every tendency: Buonarroti, the former Marquis d'Antonelle, Darthé, Lebon's ex-assistant, and Sylvain Maréchal.

All these men belonged to the Société du Panthéon, sometimes known as the 'Réunion des Amis de la République', a political club that sometimes had as many as two thousand members. In the *Tribun du Peuple*, Babeuf directed most of his attacks at this time against the Directory, which led to the closing of the club.

About March 1796, he set up the insurrectional committee, which, after working out new institutions, was to lead the 'plebeian Vendée'. This secret organization tried to win over the soldiers and workers of Paris, appointed revolutionary agents and extended its network into the provinces. A month later, the insurrectional committee joined up with a group of Montagnard members of the Convention, including Amar and Vadier, who wanted to put an end to the Directory.

Babouvism grew in importance and the plot was assuming dangerous proportions. Meanwhile Babeuf had worked out the decrees that would be necessary after a seizure of power (exclusion from political life of individuals who did not work usefully for the country, the abolition of inheritance, immediate collective enjoyment of community property, etc.).

He was denounced, the plot collapsed and its members were arrested (21 Floréal Year IV, 10 May 1797). The presence among the jurors of Drouet, deputy of the Cinq-Cents, constitutionally forced the Babouvists and their allies to be tried before a High Court. The trial began at Vendôme, on 14 Vendémiaire (5 October 1796). On 7 Prairial Year V (26 May 1797), Babeuf and Darthé, sentenced to death, stabbed themselves with a knife given them by Babeuf's son. They were nevertheless guillotined the following day. Buonarroti was to tell the story of the plot in *La Conspiration pour l'Égalité*, published in 1828. This work, read in France after 1830, was to give rise to an important neo-Babouvist communist movement among the working class.

Two days before his death, Babeuf wrote this serious, bitter letter to one of his friends:

Vendôme, 5 Prairial, Year V of the Republic.
To my worthy, sincere friend.

The jurors, my friend, are deliberating their decision, which will settle your fate and mine. From what I see, you will escape and I shall not. If my wife gives you this letter, it will join the one I wrote on 26 Messidor last year, which I did not have the opportunity, as I thought I would have at first, of sending to you, and which I have kept with me until now. Today I cannot add anything more to what I wrote then. Indeed the approach of the fatal moment closes my mind and perhaps my heart to any expression of feeling that I may have had in the past two days. I am not certain, but I did not believe that the prospect of my dissolution would cost me so dear. It is little use saying that nature is always strong. Philosophy lends a few weapons to overcome it, but one always has to pay it tribute. Yet I hope to preserve enough strength to bear, as I must, my last hour. But more must not be asked of me.

I feel an unquiet, an indifference or an absence of thought that I cannot explain; it seems that I would like to feel something for my wife and for my children, but I no longer feel anything. I can find nothing to say to you for them. I still do not know whether it is not because of the terrible presentiment of the pointlessness of anything that I can do for them, when the frightful counter-revolution must proscribe anything belonging to the republican divisions. And, anyway, this long existence in a state of unhappiness no doubt blunts those sensibilities that were at first over-exercised and it is a boundary beyond which human nature cannot go. Perhaps, too, I am taking as indifference what is not, for I blush at such a state of mind. Perhaps I think I feel nothing, because in fact, I feel too much. Excuse these disorderly thoughts; try to guess what I really mean and do what is expected of you by him who imagines that he has told you everything, assuring you that he thinks he is depositing his last words in the heart of his best friend.

I think I can console myself with the manner in which I conducted myself during the trial. Despite my disturbed state of mind, I feel that, to my last minute, I shall still do nothing of which the memory of an honest man need be ashamed. Farewell.

G. Babeuf.

APPENDICES

LIST OF PARIS PRISONS
UNDER THE TERROR

Former mansions and palaces

Grande-Force, Rue du Roi-de-Sicile
Petite-Force, Rue Pavée
Luxembourg, Rue de Vaugirard
Hôtel de Talaru, Rue de Richelieu, no 62
Hôtel des Fermes, Rue du Bouloi and Rue de Grenelle,
    Saint-Honoré
Hôtel de Dreneuc, Rue de Provence
Château de Vincennes
Conciergerie, Boulevard du Palais

Barracks and army premises

Caserne, Rue des Petits-Pères
Caserne, Rue de Sèvres
Caserne des Carmes, Rue de Vaugirard

Religious premises

Carmes réformés, known as Déchaussés or Deschaux, Rue de
    Vaugirard
Abbaye de Saint-Germain-des-Prés (chapel, refectory, cells)
Couvent de Sainte-Pélagie, Rue du Puits-de-l'Ermite
Couvent des Madelonnettes, Rue des Fontaines-du-Temple
Séminaire de Saint-Firmin, ex-Collège des Bons-Enfants, Rue des
    Fossés-Saint-Bernard
Séminaire de Saint-Lazare, Rue du Faubourg-Saint-Denis
Anglaises de Saint-Augustin, Rue des Fossés-Saint-Victor (now Rue
    du Cardinal-Lemoine)
Anglaises du Faubourg Saint-Antoine (38 Rue de Charenton)
Anglaises du Champ-de-l'Alouette (now Rue des Tanneries)
Bénédictins anglais, Rue Saint-Jacques

Collège des Irlandais, Rue du Cheval-Vert (now Rue des Irlandais)
Écossais, Rue des Fossés-Saint-Victor (Rue du Cardinal-Lemoine)
Capucins de la Chaussée d'Antin (now Lycée Condorcet)
Couvent de Picpus (annex of the Maison Coignard)

Maisons de santé

Belhomme, Rue de Charonne
Eugène Coignard, Rue Picpus (now no 4 and no 6) corner Boulevard
  Diderot
Riedain (annex Coignard), Rue Picpus
Catherine Mahaye, Jean-Baptiste Reuche, Lescourbiac and
  Lemoine, Rue des Amandiers (now Rue du Chermin-Vert)
Montprins and Desnos, Rue N.-D.-des-Champs, no 1466
La Chapelle and Romey, Rue Folie-Regnault
La Chapelle and Romey, Rue Saint-Maur (now Rue des Écluses-
  Saint-Martin and Eugène-Varlin)
Brunet, Rue de Buffon, no 4
Picquenot, Rue de Bercy
Picquenot, 48 Rue du Faubourg-Saint-Antoine, at the Petit-Bercy
Maison des Lions-Saint-Paul (now no 12)
Maison de la Citoyenne Douay, Rue Bellefonds, no 218 (now Rue de
  la Tour-d'Auvergne)

Colleges, Hospitals, Various

Salpêtrière
Bicêtre
Maison des Oiseaux, Rue de Sèvres
Collège des Quatre-Nations (?)
Collège de Montaigu
Port-Royal, known as Port-Libre, Rue Saint-Jacques
Collège du Plessis, Rue de la Bourbe (Boulevard de Port-Royal)
Dépôt de la mairie
Dépôts of the 48 sections

CHRONOLOGY

1792

12 February and 13 September: decrees concerning the sequestration of émigrés' property.
10 August: end of the Monarchy. The royal family is taken to the Temple.
2–6 September: massacres in the Paris prisons.
22 September: proclamation of the Republic.
25 October: decree ordering the banishment for life of French émigrés.

1793

21 January: execution of Louis XVI.
10 March: setting up of the Revolutionary Tribunal.
28 March: more repressive legislation against émigrés who have returned secretly.
17 July: trial of Charlotte Corday.
17 September: law on suspects.
14–16 October: trial of Marie-Antoinette.
24–30 October: trial of the Girondins.

1794

26 February–3 March: decrees of Ventôse and setting up of the People's Commissions.
14–24 March: trial of the Hébertists.
30 March–5 April: trial of Danton.
13 April: first plot in the Luxembourg and execution of the accomplices of Hébert and Danton: Dillon, Chaumette, Lucile Desmoulins, etc.
27 April: denunciation in the Convention of a plot at Bicêtre.

10 June: decree of 22 Prairial Year II divesting the Revolutionary Tribunal of the investigation of cases and altering its functioning.

16 June: condemnation of the 'conspirators' at Bicêtre.

17 June: condemnation of the 'conspirators abroad' and of Cécile Renault and her family.

June–July: repression of the pseudo-plots in the Luxembourg, at Saint-Lazare and at the Carmes.

27 July: conspiracy. Fall of Robespierre.

August–September: freeing of many prisoners.

26 October: decree temporarily restoring the enjoyment of their property to those charged with emigration who had obtained favourable reports from the administrative bodies.

1795

1 April: riots. Arrest of Collot d'Herbois and Billaud-Varenne.

April–May: trial and execution of Fouquier-Tinville.

20 May: riots, uprising against the Convention, repression.

27 October: beginning of the Directory.

1796

10 May: denunciation of the '*conjuration des égaux*' and arrest of Babeuf.

1797

May: execution of Babeuf.

4 September: coup d'état of 18 Fructidor.

CONCORDANCE TABLE of the
REPUBLICAN and GREGORIAN CALENDARS

REPUBLICAN ERA		I	II	III	IV	V
GREGORIAN ERA		1792	1793	1794	1795	1796
I Vendémiaire	September	22	22	22	23	22
I Brumaire	October	22	22	22	23	22
I Frimaire	November	21	21	21	22	21
I Nivôse	December	21	21	21	22	21
GREGORIAN YEAR		1793	1794	1795	1796	1797
I Pluviôse	January	20	20	20	21	20
I Ventôse	February	19	19	19	20	19
I Germinal	March	21	21	21	21	21
I Floréal	April	20	20	20	20	20
I Prairial	May	20	20	20	20	20
I Messidor	June	19	19	19	19	19
I Thermidor	July	19	19	19	19	19
I Fructidor	August	18	18	18	18	18

This table makes it possible, by giving the Gregorian equivalent to the first day of each of the Republican months, to convert dates from one system to the other. It concerns only the first five Republican years, the period covered by this book, but the Republican calendar remained in use, of course, until 1805 (Years XIII–XIV).

NOTES

Generally speaking, for each individual who appears before the Revolutionary Tribunal, one must refer to the files of the Archives Nationales, in particular to the trial file (series W), to the archives of the Committee of General Safety (sub-series F7) and, in addition, to series T, which relates to sequestrated property.

1. The *gêne* is a long-term imprisonment, the *fers* involved forced labour and deportation, usually to Guiana.
2. After the laws and decrees of March and April 1792, the property and incomes of émigrés were confiscated by the nation (see Chronology).
3. AN, W, 440, file 46, p. 60.
4. Minutier central, étude Dupont, LXXII, 514: Denise d'Estat, divorced wife of Tobie Gothereau de Billens, a citizen of Fribourg, was the illegitimate daughter of the procurator Joly de Fleury. She served as an intermediary in the correspondence between royalist financiers who had remained in France and their foreign counterparts. Her brother, Michel d'Estat, known as Bellecourt, kept up a correspondence with the Russian court, where he had lived for ten years. Their sister, Lucrèce, was in contact with the Spanish government, via her future husband Ocariz, and the royalist circles of West Paris and Versailles. She was nearly arrested at the same time as André Chénier.
5. A. de Lestapis, 'Un grand corrupteur, le duc du Châtelet', *AHRF*, 1953. See the letters and unpublished reports concerning the attempts by Marie-Geneviève du Châtelet to communicate with her uncle, who was in solitary confinement: AN, W 145 (216, 268–70).
6. An example of speculation among the most famous under the Revolution is the case of Rouvroy de Saint-Simon, who had profited from the facilities given by the Assembly for the payment of national property in two annuities to acquire with a small amount of capital a total of ten million in rural property. He was arrested for his relations with the Comte de Redern, the Comtesse de Stolberg, General de Flers, Louis Comte and other 'conspirators abroad'. See A. Mathiez, 'L'arrestation de Saint-Simon', *AHRF*, vol. 2, 1925, p. 571.

7. The *'fabricateurs'* (to use the word of the time) of false assignats were sent to the ordinary criminal tribunal even though their 'political' intentions were often obvious enough: a very famous example is that of Jean-François-Marie de Kératry, born at Rennes, around 1765, arrested and set free twice (April and August 1793), arrested yet again and held in solitary confinement at the Conciergerie in November 1793, sentenced to death by the Tribunal of the *département* of Paris and guillotined in August 1794. See among others A. Bouchary, *Les Faux-Monnayeurs sous la Révolution*, Paris, 1946, A. de Lestapis 'Faux assignats et émigration', *Revue des Deux Mondes*, September 1955; R. Anchel, 'Les faux assignats', *Revue de Paris*, April 1926, p. 605.

8. A former naval minister under Louis XVI, Bertrand de Molleville, a refugee in London since 1791, organized with royalists living in France a huge network for the distribution of forged assignats. One of his assistants was the Comte d'Angivilliers.

9. Chateaubriand, *Mémoires d'outre-tombe*, Paris, 1841.

10. On this subject, one may usefully refer to the *Métamorphoses, ou Liste des noms de famille et patronymiques de ci-devant ducs, marquis, comtes, barons,* 1792.

11. Any attempt to classify detainees or sentenced prisoners is difficult because of the skill with which the individuals concerned disguised their identities or invented professions that they never had any need to practise. Since facilities were given to merchants to travel abroad, many aristocrats suddenly turned themselves into merchants from 1792 onwards. At this time, Citizen Sergent Marceau was not taken in: 'You, the French émigrés,' he said, 'if recaptured on French territory under a false name and a profession that is not yours, are condemned by the law. And we see you again, disguised, hiding your names under some vulgar name in a crowd of nobles hiding their identity as you are doing, secretly armed and surrounding with mystery that court that was preparing to combat the people of Paris and to enslave the nation by handing it over to foreign armies that are merely awaiting the signal to invade our frontiers.' BHVP, ms 798, fo 200.

12. Divorce allowed women to recover their dowries, whether from a third party or from the husband's debtors. The procedure by which family arbiters were used in cases of divorce on the grounds of emigration survived until the law of 24 Vendémiaire Year III, which dispensed the applicant's spouse from citing the émigré's spouse.

13. AN, W 148 (219–231).

14. AN, W 111, L. 1 (65).

15. AN, W 153, L. 2 (48 and 49).

16. AN, W 153 (1–32).

17. AN, W 171 (15 and 37), W 124 L. 1 (86).

18. AN, W 293, no 210 and W 164, L. 2.

19. AN, W 146 (100).

20. AN, W 132 (94).

21. AN, W 138 (200).

22. AN, W 131 (152) and W 136, L. 2 (214).

23. G. Lenôtre, *Le Tribunal révolutionnaire*, Paris, 1908. On the subject of

badly guarded prisons, two escape attempts from the prison of La Force are known: those of 7 February and 18 March 1794 (BHVP, Labat, ms 863, 1022).

24. Mme Roland, *Mémoires*, coll. 'Mém. relat. à la Rév. franç.', Paris, 1821, p. 298.

25. Frédéric, Baron de Kalb, born around 1766, son of Jean de Kalb and Émilie Vanrobais, officer in Salm-Salm's regiment, owner of a copy of the *Manifeste de l'Empereur d'Autriche*, who was burnt at the stake before being executed as a deserter and émigré (14–11–1793). His last letter: AN, U 1021 (copy of the original listed as W 109, L. 3 (8), which cannot be found).

26. AN, W 132 (18): it may well be the Brest lawyer Riou de Salaün.

27. J. Epois, *L'Affaire Corday-Marat*, Le Cercle d'Or, Sables-d'Olonne, 1980. See the works on the heroine by C. Vatel. One portrait, not the one by Hauër, was, according to Ferrières-Sauvebeuf (AN, F⁷ 4706), executed at the Tribunal by Citizen Darnaud: does it need to be compared with the anonymous sketch by Vinck 5366?

28. Dauban, *Les Prisons de Paris*, Paris, 1870, p. 270.

29. Fleury, *Mémoires*, Paris, 1844, II, p. 195.

30. Dauban, p. 285. Anne-Marie Gauthier de Montgeroult de Coutances, to use her maiden name, was the mistress of the deputy Julien de Toulouse, and served as an intermediary in the correspondence between the Comte de La Châtre, in London, and royalists who had remained in Paris. Cf. A. Mathiez, *La Corruption parlementaire* . . ., pp. 206–7 and AN, BB 3 (52, 66 and 67).

31. P. Caron, *Rapports des agents secrets* . . . II, p. 208 (See Roman d'Amat, notice by Victor de Broglie (1756–1794), a member of the Constituent Assembly, army officer with the rank of Brigadier, who returned from emigration in 1793 to protect his property. He was then arrested as he was trying to escape to Switzerland. He was sentenced to death as one of Dumouriez's accomplices.

32. Dauban, pp. 359 ff.

33. AN, W 111, L. 3 (20).

34. Dauban, pp. 354 ff.

35. A. Mathiez, 'Dernières lettres de Momoro', *AHRF*, V, 1912, p. 396 and IX (1917) p. 544. Cf. A. Tuetey, X (1913) biographical notice. Sophie Momoro represented the goddess Reason at Saint-Sulpice. She was the daughter of the engraver and founder Fournier the younger. Her husband, Antoine-François, had been admitted in 1787 to the community of booksellers. A citizen of the Théâtre-Français section, he printed the *Journal de Club des Cordeliers* at his premises, 7 Rue Serpente. As an administrator of the *département*, he dealt with émigrés' cases. With his brother, a member of the office concerned with checking certificates of non-emigration, they signed forged certificates for returned émigrés.

36. Dauban, p. 420.

37. Louis-François, Comte de Ferrières-Sauvebeuf, born in 1762, murdered in 1814, AN, F⁷ 4706. (See O. Blanc, 'Les indices de la Révolution', *L'Histoire*, December 1983).

38. A. de Coigny, *Journal*, p. 145 and C. Velay, *Le Duc de Lauzun*, Buchet-Chastel, 1983.

39. AN, W 134 (40): a second letter (item 66) is addressed to his father.

40. G. May, *Madame Roland and the Age of Revolution*, New York and London, Columbia University Press, 1970 and A. Le Corbeiller, *Le Calvaire de madame Roland*, Paris, 1942.

41. AN, F⁷ 4704 (Ferniot) and W 152, L. 1 (179): unpublished information on the du Barry conspiracy.

42. H. Lyonnet, 'Une prison pour comédiennes', *La Nouvelle Revue*, 4ᵉ série. t. 45, 1920, p. 166; 'Comédiens révolutionnaires', *La Nouvelle Revue*, t. 51–53, 57, 59, etc. (1921–1925).

43. AN, BB³ 68 (148): mother-in-law of the deputy Regnault de Saint-Jean d'Angély, of the writer Arnault and the rich merchant Buffaut, she was more royalist than the whole family combined. As Cazalès' mistress, she was whipped by the people at the Palais-Royal in 1791. According to a denunciation of 1793 she plotted, at her home in the Rue Neuve-Sainte-Catherine, with the deputy Osselin, governor of Pondichéry Laumur and his sister Françoise d'Eprémesnil, who were all three guillotined. She seems to have made several journeys under the Directoire to assist the re-establishment of Louis XVIII, of whom her husband had been first valet de chambre.

44. BHVP, entry register of Sainte-Pélagie, ms. 997.

45. J.–A. Roucher, *Consolation de ma captivité, ou Correspondance de Roucher*, Paris, Agasse, Year VI, 1797. He was guillotined on the same day as André Chénier, another royalist poet.

46. Abbé J. Gaston, *Une prison parisienne sous la Terreur . . .*, Champion, Paris, 1909 and 1911.

47. Foignet, *Encore une victime*, Paris, Vachat, undated.

48. A. de Lestapis, *La Conspiration de Batz*, Sté Et. Robesp., Paris, 1969.

49. AN, W 78, pl. 2, p. 141. Daughter of Madame d'Eprémesnil's first marriage and detained with her, Michèle Thilorier married the Baron de Batz under the Empire.

50. A. Roland, *La Famille Sainte-Amaranthe,* Paris, Goupil, 1867 and Lefevre Saint-Ogan, 'Les dames de Sainte-Amaranthe', *La Nouvelle Revue,* vol. 30 and 31 (1904). Lastly, see the many denunciations of 1792 and 1793, by which we learn that the forged assignats coming from abroad were brought into circulation by the gaming house (AN, AF IV (1470), F⁷ 4775¹⁰, BB³ 73 (104), etc.).

51. P. Bru, *Histoire de Bicêtre*, Paris, 1890.

52. W 165, L. 2 (113), See *Le Moniteur*, vol. XX, p. 324.

53. Several prisoners knew the secret – which has still not been divulged – surrounding the theft, in September 1792, of the crown jewels.

54. L. Blanc, *Histoire de la Révolution française*, Paris, Langlois, 1847–62.

55. *Almanach des prisons*, Year III, 3rd edition, p. 133.

56. Dauban, pp. 235 ff. Anne-Louise-Reine-Jeanne Baillon, daughter of an intendant of Lyon, married the Comte d'Ormesson, who, for obscure reasons, had her imprisoned by *lettre de cachet* under the *ancien régime*.

57. Armand Martial Joseph Herman, a former judge of the district court of Arras, was president of the Revolutionary Tribunal from Brumaire to

Germinal Year II, then commissioner of the Civil Administrations for Police and Tribunals. He was a joint defendant at the trial of Fouquier-Tinville and was sentenced to death.

58. *Papiers inédits trouvés chez . . . Vadier,* coll. 'Mém. relatifs à la Révolution', Paris, 1828, vol. 3, pp. 341–4. See Bourgin, 'La commission des administrations civiles. Police et Tribunaux', *AHRF,* 1930, p. 176.

59. Duras (Duchesse de), 'Souvenirs', *Revue historique,* 1889, I, p. 121.

60. AN, F⁷ 4704 (Ferniot).

61. On Courlet de Boulot, who was involved in selling forged assignats and in the plot at Le Plessis, see AN, F⁷ 4674 and W 187, L. 1 (88), W 434 (no 974), W 145 (292), W 165, L. 1 (81) and L. 3 (143), W 149, L. 3 (49). See 'Procès Fouquier', *Bulletin du Tribunal,* no 7, p. 3 and no 11, p. 2. A report by the police officer Faro, dating from 4 Thermidor, Year II, concerns a letter announcing a 'plot' in the prison of the Madelonnettes. 9 Thermidor intervened before the supposed authors of the 'plot' were sentenced and executed (*Papiers trouvés . . ., op. cit.,* vol. 2, p. 417).

62. This is a reference to Jean Henriot, aged thirty-eight, born at Houilles (Seine-et-Oise). His sentence of deportation was quashed on 9 Floréal Year V. The term 'to innoculate' a prison was used when attempts were being made to provoke an uprising of the detainees.

63. *Mémoires sur les prisons,* I, p. 282.

64. *Mémoires sur les prisons,* p. 285.

65. AN, W 111, L. 3 (35), W 150 (18 and 19), W 178 (99): by decree of 24 Ventôse Year II, all letters to or from detainees were intercepted (Tuetey, XI (75)).

66. Savine, pp. 162–3.

67. On P.A.N. Pépin Desgrouettes, see: AN, F⁷ 4774⁶⁶ (V), F⁷ 4665 (IV) and I. Bourdin, *Les Sociétés populaires,* 1937.

68. Dauban, pp. 390–2 ff.

69. P. Bart, 'L'arrestation de Frenck', *AHRF,* VII, p. 101.

70. Dauban, p. 395.

71. Dauban, p. 372.

72. Nicolaï (Mme de), 'Mémoires', *Mercure de France,* 15 March 1939, p. 619 and 'Souvenirs', *La Nouvelle Revue,* vol. 91, 1894, p. 475.

73. Nicolaï, p. 620.

74. Roman d'Amat, notice by Alexandre de Beauharnais, deputy for Martinique in the States General, accused of complicity with General Custine, guillotined for high treason. See the farewell letters of two other generals sentenced for treason: Dortoman: AN, W 131 (197) and Lamarlière: AN, W 121, L. 2 (64), W 123, L. 1 (64) and W 171, L. 2 (39).

75. *Almanach des prisons,* Michel, Paris, Year III, p. 155.

76. See p. 205.

77. See p. 192.

78. Roman d'Amat, notice by Louis-René Quentin de Richebourg, Chevalier de Champcenetz (1760–94), arrested with the royalist booksellers and publishers Gattey, Lesclapart, Weber, etc.

79. Dauban, p. 374: these verses were dedicated to a certain Demoiselle de Croiseille.

80. In prison slang, when an individual arrived, usually '*ganté*' (wearing

gloves, i.e. handcuffs), one '*allumait le miston*' (he was scrutinized atten-tively) and, sometimes, after entering his name in the entry register he was sent to the '*houzard*' ('hole').

81. Savine, p. 180.
82. Dauban, p. 141.
83. Savine, p. 178.
84. *Almanach des prisons*, Year IV, p. 56.
85. Dauban, pp. 125 and 153.
86. Caron, II, p. 252.
87. Dauban, p. 127, pp. 155 ff.
88. AN, U 1020: copy of the letter written by Gabriel-Nicolas-François de Boisguyon, born at Châteaudun. He served as adjutant general under the orders of Beysser.
89. AN, W 145 (196).
90. Dauban, p. 183.
91. P. Caron, *Rapports des agents secrets*, VI, p. 313 (see also the Mémoires of Bergnot and Riouffe).
92. See Bault, *Récit exact de la captivité de la reine*, Paris, 1817, Pierre, 'Marie-Antoinette à la Conciergerie', *Revue des questions historiques*, 1897.
93. AN, W 194. The Paris Revolutionary Tribunal passed in all 2,639 death sentences, if one includes the victims of the 'Tribunal of 17 August' 1792. Several individuals counted among those sentenced to death were never actually executed: especially pregnant women. The effects of the Terror, particularly in Paris, were deliberately exaggerated by the royal-ists, with the blessing of the Thermidorians. By way of comparison, the Terror was less bloody than the repression of the Commune in 1871, which, in Paris alone, amounted to 20,000 executions. It was infinitely less terrible than the Russian Revolution of 1917–21, the White Terror of 1936–39 and, still less, the Nazi Brown Terror that spread first over Germany, then over Europe.
94. See J. Godechot, *Les institutions de la France sous la Révolution et l'Empire*, PUF, Paris, 1968, p. 386.
95. AN, W 121 (67): as Commissioner for War, Bonnefoy was entrusted with the task of buying horses for the army. He was sentenced to death for misappropriation of public funds.
96. AN W 171: Louis-Charles de Faverolles, formerly Dumouriez's aide-de-camp.
97. AN, W 171 (75): Agathe Jolivet, separated wife of the Lyonnais lawyer Barreau de Crécy.
98. Caron, II, p. 141.
99. Dulac, *Le Glaive vengeur*, Paris, Year II.
100. AN, W 171 (101); Caron, II, 323: also for Federalism, Citizen Sourdille Lavalette was executed on 12 Ventôse, Year II. His letter: AN, W 123, L. 1 (30).
101. AN, W 123, L. 1 (79); W 116 (46).
102. Caron, IV, p. 260.
103. Caron, I, p. 187, II, p. 36, V, p. 13, 39, 159, 272, VI, p. 322, etc.: see index 'Executions'.
104. Duras (Duchesse de), *Souvenirs*, p. 295. This account by the Abbé

Carrichon concerns the execution of his grandmother, his mother, Mme d'Ayen, and the Vicomtesse de Noailles, his sister.

105. Caron, VI, p. 322.
106. Caron, VI, p. 272.
107. Caron, V, p. 53.
108. G. Perier de Feral, *La Maison d'arrêt des Oiseaux d'après les Souvenirs de captivité du président de Dompierre d'Hornoy*, Paris, 1955.
109. *Pièces originales du procès de Fouquier-Tinville et de ses complices . . .*, impr. d'Hacquart, Paris, Year III.
110. Hornoy (président d'), Mémoires, *Fédération des Sociétés historiques et archéologiques de Paris et de l'Île de France*, vol. IV.
111. AN, W 111, L. 2 (28).
112. AN, W 154, L. 2 (20) and W 154, L. 1 (86): Louise Cécile Quévrin, known as Lusigny, born at Montdidier (Somme) around 1762.
113. AN, F⁷ 4673 (645), W 121, L. 1 (100), W 141 (155), W 148 (6 and 7), AF+ II 294 f⁰ 106, BHVP, ms 997 (register of Sainte-Pélagie), etc. A portrait and the princess of Monaco's plait of hair were exhibited at the Musée Carnavalet in 1934 during an exhibition devoted to the Revolution.
114. A. de Lestapis, 'Tallien, le héros du neuf', *Revue des Deux Mondes*, June, 1961.
115. A. de Coigny, *Journal, op. cit.*, p. 105.
116. L. Lecointre, *Les Crimes des sept membres des anciens comités de salut public*, 20 Frimaire, Year III, *Plaidoyer de Lysias contre les membres des anciens Comités . . .*, Paris, Year III.
117. Foignet, *op. cit.*, p. 41. Up to 14 September 1793, the date of its renewal, the Committee of General Safety was not solely responsible for serious political crime. The Girondins, who distrusted it, had set up alongside it, several commissions, each having a specific responsibility: the Commission of the 24 to list the papers of the Committee of Surveillance of the Commune of 10 August, the Commission of the 12, to list the papers of the *amoire de fer*, the Commission of the 21 to present the document outlining the crimes of Louis Capet, a new Commission of the 12, which, on 18 May 1793, was made responsible for suppressing plots in Paris against the Convention. The 'Grand Committee of General Safety', reduced to twelve members, was given the task of preparing the case for the prosecution in the trials of the Girondins and Federalists. They investigated the long, complicated affair of the Compagnie des Indes, which lay at the root of the trial of the Hébertists and Dantonists. The Committee of Surveillance of the *département* of Paris was, from 31 May to the middle of 1794, directly dependent on the Committee. The police bureau set up in the Committee of Public Safety in the spring of 1794 was one of the main causes of its rivalry with the Committee of General Safety. See G. Lefebvre, 'La rivalité du Comité de salut public et du Comité de sûreté générale', *Revue Historique*, 1935, p. 336 and A. Mathiez, 'Les divisions dans les comités à la veille de thermidor', *Annales révolutionnaires*, 1915, p. 70.
118. A Mathiez, *La Corruption parlementaire . . .*, Paris, 1917–18, 2 vols.
119. AN, F⁷ 4668 (dossier Laubespin), BB³ 68.

120. AN, W33 (procès-verbal d'interrogatoire), W 363, dos. 787, t. 237 and 1610.

121. *Mémoire justificatif pour le citoyen Mesnil-Simon* (BHVP: 109 576).

122. AN, F' 4774⁸ᵁ (Pottier de Lille), 20 Thermidor Year II.

123. Sainte-Beuve, *Nouveaux Lundis*, vol. IV.

124. Mme Roland, *Mémoires*, coll. 'Mém. rel. Rév. franç.', Paris, 1821, p. 189.

125. AN, W 189 (42).

126. Mme Roland, *op. cit.*, p. 191.

127. AN, W 145 (397) and Mme Roland, *op. cit.*, p. 190.

128. AN, W 134 (158): Marie-Gabrielle Chapt de Rastignac, Marquise du Mas de Paysac, mother of Mme de Fausse-Landry, author of accounts of the September massacres. Her active correspondence with persons abroad and her journeys to the Netherlands brought her to the scaffold.

129. F. Foiret, *Une corporation parisienne*, Champion, Paris, 1912; see also Minutier Central, Denis de Villières, 14 Nivôse Year II: charge against Roettiers Antoinette-Catherine Hermant. On the inventory of property left at the Roettiers' residence: BHVP, ms. 762, f° 25.

130. R. Arnaud, *La Débâcle financière de la Révolution*, Cambon (1756–1820), Paris, Perrin, 1926. Mehée de la Touche, *Coup d'œil d'un aveugle sur l'administration du contrôleur général Cambon*, 1794.

131. J. Lafitte, *Mémoires* (1767–1844), published by Paul Buchon, Firmin-Didot, Paris, 1922.

132. J. Bouchary, *Les Manieurs d'argent*, vol. II, p. 38. On Perrégaux, see Lhomer, *Le Banquier Perrégaux et sa fille la duchesse de Raguse*, Paris, 1925, and above all J.–L. Rieser, *Les Relations franco-helvétiques sous la Convention*, Dijon, 1927.

133. A. de Coigny, *op. cit.*, p. 123.

134. J.–B. Dubois, known as 'Dubois d'Ossonville' (1753–1833), was attaché to the Comte de Sallaberry under the *ancien régime*, then opened a café in Paris at the beginning of the Revolution. He was appointed an officer of the peace (November 1791) and joined Louis XVI's secret police. As an agent of the Committee of General Safety in 1793–4, he was responsible above all for prosecuting forgers. After the fall of Robespierre, he became a Thermidorian, but was nevertheless deported to Cayenne, from which he escaped. He turned up successively in Hamburg, London, Madrid, Olmütz, then entered Bonaparte's secret police and was nearly shot for high treason. Far from being investigated under the Restoration, the former 'terrorist' ended his days peacefully as inspector of police for the Île Saint-Louis quarter. (See the Memoirs of Durfort de Cheverny and of the Comte de Moré, as well as Charles d'Héricault, 'Fragments des Mémoires de Dossonville', *Revue de la Révolution*, 1884.)

135. BHVP, ms 775, f° 168.

136. AN, W 152, L. 2 (227).

137. Estat (Lucrèce d'), sister of Mme de Billens, first the mistress, then the wife of the chargé d'affaires Ocariz, who acted as Spanish ambassador in Paris after 10 August 1792. Lucrèce d'Estat was nearly arrested at Passy at the same time as André Chénier. In 1793, after the arrest of the Abbé

d'Espagnac at her house in the Rue Caumartin, she was charged with burning the correspondence between Dumouriez and the abbé.

138. Lavaud, *Les Campagnes d'un avocat*, Paris, 1819. The escape of the Abbé d'Espagnac was assisted by Police Inspector Louis Jouenne (Labat).
139. A. de Lestapis, *La 'Conspiration de Batz'*, Paris, 1969.
140. Seilhac, *L'Abbé Marc-René Sahuguet d'Espagnac*, Tulles, 1881 and *Bull. Sté. hist. de Paris et de l'Ile-de-France*, 1934, p. 28.
141. AN, AF, II 292, f° 113 (17 August 1817).
142. AN, F⁷ 4673, *pièce* 459 (25 Floréal Year II).
143. François-Elie Ducoster was arrested with the wife of his partner Laplaigne in Messidor and sent to Saint-Lazare. He is mentioned in connection with Swiss citizens living in Paris under the Terror in Barthélemy's correspondence. See also Ferrières-Sauvebeuf's denunciation (F⁷ 4706).
144. On Romey's connections, one must explore the *Minutier central*, which still houses many unknown documents on his relations with Swiss businessmen and financiers and with the counter-revolutionaries.
145. AN, W 328, dos. 541, see Foiret, *Une corporation . . . op. cit.*
146. AN, F⁷ 4706 (Ferrières-Sauvebeuf), La Feuillide, alias Cappot de Feuillide.
147. E. Daudet, 'Magon de la Balue', *Revue des Deux Mondes*, 15 March and 1 August 1911. Shortly before 30 Germinal Year II, the Magons were held at the *maison de santé* in the Rue Saint-Maur: their portfolio of stocks and shares, which could not be found after their execution, might have been entrusted to Citizen Romey (BHVP, Labat, f° 135, 178, 221). See Berryer, *op cit.*
148. A. Doyon, *Maximilien Radix de Sainte-Foix (1736–1810)*, Paris, 1966. It will be noted that the administrator of police, François Lafosse, wrote to Fouquier-Tinville on 28 Nivôse Year II on the subject of the *maison de santé* that he wanted to open with his sister-in-law at Bercy. The establishment did not have a long life. Lafosse was guillotined on 29 Prairial, Year II with the 'Conspirators from abroad'. AN, W 111, L. 3.
149. Géant (17 Floréal Year II), AN, W 123, L. 1 (131), W 147 (122), W 124, L. 1.
150. Poutet (17 Floréal Year II, AN, W 147 (89), W 116, L. 3 (54), W 178, L. 2 (3 and 4).
151. Collignon (9 Germinal Year II), ms AN, W 171 (100). Paquet (R.), *Bibliographie analytique de l'Histoire de Metz pendant la Révolution*, Picard, 1926, pp. 712–930.
152. Morisset (25 Germinal Year II), ms. AN, W 147 (14). Barnier (C.), 'Montargis pendant la Révolution', *Bull. de Montargis*, 1922, pp. 165–6.
153. Courtonnel (16 Pluviôse Year II), ms. AN, W 115, L. 2 (17).
154. Grassin (17 Ventôse Year II), ms. AN, W 134 (30). Grassin, *Souvenirs de Famille*, undated. (BN: 8° Ln³ 1572); Cornillon (J.), 'Une famille noble de Saint-Géraud Le Puy pendant la Terreur', *Amis de Montluçon*, 16ᵉ année, ms. pp. 58–89.
155. Collin (17 Floréal Year II), ms AN, W 146, L. 3 (6). Paquet (R.), *Bibl. anal. de l'histoire de Metz . . .*, 1926. Poulmaire (M.), *Mémoires de l'Acad. de Metz*, 1881–82, pp. 259–320.

156. Homme inconnu, ms. AN, W 121, L. 1 (146).

157. Laviolette (18 Nivôse Year II), ms AN, W 194 (55) and W 194 (56), vol. 622, Riouffe, Paris de l'Épinard.

158. Harelle (9 Germinal Year II), ms. AN, W 168 (134).

159. Paisac (Antoinette Albisson, wife of) (7 Messidor Year II), ms. AN, W 153 (182), W 152, L. 2 (173); W 146, L. 1 (15); W 139, L. 1 (3), W 124 (124); W 150, L. 2 (178); W 115 (150). A. Lods, 'L'arrestation de Rabaut de Saint-Étienne', *La Révolution française*, t. 45, Paris 1903, p. 354.

160. Gueau-Reverseaux (24 Pluviôse Year II), ms. AN, W 134 (53, 68, 69, 70), W 116 (43) Z^{1j} 1053. Gruder (V.R.), *The Royal Provincial Intendants, a Governing Elite in the Eighteenth Century*, N.Y., 1968. Bluche (F.), *Les magistrats au Grand Conseil au XVIII^{e}s.*, Annales litt. univ. Besançon, Paris, 1966.

161. Bottagne, ms. AN, W 171 (47).

162. Paillot (14 Pluviôse Year II), ms. AN, W 134 (35). Babeau (A.), *Histoire de Troyes pendant la Révolution, 1787–1792*, Paris, 1873, vol. 2; Paillot (R.) *Journal d'un émigré*, Brussels, 1909, Babeau (A.), *Histoire de Troyes pendant la R.F.*, Paris, 1874.

163. Duplain (21 Messidor, Year II) ms. AN, W 146, L. 2 (105), F^7 4694. *Notes tirées d'un portefeuille anglais* (BHVP: 106 907). Lablée, *Relations de ce qui s'est passé au Luxembourg*, Paris, 1823.

164. Saint-Laurent, ms. AN, W 116, L. 2 (3).

165. Beaulieu de Surville (9 May 1793), ms. AN, W 134 (111). Le Bihan, Dulac.

166. La Rouërie, Bibl.: Pocquet du Haut Jusse, 'La Rouërie a-t-il été le père de la chouannerie?', *AHRF*, 1967. See Index of *Stè hist. et archéo. de l'arr. de Saint-Malo*.

167. Groult de la Motte (18 June 1793), ms. AN, W 134 (94), W 134 (105).

168. Moëllien (18 June 1793), ms. AN, W 134 (96).

169. Fontevieux (18 June 1793), ms. AN W 134 (109). Roman d'Amat, vol. X. Lasseray, *Les Français sous les treize étoiles*, Paris, 1935, p. 216.

170. Morin de Launay, ms. AN, W 134 (93).

171. Vincent, ms. AN, W 134 (91 and 126). J. Haize, *Un lieutenant du marquis de la Rouërie, G. J. Vincent*, Saint-Servan, Haize, 1906.

172. Lamotte-La Guyomarais, ms AN, W 134 (103).

173. T. Courteaux, *Hist. généal. de la famille Pontavice*, Paris, 1901, Pontavice, ms. AN, W 134 (98–102) Labat.

174. Locquet de Grandville, ms AN, W 134 (24 and 104). E. Fournier, *Une Malouine au temps de la Révolution*, 1922.

175. La Fonchais, ms. AN, W 117 (46). Levot, *Biographie bretonne*, vol. 2, 1857, pp. 97–100. Bordeaux (H.), *Les Trois sœurs des Isles*, Paris, 1952. Le Bastart de Villeneuve (P.), *André Désilles*, Nel, Paris, 1977.

176. Picot-Limoëlan, ms AN, W 134 (92). D. Darrah, *Conspiracy in Paris*, Expo-Press, New York, 1953.

177. Berger (13 September 1793) ms AN, W 136 (137).

178. Rutant (5 October 1793), ms AN, W 134 (36). Rutant (A.), *Pétition*, Nancy, 1793, BN, 8° LN ^{27} 18145.

179. Gorsas (7 October 1793), ms AN, W 123 L. 1 (59). Gorgeix (S.), A.-J. Gorsas, *Informations Historiques*, 1953, 5, pp. 179–83. Kuscinski, p. 299.

Le Bihan, p. 229. Michaud, Robert and Cougny, vol. 3, p. 208.

180. Barbot (20 Vendémiaire Year II), ms. AN, W 123, L. 1 (60), W 177 (18). S. Lacroix, *Actes de la Commune de Paris*, vol. VI, p. 348 and vol. VII, p. 658; *Compte rendu aux Sans-Culottes*. Dulac, *Le Glaive vengeur*.

181. Marie-Antoinette (16 October 1793). Tourneux, I (4180–4186); IV (21220–21230).

182. Wormeselle (12 Brumaire Year II), ms AN, W 131 (172), W 132 L. 1 (52), W 123 L. 1 (66). Labadie (E.), *La Presse bordelaise pendant la Révolution*, Bordeaux, 1910. *Journal de Bordeaux et du département de la Gironde*. Forrest (A.), *Society and Politics in Revolutionary Bordeaux*, Oxford University Press, 1975, p. 126.

183. Lemoine (12 Brumaire Year II), ms. AN, W 134 (51), W 132, L. 1 (52). Forrest (A.), *Society and Politics in Revolutionary Bordeaux*, Oxford University Press, 1975, p. 126. *Le Moniteur*.

184. Gouges (13 Brumaire Year II), ms. AN, W 131 (192). Blanc (O.), *Olympe de Gouges*, Syros, Paris, 1981.

185. Coutelet (14 Brumaire Year II), ms AN, W 134 (29). Gaulot (P.), *Les Petites Victimes de la Terreur*, Plon Nourrit, Paris, 1912, p. 34.

186. Kolly (3 May 1793), ms AN, W 134 (38), W 123 (73), W 81, L. 3 (1); AF^{11*} 286, 1637, 1683, 1685. Gaulot (P.), *Madame de Kolly*, Rev. Hebd. 2e serie, 4e année (VII and VIII); Seligmann (E.), *Mme de K. Une conspiration politique et financière*, Paris, Juven, 1904, Bouchary, *Les Manieurs d'argent*, vol. II, Paris, 1939. Le Bihan, Dulac, etc.

187. Gorneau (13 Frimaire Year II), ms. AN, W 123 L. 1 (6), W 116 (144). Beyrrier (P.R.), *Souvenirs*, Paris, 1840.

188. Dufresne (13 Frimaire Year II), ms. AN, W 123, L. 1 (7 and 80), Tuetey, vol. X.

189. Léonard ms. AN, W 131 (169) and AF^{11} 48, 371, 18, F^7 4774^{17}, D 4: Bouchary, *Faux-Monnayeurs sous la Révolution*, Paris, 1946. Condemned for the same reasons, Citizen Dubiez was executed on 5 Germinal Year II. His last letter: AN, W 147 (102).

190. Pinard (19 Frimaire Year II), ms. AN, W 134 (131).

191. Rigaud (19 Frimaire Year II), ms. AN, W 131 (39). Caron, vol. VI, p. 310.

192. Serpaud (25 Frimaire Year II), ms. AN, W 134 (77), W 195 (168).

193. Blouet (25 Frimaire Year II), ms. AN, W 134 (37), W 131 (86). Foiret, *Une corporation parisienne pendant la Révolution*, Paris, 1912.

194. Clément (6 Nivôse Year II), ms. AN, W 134 (163). Tuetey, vol. IX, 982 and 983, Caron, vol. II, p. 298.

195. Dietrich (8 Nivôse Year II), Riouffe, *Mémoires d'un détenu*, 2nd ed., Paris, Year III, p. 193. Mathiez (A.), *Un complice de La Fayette*, AHRF, p. 389 and 471. Roman d'Amat, vol. XI.

196. Custine (14 Nivôse II), ms. AN, W 141, L. 1 (15 ff). *Mémoires sur les prisons*, vol. 1, pp. 133–5. Roman d'Amat, vol. IX.

197. Charras (11 Pluviôse Year II), ms. AN, W 171, L. 2 (24), W 115, L. 3 (64), W 121 (154), F^7 4641, T 1683.

198. Roettiers (11 Pluviôse Year II), ms. AN, W 115, L. 1 (142).

199. Vernon (chanoine), *La Petite Vendée Briarde, ou Coulommiers sous la Terreur*. E. Dessaint, *Coulommiers sous la terreur* (BN, 8° Lk^7 43915).

Marolles, *Lettres d'une mère, épisodes de la Terreur (1791–1793)*, Paris 1901.
Vovelle (M.), *Religion et Révolution. La déchristianisation de l'an II.*
Hachette, Paris, 1976.

200. Blancheton, AN, W 134 (34).
201. Deltombe, AN, W 134 (23).
202. Igonnet, AN, W 134 (53 and 54).
203. Prévost de la Plumasserie, AN, W 134 (71).
204. Merlin, AN, W 123, L. 1 (63).
205. Maulnoir, AN, W 123, L. 1 (84).
206. Martin, AN, W 134 (75).
207. Ogier de Baulny, AN, W 134 (72).
208. Troussebois (19 Pluviôse Year II), ms. AN, W 123, L 1 (81), F^7 4434, Raoul Armand, *Sous la rafale*, Paris, 1913.
209. Millin-Labrosse (23 Pluviôse Year II), ms. AN, W 134 (161), W 115, L. 3 (54).
210. Fourcault de Pavant (2 Ventôse Year II), ms AN, W 135 (140), AF+ II 294, Le Bihan; Foiret; Houdard (J.), *État du notariat français à la fin du XVIIIes.*
211. Maussion (6 Ventôse Year II), ms AN, W 134 (65), W 145 (258), W 193 BHVP, ms. 775, Fol. 197-213. Ardascheff (P.), 34, 42–3, 56; Douarche, I, p. 115, Berthe, Maussion (Mlle de), *Mémoires*, P. 1980, Le Bihan, Caron, etc.
212. Prunelle (12 Ventôse Year II), ms. AN, W 134 (61).
213. Villemain (7 Germinal Year II), ms. AN, W 134 (25, 49, 55–8, 156–60). W 115, L. 2 (36), W 146, L. 3 (30), W 145 (233). Soboul (A.), *Les Sans-Culottes*, Paris, 1966. Caron (P.), vol. I, pp. 330–1.
214. Poiré (9 Germinal Year II), ms. AN, W 134 (27). Soboul (A.), *Les Sans-Culottes*, Seuil, Paris, 1966, p. 50.
215. Gattey (25 Germinal Year II) ms AN, W 152, L. 2 (27). Calvet (H.), *Un instrument de la Terreur . . .*, Paris, 1941. Begis (A.), 'Persécution des libraires pendant la Terreur', *Le livre, bibl. rétrosp.*, V, 1884, p. 177.
216. Lavoisier (19 Floréal Year II), ms AN, W 153, L. 2, pp. 16 and 42. Berrier (A.P.), *Souvenirs . . . de 1774 à 1838*, Paris. Dujarric and Chabrier, *La Vie et l'Oeuvre de Lavoisier*, Michel, Paris, 1959.
217. Lubomirska (3 Floréal Year II), ms AN, W 152 (201), W 150 (204), W 136, L. 2 (149), W 116 (40), W 115, L. 2 (170), W 115, L. 2 (26). C. Stryenski, *Deux victimes de la Terreur*, Paris, Girard et Villevelle, Paris, undated.
218. Salm-Kyrburg (5 Thermidor Year II), ms. AN BB^3 68 (197). Wendel (H.), Deux Salm, *La Révolution Française*, October 1934, p. 325. Thirion (H.), *Le Palais de la Légion d'honneur . . . précédé d'une notice sur le prince de Salm*, Versailles, 1883.
219. Paville (4 Prairial Year II), ms. AN, U 1021, T 704. Baragnon (L.), *Abrégé de l'histoire de Nîmes*, Nîmes, 1831–5. Durand (A.), *Histoire religieuse du département du Gard pendant la Révolution*, Nîmes, 1918.
220. Dufouleur de Courneuve (16 Prairial year II), ms. AN, W 134 (50), W 116 (94), Foiret, Le Bihan, etc.
221. Raucourt, ms. AN, W 124, L. 2 (124).
222. Gouy d'Arsy (5 Thermidor Year II), *Lettre de M.G. . . . D'A . . . alors*

détenu dans la maison des Carmes, addressée à son épouse, undated, 8°, 23 p.
BN, Lb⁴¹ 3963. Boissonnade (L.), *Saint-Domingue à la veille de la Révolu-tion,* Paris, 1906, p. 52. Debien (G.), *Les Colons de Saint-Domingue et la Révolution. Essai sur le club de Massiac,* Paris, 1953, p. 59; Le Bihan, p. 231. Robert and Cougny, p. 227. Michaud.

223. Fouquier-Tinville (17 Floréal Year III), ms. AN, W 479, no 550, p. 41; W 118 (between 4 and 31); W 123, L. 2 (88); W 129, p. 16; W 152, L. 1 (108). A. Dunoyer, *Fouquier-Tinville,* Paris. P. Labracherie, *Fouquier-Tinville,* Paris, Fayard, 1961.

224. Babeuf (5 Prairial Year V), ms. Bibl. Hist. Ville de Paris, ms. 774, F° 250 and ms. 1214, F° 76. Bibl.: decennial tables of the *Annales Historiques de la Révolution française.* See also Goujon's beautiful farewell letter, published after his death (he was sentenced to death with Babeuf).

GENERAL BIBLIOGRAPHY

ANONYME, *Les Hommes de la Terreur*, Paris, 1854.

ANONYME, *Tableau historique de la maison Lazare*, Paris, 1828.

ARDASCHEFF (P), *Les Intendants de province sous Louis XVI*, Geneva, 1909.

AUDOUIN (X), *L'Intérieur des maisons d'arrêt*, Paris, 1795.

AULARD (FA), *La Société des Jacobins*, Paris, 1889–1897.

BAULT (Vve), *Récit exact des derniers moments de la captivité de la Reine*, Paris, 1817.

BEAULIEU, *Essai historique sur les causes et les effets de la Révolution*, 1801.

BELLONI, *Le Comité de sûreté générale*, Paris, 1927.

BECQ DE FOUQUIÈRES, *Œuvres en prose d'André Chénier*, Paris, 1881.

BERRYER (PN), *Souvenirs de 1774 à 1838*, Paris, 1839.

BEUGNOT (comte), *Mémoires*, Paris, 1866.

BILLARD (M), 'Les maisons de santé sous la Terreur', *Chronique Medicale*, 1912.

BILLARD (M), *Les Femmes enceintes devant le Tribunal révolutionnaire*, Paris, 1909.

BIZARD et CHAPON, *Histoire de la prison de Saint-Lazare*, Paris, 1925.

BLANC (L), *Histoire de la Révolution française*, Paris, 1865.

BLUCHE (F), *Les Magistrats du Grand Conseil*, Paris, 1966.

BOHM (comtesse de), *Les Prisons en 1793*, Paris, 1830.

BONNEMAIN, *Les Chemises rouges*, Paris, Year VII.

BOUCHARY (J), *Les Manieurs d'argent à Paris à la fin du XVIIIe siècle*, Paris, 1939–1943.

BOUCHARY (J), *Les Faux-Monnayeurs sous la Révolution française*, Paris, 1940.

BOULOISEAU (M), *La République Jacobine*, Paris.

BRU (P), *Histoire de Bicêtre*, Paris, 1890.

Calvet (H), *Un instrument de la Terreur à Paris, le Comité de salut public ou de surveillance du département de Paris*, Paris, 1941.

CARON (P), *Tableaux de dépréciation du papier-monnaie*, impr. Nale, Leroux, Paris, 1909.

CARON (P), *Paris pendant la Terreur. Rapport des agents secrets du ministre de l'Intérieur*, Paris, 1910–1949 (6 vols. + index).

CHAUSSINAND-NOGARET (G), *Gens de finances au XVIIIᵉ siècle*, Bordas, Paris, 1972.

CIORANESCU (A), *Bibliographie de la littérature française du XXVIIIᵉ siècle*, CNRS, Paris, 1969.

COBB (R), *La Protestation populaire en France (1789–1820)*, Calmann-Lévy, Paris, 1975.

COBB (R), *Terreur et subsistances (1793–1795)*, Clavreuil, Paris, 1965.

COIGNY (A de), *Journal*, presented by A-M Grangé, Paris, 1981.

CONAN, *La Dernière compagnie des Indes*, Rivière, Paris, 1942.

COURET (E.), *Histoire complète de la prison politique de Sainte-Pélagie*, Paris, 1895.

DURAS (duchesse de), *Journal des prisons de mon père . . .*, Paris, 1889.

DAUBAN (C-A), *Les Prisons de Paris sous la Révolution*, Paris, 1870.

Débats de la convention nationale, Paris, 1828, 5 vol. in-8°.

DELAUNAY (P), *La Prison de Port-Libre*, Paris, 1909.

DOUARCHE, *Les Tribunaux civils de Paris pendant la Révolution*, Paris, 1905–1907.

DOUCET-SURINY, *Mémoire sur trois arrestations . . .*, Prairial Year III.

DOWD (D-L), *Security and secret police during the reign of Terror*, 1956.

DU BLED (V), *La Société dans les prisons de Paris pendant la Terreur*, Paris, 1892.

DUSAULCHOY, *L'Agonie de Saint-Lazare*, undated.

ELIOTT (G-D), *Mémoires sur la Révolution française*, Paris, 1861.

FELKAY (N), *En prison sous la Terreur. Souvenirs de Billecoq*, Sté Et. Rob., Paris, 1981.

FLEURY, *Mémoires*, publ. by Lafitte, Gosselin, Paris, 1844.

FOIGNET, *Encore une victime, ou Mémoires d'un prisonnier . . . des Anglaises*, undated.

FOIRET (P), *Une corporation parisienne pendant la Révolution*, Paris, 1912.

GASTON (abbé J), *Une prison parisienne sous la Terreur: le couvent des bénédictines anglaises du Champ-de-l'Alouette*, Paris, 1909.

GODECHOT (J), *La Contre-Révolution. Doctrine et action (1789–1804)*, PUF, Paris, 1961.

GODECHOT (J), *Les Institutions de la France sous la Révolution et l'Empire*, PUF, Paris, 1951.

GOODWIN (A), 'The underworld of the French revolutionary Terror', *Memoirs and proceedings of the Manchester and Philosophical Society*, 1954–1955.

GRUDER (V-R), *The royal provincial Intendants, a governing elite in 18th century*, New York, 1968.

HAUTERIVE (E), *Mouchards et Policiers*, Paris, 1930.

HAUTERIVE (E), *Figaro policier*, Paris, 1927.

HERLAUT (Gal), *Le Général rouge, Ronsin*, Paris, 1856.

HESDIN (R), *Journal of a spy in Paris during the reign of Terror*, J. Murray, London, 1895.

JANZE (A de), *Les Financiers d'autrefois*, Paris, 1886.

JACOB (L), *Les Suspects pendant la Révolution (1789–1794)*, Paris, 1952.

JACOB (L), *Hébert, le père Duchêne*, Paris, 1950.

Jugements du tribunal révolutionnaire, Paris, 1793–1795.

LABAT (L), Bibl. Hist. Ville de Paris, mss 816 to 856.

LA CHABEAUSSIÈRE, *Les Huit mois d'un détenu aux Madelonnettes*, Year III, 8°.

LACROIX (S), *Le Département de la Seine pendant la Révolution*, Paris, 1904.

LA LAURENCIE (J de), *Une maison de détention sous la Terreur, l'hôtel des bénédictins anglais*, Paris, 1905.

LAMBEAU (L), *Une prison parisienne dans la rue des Lions-Saint-Paul*, Cité, XIV, 1919, p. 201.

LAVAUX, *Les Campagnes d'un avocat*, Paris, 1819.

LE BIHAN (A), *Francs-Maçons parisiens du Grand-Orient de France*, Paris, BN, 1966.

LEGRAND (L), 'L'Hospice du Tribunal révolutionnaire', *Rev. question historiques*, July 1890.

LESTAPIS (A de), *La 'conspiration de Batz'*, Sté des Et. Robespierristes, Paris, 1969.

MAITRON (J), *Dictionnaire biographique du mouvement ouvrier français (1789–1864)*, Ed. ouvrières, 1964.

MALLET DU PAN, *Mémoires et Correspondance*, Paris, 1851.

MARICOURT (A de), *Prisonniers et Prisons de Paris pendant la Terreur*, Paris, 1924.

MATHIEZ (A), *La Vie chère et le mouvement social sous la Terreur*, Paris, 1927.

MATHIEZ (A), *Un procès de corruption . . ., l'affaire de la Cie des Indes*, Paris, 1920.

MEYER (J), *La Noblesse bretonne au XVIIIe siècle*, Flammarion, Paris, 1972.

MICHAUD, *Biographie Universelle*, Desplaces, 2nd ed, Paris, 1854.

MITCHELL (A), *The underground war against Revolutionary France*, Clarendon, Oxford, 1965. Moniteur (1789–1797).

PAREIN (PM), *Les Crimes des parlements ou les Horreurs des prisons judiciaires dévoilées*, Paris, Girardin, 1791.

Paris de l'Epinard, *Mon retour à la vie après quinze mois d'agonie*, undated.

Paroy (comte de), *Mémoires*, publ. Charavay, Paris, 1895.

Pinasseau (J), *L'Émigration militaire*, Picard, Paris, 1957.

Poisson, *Les Fournisseurs aux armées sous la Révolution*, A. Margraf, Paris, 1932.

Pottet (E), *Histoire de la Conciergerie*, Paris, 1887.

Pottet (E), *Histoire de Saint-Lazare*, Paris, 1912.

Proussinalle, *Histoire secrète du Tribunal révolutionnaire*, Paris, 1815.

Richard (G), *La Noblesse d'affaires au XVIIIᵉ siècle*, A. Colin, Paris, 1974.

Rieser (J-L), *Les Relations franco-helvétiques sous la Convention*, Dijon, 1927.

Riouffe, *Mémoires d'un détenu*, Paris, 1923.

Robert and Cougny, *Dictionnaire des Parlementaires français*, Paris, 1889–1891.

Roland (Mme), *Appel à l'impartiale postérité*, Paris, 2 vol, s.d., 8°.

Roland, *Mémoires*, Mercure, Paris, 1966.

Saint-Edme (E T Bourg, dit); Description historique des prisons de Paris . . ., Paris, 1828.

Ste-Claire Deville (P), *La Commune de l'an II*, Paris, 1946.

Savine (A), *Les Cachots de Paris sous la Terreur*, Paris, 1911.

Senar, *Mémoires*, pub. A. Dumesnil, Paris, 1824.

Six (G), *Dictionnaire biographique des généraux*, Paris, Saffroy, 1924.

Soboul (A), *Les Sans-Culottes parisiens de l'an II*, Paris, 1958.

Sorel (A), *Le Couvent des Carmes . . . pendant la Terreur*, Paris, Didier, 1864.

Tuetey (A), *Les Prisons de Paris en 1792*, Paris, 1902.

Tuetey (A), *Répertoire des sources manuscrites de l'Histoire de Paris pendant la Révolution*, impr. nouvelle, Paris, 1890–1913.

Vigée, *La Nouvelle Chartreuse ou ma détention à Port-Libre*, Year III.

Vovelle (M), *La chute de la monarchie 1787–1792*, Paris, 1972.

Walter (G), *Actes du Tribunal révolutionnaire*, Mercure, Paris, 1968.

INDEX